DR. COCKTAIL

DR. COCKTAIL

50 SPIRITED INFUSIONS
TO STIMULATE THE MIND AND BODY

ALEX OTT

RUNNING PRESS
PHILADELPHIA · LONDON

Books published by Running Press are available at special discounts for bulk
purchases in the United States by corporations, institutions, and other organizations. For
more information, please contact the Special Markets Department at the Perseus Books
Group, 2300 Chestnut Street, Suite 200, Philadelphia, PA 19103, or call (800) 810-4145, ext.
5000, or e-mail special.markets@perseusbooks.com.

ISBN 978-0-7624-4568-4
Library of Congress Control Number: 2012938261

E-book ISBN 978-0-7624-4694-0

9 8 7 6 5 4 3 2 1
Digit on the right indicates the number of this printing

Designed by Joshua McDonnell
Edited by Cindy De La Hoz
Typography: Avenir, Bembo, Haymer, and Mensch

Running Press Book Publishers
2300 Chestnut Street
Philadelphia, PA 19103-4371

Visit us on the web!
www.runningpress.com

"WHY TRY TO EXPLAIN MIRACLES
TO MY KIDS WHEN I CAN JUST
HAVE THEM PLANT A GARDEN?"

—MY FATHER, 1979

CONTENTS

ABOUT ALEX

World-renowned alchemist and mixologist Alex Ott learned the life of a nomad from his globe-trotting mother and father, a nutritionist and musician, respectively, who exposed young Alex to a vast array of adventures. From playing with lions in Africa to exploring the Atlas mountains, surfing with dolphins, and fighting off nature's elements in the rain forest, Alex learned how to get the most out of life. His journeys provided him with the unique ability to experience the flavors of foreign lands and taste all the fruits of the earth.

Alex began his career in mixology at age fourteen and learned the tricks of the trade under the tutelage of Heiko Beck and Thomas Kothe, owners of one of Europe's most creative cocktail bars. After getting his bachelor of science in organic chemistry and further cultivating his craft, Alex launched the exotic cocktail menu for the famed Buddha Bar in Paris. The process inspired Alex to delve deeper into the art and science of drink alchemy and to develop his unique approach to infusing fresh fruits, spices, and herbs into elixirs used to stimulate the mind and body.

For the next few years, Alex continued traveling and experiencing foreign cultures, tastes, and scents. After surviving a harrowing plane crash in Thailand in 1998 that killed 101 passengers, Alex had a renewed sense of dedication to all of the passions in his life, including art, surfing, film production, nature preservation, and flavor alchemy. Alex's path led him to New York City, where he made a name for himself at the fusion eatery Sushi Samba. Acclaimed for his unconventional drink mixes, Alex landed roles as himself in the HBO series *Sex and the City* and earned titles such as "Bartender of the Year" and "Best Mixologist in America" from national publications.

Since then, Alex has worked with more than fifty major spirits brands, including Svedka Vodka, Gallo Wines, and Möet Hennessy. He has created cocktail menus for high-end establishments and events such as the Oscars, produced Tom Ford fragrances, invented space travel beverages for NASA, and helped conjure the hangover prevention drink Mercy. From twenty years of experience in food and drink science, Alex has developed a one-of-a-kind approach to cocktails. In this book he shares his knowledge of botanicals, juices, herbs, and spices to awaken the world to the effects and benefits of earth's finest offerings.

THE
SEPTEMBER
SESSIONS

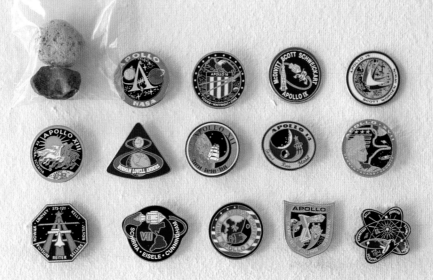

YOUR GUIDE TO DR. COCKTAIL

"THERE HAVE BEEN TWO GREAT REVELATIONS IN MY LIFE: THE FIRST WAS BEBOP, THE SECOND WAS HOMEOPATHY."

—DIZZIE GILLESPIE, MUSICIAN

I couldn't have said it better. My grandmother introduced me to herbs when I was five years old. I learned how to pick them, plant them, and incorporate them into food. My father taught me how to grow six different varieties of cherries on one tree. My mother introduced me to essential oils, perfumes, and cosmetics. I spent most of my childhood traveling the world, experiencing scents, flavors, and food from Africa to India, Asia to Australia, Europe to the South Pacific. It wasn't my choice, but boy am I happy my parents dragged me around. I embarked on a quest to collect and catalogue as many flavors and scents from foreign cultures as possible. A plethora of taste bud and olfactory experiences provided me with insight on what is mixable, edible, dangerous, and most importantly, what can stimulate and benefit us in a positive way.

We are bombarded with flavors and scents every day. These experiences can be stored with surprising vividness for a very long time, and on being re-experienced can evoke strong and sudden emotions. (See the chapter on memory-evoking libations, page 146.) Scent is but one of my main ingredients in the recipes of this book. Mixed in with extraordinary flavors in surprising combinations lie secret ingredients that have been used in homeopathic potions for 4,000 years to affect us in beneficial ways.

Just think about how certain foods make us feel a certain way. With just a few trips to your local market you can improve your overall health and even influence others. Do you ever dream of stimulating your friends, customers, or business partners by simply fixing them a special drink? Would you like to seduce your date and make him or her feel like they're on cloud nine, or relieve someone's stress without medications? Or drink socially for six hours without any hangover? I'm glad to be of service!

Many conditions and states of mind for which we turn to modern medicine can be treated naturally with everyday items from your kitchen. Ever tried fennel for anxiety or celery to help you focus? Basil and almond are known to boost fertility. Natural antihistamines found in fig, fennel, grapefruit, and thyme can prevent allergies. Drinking damiana tea can induce erotic dreams and a libido boost. Get smarter with gingko and lecithin. Papayas can banish parasites. And did you know you can help regulate your body temperature with pears?

Homeopathic or herbal medicine may, in many cases, prove to be more economical, more effective, and safer than pharmaceuticals—all with fewer side effects. The average MD has about an hour of nutritional training during eight years of medical instruction. Doesn't this make you wonder? How can someone heal you if they know little about substances that people have been digesting and using in herbal medicine for thousands of years? The two biggest industries on the planet are the food industry (the guys that make us sick, give us allergies, insomnia, cancers, and ulcers), and on the other side the pharmaceutical industry, which tries to heal us but also wants to make money. Most drugs are not really helping the healing process or underlying cause of why we get sick. Simply stated, we get sick from eating artificial and genetically modified foods. What we put into our bodies has a direct effect on how we feel, how long we live, and how we live.

Fruit, vegetables, herbs, and spices contain a concentrated hydrophobic liquid containing volatile aroma compounds, phyto-chemicals, essential oils, bio-flavonoids, antioxidants, vitamins, and many more things that I will discuss later in the book. These "ingredients" pack a powerful punch. They have a direct effect on our central nervous system and activate an anatomically and biochemically defined pleasure circuit in the brain. All evoke neural signals that converge on a small group of interconnected brain areas called the medial forebrain pleasure circuit. This pleasure circuitry can also be co-opted by artificial activators like alcohol. Certain types of alcohol have been with us for a long time. Beer and wine since 2000 BC and gin since 1650 (originally invented to treat Bright's disease, "female complaints," and urinary problems).

Most of us like immediate pleasure sensations to relax and even perhaps drink our problems away. American author William S. Burroughs expressed, "Our national drug is alcohol. We tend

PICAL MELON
LAC-08-22

PISTACHIO

Ingre
trigly
natur
potass
sodium

Bakto Flavors, LLC
North Brunswick, NJ USA
www.baktoflavors.com

NET 29 mL (1 FL OZ)

Aura Cacia

pure aromatherapy

Wild
Chamomile

100% PURE ESSENTIAL OIL

CALMING

NET .5 FL OZ (15mL)

pinepple lychee

green tea fig

ginger plum

Timbukt
Sandalw
Essence

تشوهلي
Patcho

to regard the use of any other drug with special horror." I have better news for you: This book is not about the alcohol but more about the natural spices, herbs, and flavor compounds used in the cocktails. Based on my research and decades of hands-on experience in the fields of food science, biochemistry, and culinary alchemy, the recipes in this book are a unique repertoire of carefully crafted, mood-altering concoctions—most containing our beloved spirits.

Throughout these recipes I will explain almost every ingredient by its country of origin, use, function, and the after-effect it has in conjunction with the featured cocktail elixirs. Above all, I will show you that with a combination of particular ingredients, I can make you hungry, de-stress you, prevent your hangover, hold back aging, enhance your libido, wake you up, relax you, and even evoke long-lost memories. You can do this by simply combining everyday items from your refrigerator, spice rack, and pantry and transforming them into delicious and effective potions for any occasion or time of day.

I hope you enjoy the drinks, the garnishes, the newly found tastes, and most of all the delicious benefits—bottoms up!

SAFETY FIRST

"Let your food be thy medicine" said Hippocrates, the Father of Medicine, who compiled a list of more than four hundred herbs and their uses. While modern medicine is barely a century old, natural nutritional substances are the oldest form of medicine known to man. From my years of research, consulting with numerous Ph.D.s and herbalists, it's clear that all medicines, natural or synthetic have their risks. To benefit from using herbs, you need some basic background information.

Misidentifying herbs is a classic killer, so make sure you get herbs from the store. You don't want to orphan your kids because the poison hemlock in your garden looked like parsley! Pregnant women should consult their obstetrician before taking herbs because certain ones can increase the risk of miscarriage. People taking anti-depressants and MAO Inhibitors should consult their physician as well because those medicines interact badly with wine and certain foods.

Use caution when ingesting any herb or spice for the first time. Always read the fine print on labels, be it chamomile tea or wormwood. I made

sure to use only the most common and typically harmless spices and herbs in the cocktails collected in this book, but people can be allergic to anything. If you experience difficulty breathing within thirty minutes of trying a new herb or spice, seek emergency aid. I am not trying to scare you. These are very rare situations.

Since this is a book filled with recipes using many fine and healthful ingredients, I do not advise you to ruin it by mixing in a marketed energy drink or the next artificially flavored high-fructose corn syrup schnapps. The chemicals in cordials, bitters, and artificially flavored infusions are more harmful than you think. In general, stick to natural ingredients, particularly if you work in a bar or restaurant. Not only will it save 80 percent in liquor costs, but you can almost guarantee that you or your customer will not wake up with nausea and a pounding headache.

Lastly, one of the least-known facts among average consumers about our food hierarchy is that most herbs, spices, and teas are not approved by the FDA (Food and Drug Administration). Shocking, isn't it? Though herbs have successfully been used for thousands of years to heal ailments, herb marketers would need to spend up to $200 million proving to the FDA that an herb can claim medicinal benefits. No one can patent the benefits of a plant, so who has that kind of money? The big drug companies do. So don't be afraid of chamomile—a reliable sedative and stomach settler—simply because it has not been approved by the FDA. Politics aside, please approach all libations with caution and drink responsibly!

SHOPPING TIPS

The reason it's so easy for me to make these delicious and working elixirs is the olfactory experiences I have accumulated in my brain—that and the incredibly easy access to the ingredients. For a moment think of yourself as MacGyver—you know, that guy from TV who can build an atom bomb out of a paper clip. I want you to be that person. Go into your kitchen and raid your refrigerator, spice rack, pantry, and freezer. I almost always use common ingredients that are safe, effective, and relatively inexpensive. You probably already have many of them in your kitchen or can get them at the local market.

The difference in the price of products among

markets is usually determined by distance between their suppliers, product quality, and (usually in the case of major supermarket chains) by how much money they want to make. I'm not picky about blemishes or bruises on my fruit when I get twenty lemons at a produce shop for 99 cents. That's right. Just because my Honeycrisp apple doesn't reflect light, it is not less flavorful or loaded with any fewer nutrients. I get watermelons for $3, cilantro for 65 cents a bunch, and raspberries for $1.50 instead of $7.50 at the supermarket. There are alternatives to the big stores.

Every town has its little secret store, some old run-down bodega or dilapidated gas station that carries guava juice, fresh oranges, or even a bottle of gin or tequila. Years of working as a brand ambassador for spirits companies made me a local explorer. I recommend a thorough exploration of your city or town to discover the best places to purchase relatively exotic ingredients or last-minute items for your cocktail party. You'd be surprised what you can find in any town.

Lastly, I have a couple of tips regarding two essential tools of my trade: the muddle stick and the cocktail shaker. Muddling or mashing is one of the most commonly used techniques in modern mixology, to extract the essential oils from ingredients. The muddle stick is one of our best friends. It replaces the blender and is very inexpensive. When shopping, go for the thickest and heaviest one because the less wrist power you have to use when muddling the easier it will be on your arm.

Cocktail shakers are used in most of the recipes in this book. The professional Boston Shaker comes in two parts: the tin and the shaker glass. The glass will be wedged into the metal part and can be opened by simply tapping against the side of the shaker. Then a strainer is placed on top of the glass and the cocktail can be strained into a glass. Most stores sell all-in-one shakers, which most non-professionals find easier to use. These consist of three parts: the glass bottom, the middle stage that contains strainer holes, and a top that covers the middle stage. After shaking, you simply lift the top and strain the drink out. The downside of average shakers is that they're sometimes impossible to take apart when the cold shrinks the metal so much that you get very frustrated trying to open it. I call it the "He-Man Effect." My advice is to go to a kitchen store and ask for the professional Boston Shaker.

I took this picture of my parents in Kenya when I was seven years old. It reminds me of our wonderful breakfasts together. My favorite was apricot jam with butter spread on toast. To this day, the combination takes me back to moments like this. It's my personal "Time Travel Flavor."

APPETIZING LIBATIONS

This chapter deals with the power of aromatic herbs, bitters, and spices. A number of plant foods supply generous amounts of minerals that stimulate the appetite and comfort the digestive tract.

THE ARABESQUE

Reminiscent of fairytales from Morocco, Algeria, or India, this potion is perfect as a refreshing drink and appetite stimulant. Originally created for the first Buddha Bar in Beirut, Lebanon, it was meant to be served as a complimentary shot that helps put customers in the mood to eat. Serve this cocktail about fifteen minutes before you want to achieve the desired effect, or simply enjoy as a refreshing drink to transport you to the East.

2½ ounces pear nectar (Looza and Kerns brands are great)

2 ounces Svedka Clementine Vodka

1 ounce mango nectar

½ ounce fresh lemon juice

Pinch of curry

Dash of grenadine

DIRECTIONS:

Combine all ingredients in a cocktail shaker filled with ice. Shake vigorously, with fast and short motions, for at least 8 seconds to achieve the perfect blend and coldness. Strain into a martini glass.

GARNISH: ORANGE-SKIN STAR

Try making a unique orange-skin garnish using a star-shaped cookie cutter. Use a knife to cut off the top an orange, then carve out the flesh of the orange peel with a spoon. From the inside of the peel, use your cookie cutter to stencil out heart-shaped orange skin garnishes. Make a small incision on the orange peel and place it on the rim of your cocktail.

ACTIVE INGREDIENTS: CURRY AND LEMON

Curry contains natural fragrances that begin working on your appetite as soon as they hit your nose. It is a blend of many spices with a base of the almighty turmeric. These spices help stimulate secretions of saliva and stomach acid.

Lemon juice and zest, which I use to give this drink a refreshing after effect, is high in vitamin C and contains bioflavonoids with proven power to lower blood pressure.

JAGMANDIR

Jagmandir is a lake palace in Udaipur, India. I have worked some of the most amazing events there for my friend Padmaja, who happens to be that palace's princess. I source all my ingredients from the town outside the palace walls. This cocktail is designed as an appetizing and healing potion. Sandalwood and turmeric are the featured aromatic herbs.

1 ounce liquefied honey
1½ ounces New Amsterdam Gin
3 ounces cranberry juice
½ ounce fresh lime juice
2 pinches of sandalwood
Pinch of turmeric

DIRECTIONS:

Make liquefied honey by dissolving 1 part honey in 1 part hot water. Refrigerate to cool. Next, combine all ingredients in a cocktail shaker filled with ice. Shake vigorously and strain into a champagne flute.

GARNISH: LIME SPIRAL

Place a lime on a cutting board and use a knife to cut off one end. Place the knife at a 45 degree angle on top of the lime and start cutting within the first half of the lime, pushing and rotating the fruit away from you with every cut. After 3 rotations, cut through and sever the garnish from the rest of the lime. Pull it apart like a slinky and place it over the entire glass.

ACTIVE INGREDIENTS: SANDALWOOD AND TURMERIC

Sandalwood comes from the Agar tree in India and has been used for thousands of years. It is usually gun powdered (rolled into tight pearls) and used for incense or as an antiseptic good for repairing mucus membranes and the digestive tract.

Turmeric, once called the poor-man's saffron, is a kitchen staple in India. It owes its curative nature to the chemical curcumin, a compound rich in antioxidants and anti-inflammatory properties. It has been shown to improve organ health without the side effects of both prescription and over-the-counter pain relievers.

RAVENOUS

This amazing potion is perfect to enjoy both before and during a meal, particularly a meal containing meat.

2½ ounces grapefruit juice
1½ ounces Svedka Citron Vodka
1 ounce pineapple juice
Pinch of sea salt
Dash of fresh lemon juice

DIRECTIONS:

Combine all ingredients in a cocktail shaker filled with ice. Shake and strain into an ice-filled rocks glass or tumbler.

GARNISH: GRAPEFRUIT SLICE

For the Ravenous, our garnish will be a folded grapefruit slice. Think of it as fruit origami. Cut the grapefruit in half and cut off a thin slice from the middle. Fold the slice in half and then fold it again until you have a triangle with 4 folds. Holding the folds together, cut an incision about ½" into the flesh part, cutting through all layers. Place the garnish on the rim of the glass.

ACTIVE INGREDIENTS: GRAPEFRUIT AND SALT

Grapefruit juice contains considerable bio-flavonoids, which are necessary for the maintenance of small blood vessels. These flavonoids also help to set the body's thermostat higher in order to burn away excess stored fat.

Certain substances increase our appetite and salt is one of the most powerful. The reason for this lies in the part of our brain called the appestat. The appestat monitors our nutrient levels in the blood. When all of these nutrients are present at their proper levels we feel satisfied and balanced. By adding additional salt, the appestat compels us to compensate by bringing back a balance of nutrients. Hence, our appetite is stimulated. That's one reason we can't snack on just one pretzel or potato chip!

VORACIOUS

This refreshing summer cocktail—designed especially for the ladies—increases the appetite. It's a derivative of one of the best-selling martinis in Manhattan, the Nina Fresa. Originally designed for the fusion restaurant Sushi Samba, this drink features the savory aromatic herb basil and the sexy strawberry. You can also use this mix as a marinade for fish, especially salmon.

Sprig of basil
3 strawberries
1½ ounces New Amsterdam Gin
½ ounce guava juice (Goya is great)
2 teaspoons fresh lime juice

ACTIVE INGREDIENTS: BASIL AND GIN

Estragole is the main component in basil and boosts the metabolism. It causes an overall increase in appetite. Basil also contains large amounts of E-beta-caryophyllene, which aids digestion and treats bowel diseases.

Regarding the spirit content of this potion, I chose gin, which was originally invented to treat Bright's disease, upset stomach, and menstrual cramps. Its main flavor component is juniper, which acts as another aromatic herb and appetite stimulant.

DIRECTIONS:

First we must muddle to extract the flavor (and therefore chemicals) from the basil and strawberries. We tend to the basil first because it doesn't produce much juice. If we started with the strawberries we would have a hard time mashing the basil because the strawberry juice in the glass would prevent us from having a semi-solid base on which to muddle the basil.

Place the basil sprig in a shaker glass and pound the leaves 7–10 times with a muddle stick. Be careful not to rip the leaves and stems when you muddle because besides extracting the essential oils, muddling can also release the chlorophyll in plants, creating an element of bitterness in your drink. When finished, put your nose to the glass and smell. If you are satisfied with the strength of the basil scent, stop. If it's too weak, muddle a bit more.

Next, cut the strawberries in half and remove the green leaves from the tops. Add the strawberries to the glass and muddle again.

Once you have created a good strawberry mash, combine all other ingredients with ice and shake vigorously. Strain into a martini glass.

GARNISH: STRAWBERRY AND BASIL

This garnish will be fairly simple: simply cut a small incision into the bottom of a strawberry and squeeze it onto the rim of the martini glass. Float a basil leaf on top of the liquid for an extra olfactory experience.

GHOSTBUSTER

This cocktail was designed in India. I use it to expel bad ghosts in the digestion and stimulate the appetite at the same time. This is a perfect martini to pair with poultry and fish.

2 sage leaves
3 ounces pear nectar
2 ounces Svedka Vodka
Dash of fresh lemon juice

DIRECTIONS:

Place sage leaves in the bottom of a shaker glass and gently pound on them a few times with a muddle stick. Without your nose even being close to the glass you'll detect the scent of sage. Add ice and all remaining ingredients to the glass and shake vigorously. Strain into a martini glass.

GARNISH: SAGE AND PEAR SLICE

For the garnish we again use sage for an extra olfactory experience. Simply float the leaf on top of the liquid after clapping it in between your hands to release extra oils. Next, go for a dynamic visual by cutting a pear slice and placing it on the rim of the glass.

Sage contains bitter compounds that have been used as an appetite enhancer since the Middle Ages. One of these compounds, alpha-pinene, causes slight water loss in your body, thus leading to an increase in appetite. Sage is also beneficial to the liver. The essential oils in sage cause mucus thinning, which relieves indigestion and stimulates the appetite. For our drink, muddling just two fresh leaves flavors the potion and produces our desired effect.

ANTI-STRESS COCKTAILS & MENTAL HEALTH ELIXIRS

Stress and anxiety is the immune system's number-one enemy. Both create imbalances by raising the level of the stress/anxiety hormone cortisone in the blood. Emotional and physical stress can be reduced by ingesting delicious potions of calming herbs. I consider this chapter to be most important of all in this book, as it speaks to every one of us.

About thirteen years ago, while living in Thailand, I boarded a plane to take me from Bangkok to Surat Thani. Little did I know this flight would change my life forever. Following the most turbulent ride I've ever experienced, the plane crashed into a hill and exploded. Being one of forty-five lucky survivors of this harrowing disaster that killed 101 passengers, I was left with extreme post-traumatic stress. For the next three years, I tried everything physicians told me to take to relieve my anxiety of flying, heights, and the recurring nightmares I began having.

I was convinced that my traumatic survival aggravated just about any physical or emotional problem I encountered over the coming years. I lived in the most remote parts of the world in order to meditate and "find myself." It took me about two years to feel somewhat comfortable enough to approach an airport without getting sweaty palms, elevated heart beats, and chest pain. Then my friend Arthur, who happens to be the doctor that saved my life by helping me cope with my anxiety after the crash, introduced me to a short-acting drug that belongs to a group of benzodiazepines. It works by decreasing abnormal excitement in the brain. He said, "Pop one an hour before takeoff and you won't be as nervous anymore."

Boy, was he right! The next time I was at the airport, as I sat at the gate waiting for my plane, I sensed a dramatic shift in attitude. My spine began to tingle and I began to relax. For the first time in years I was able to sleep—and drooled like a sheep dog! Upon arrival at my destination, I picked up my suitcases from the baggage claim and waited for my driver. I checked into my hotel, had dinner with a client, went back to my room, and passed out. The next morning I woke up feeling slightly buzzed and wondering where exactly I was. After rummaging through my pockets, I found several business cards. I then checked my e-mail and saw that people sent me e-mails that said, "It was such a pleasure talking to you on the plane yesterday. Let's keep in touch." I tried to patch together the day's events, but I couldn't. After replying to the e-mails, I found out that I supposedly had scintillating conversations with a couple of my fellow passengers. What? Me? I can't even order water on a plane without taking my eyes off the window! I later found out that my meds were amnestic, meaning they are known to cause temporary (though harmless) episodes of "What the Hell Happened Last Night?" I got scared and promised myself to stop taking them. After ten years of occasionally taking a few here and there, I found some alternative and natural elixirs to take away my fear.

About 15 percent of the general population suffers from anxiety disorders. My hope is that the following recipes will help a few of us take control, whether your anxiety is triggered by a school exam, Obsessive Compulsive Disorder (OCD), or if, like me, you have survived traumatic events. Aromatherapy and inhalation of essential oils such as chamomile, lavender, and thyme have been proven to calm and detangle nerves. Breathing exercises, meditation, and tai chi also promote relaxation. In addition to these natural forms of relief, the following are my top anti-anxiety elixirs.

PARISIAN GEISHA

This, my favorite anti-anxiety libation, also induces erotic dreams. All of my close friends have been treated to it at one time or another. It's a recipe I have played with and evolved to a point where friends find it hard to leave my house without asking for a to-go cup. The spirit used is bourbon, but it can be substituted with cognac or other brandies.

DAMIANA TEA:

8 ounces water

1 damiana tea bag

1 teaspoon sugar

PARISIAN GEISHA:

3 ounces damiana tea

1½ ounces bourbon (I prefer Woodford Reserve)

6 raspberries (or blackberries)

Juice of half a lemon

GARNISH: ROSE PETAL

Our froth on this cocktail provides a perfect base to float a rose petal. Buy a nice red rose. Holding the top of the petal bulb, pull off the green stem. You will notice that all petals instantly come apart and provide you with about 25 usable rose petals. Simply place the petal on top of the froth. Add a water drop on the petal for an extra visual effect.

DIRECTIONS:

DAMIANA TEA: Boil the water in a small saucepan. Once the water boils, add the damiana tea bag and sugar. Reduce heat and stir. Simmer for 10 minutes. Cool before continuing the recipe.

PARISIAN GEISHA: Note there is no need to muddle the raspberries in this recipe. Every pod of the berry has a seed that when cracked releases bitter compounds. Raspberries are quite fragile and will disintegrate while shaking. Combine the ingredients with ice in a cocktail shaker and shake vigorously for about 8 seconds. Strain into a cognac snifter.

The top of the liquid in this cocktail will have a beautiful white froth that's created through the interaction of chemicals and the physical stress on them when shaken. People often add egg whites to provide froth and texture. With the risk of salmonella from raw eggs, I prefer to use simple substitutes. In some cases, teas and citrus fruits or berries create a natural and sometimes colorful froth.

ACTIVE INGREDIENTS:
DAMIANA AND RASPBERRIES

Damiana (turnera diffusa), known as the lover's herb, is a shrub native to Central and South America and the Carribean. The leaves have traditionally been made into tea or incense that has relaxing and libido-boosting effects. Damiana can also be used as a smokeable incense, making it a great way to help quit smoking. Yes, folks, it is legal to roll up a damiana joint and smoke it in public. Its flavor is pleasantly sweet and will remind you of chamomile.

The juice of red and black raspberries is great against anxiety, hypertension, STDs, motion sickness, and hypoglycemia.

TRANQUILI - TEA

My grandmother suffered from severe migraines and stress raising a ton of children, dealing with the war, and generally looking after everybody. My mother took after my grandmother and also suffered from migraines and stress from running her own business. Whenever they needed to calm down, they drank chamomile tea. I can still smell the scent and it calms me down today just thinking about it. This drink is dedicated to the strong women of my family.

CHAMOMILE TEA:

  8 ounces water

  1 chamomile bag

  3 teaspoons sugar

TRANQUILI-TEA:

  3½ ounces chamomile tea

  2 ounces armagnac or cognac (I prefer Hennessy for this but any VS or VSOP will do)

  2 ounces apple cider (or apple juice)

  Splash of fresh lemon juice

DIRECTIONS:

CHAMOMILE TEA: Boil the water in a small saucepan. Once the water boils, add the chamomile tea bag and sugar. Reduce heat and stir. Simmer for 10 minutes. Cool before continuing the recipe.

TRANQUILI-TEA: Combine all ingredients in a cocktail shaker filled with ice. Shake vigorously and strain into an ice-filled rocks glass.

This cocktail can be served hot. Instead of shaking, combine all ingredients in a small sauce pan with a lid and heat slowly. Serve in a tea glass.

> **GARNISH:** APPLE SLICE
> The strong and calming scent of this potion could stand alone as a garnish, but a slice of apple will look lovely on the rim of this natural sedative.

ACTIVE INGREDIENTS:
CHAMOMILE AND ARMAGNAC

Chamomile relaxes the muscles in the body, particularly muscle spasms caused by stress. A main compound in chamomile is apigenin. In the central nervous system, apigenin reacts the same way a pharmaceutical tranquilizer such as valium would, thus relaxing the mind and body without the side effects or risk of addiction. It also works as an excellent sleep aid. Another important compound in chamomile, azulene, is a blue crystalline substance that has been used since early Roman times as a calming aid for heartbreak. Because anxiety can also wreak havoc on your digestion, the anti-inflammatory capabilities of this tea are very useful. Chamomile stimulates the secretion of digestive juices and can even prevent ulcers.

Armagnac is a distinctive brandy from the Armagnac region in southwest France, where for centuries it's been consumed for its therapeutic benefits.

PIPER METHYSTICUM

This is not your grandfather's drink. Wait! Yes it is, but not commonly known for all the wonderful things it can do to your body. I designed this cocktail as a powerful, concentrated shot to act as an emergency potion for those who desire quick relief from stress, a calm mind, and immediate tranquility.

1 ounce liquefied honey
2 ounces whole milk
½ ounce single malt scotch
1 teaspoon kava root powder

DIRECTIONS:

Make liquefied honey by dissolving 1 part honey in 1 part hot water. Refrigerate to cool. Next, prepare kava tea by steeping the powder for about 10 minutes in the cold milk. Combine all ingredients with ice in a cocktail shaker. Shake vigorously for about 8 seconds and strain into a shot glass.

GARNISH: COOKIE OF YOUR CHOICE
It is recommended to have something in your stomach with this shot, so use your favorite cookie for dipping and as a chaser. For me, macadamia nut and chocolate chip cookies work wonders.

ACTIVE INGREDIENT: KAVA
Pacific islanders gave piper methysticum the name kava. It's a hearty perennial which often grows up to three yards or more. The rootstock contains psychoactive substances known as kavalactones. After you purchase the kava root powder (at your local spice store or a health food store), the best way to extract the kavalactones is to soak it in fatty milk. Cow's milk, soy milk, or coconut milk are your best choices and make a tasty drink. When making kava tea, no heat should be used because the active ingredients in kava are destroyed at the high temperatures normally required to make tea. Drinking this infusion relaxes the muscles and creates a state of mild euphoria in the body.

INTERGALACTIC PEACE PIPE

A version of this sweet, savory, flavorful potion dates back to the Middle Ages. I created my concoction of fennel, anis, and honey a few years ago, out of pure desperation to cure and relieve my friend from stress and gastrointestinal problems by rummaging through his spice rack and refrigerator at 4 AM. Back then he was a stressed-out rock star nourished by every drug you can think of. Since then he has become one of my converted friends.

5 fennel leaves

3 ounces cranberry juice

1 ounce grenadine

½ ounce fresh lemon juice

½ teaspoon ground anise

3 pinches of ground ginger

3 ounces light beer (try a German light beer such as Warsteiner, or Japanese Sapporo)

DIRECTIONS:

Place the fennel leaves in a shaker glass and use your muddler to extract the flavor and oils. Add the cranberry juice, grenadine, lemon juice, anis, ginger, and ice to the cocktail shaker. Shake and strain into an ice-filled pilsner glass until it's ¾ full. From 6 inches above the rim, pour the light beer on top of the mixture, creating a foam on top. This aids through an olfactory experience and the calming effect of inhaling hop scent. It also creates a beautiful gradation of color from dark red in the bottom of the glass to a light pink/yellow hue on top.

ACTIVE INGREDIENTS: FENNEL AND ANIS

Anxiety causes gastrointestinal upsets which leads to more anxiety. Fennel is commonly used to heal digestive problems. It contains phytoestrogens that fight against PMS hormonal imbalance in women. Fennel calms the nervous system and is an antispasmodic, which makes it effective in preventing muscle spasms related to stress.

Anis is our second soldier against stress and anxiety in this elixir. Its powerful compound, eugenol, controls the release of neurotransmitters in the brain and has antidepressant effects similar to anti-depression medications. Anis also contains the volatile oil anethol, which relaxes the stomach and stimulates gastric juices.

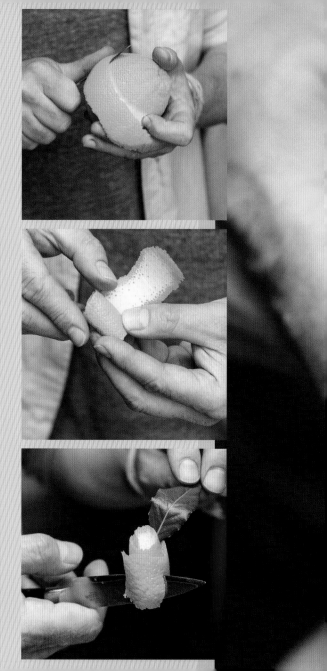

GARNISH: ORANGE SKIN ROSE

This is a great billboard for your drink that can easily be created by using a fruit knife or a potato peeler. Start by slicing off a 1"-wide and 4"-long piece of orange skin. Because of the area the skin was removed from, it will automatically tend to form a spiral on its own. Just go with the direction it's taking you naturally and complete the form by tightly rolling it into the shape of a rose. With your thumb on the end of the peel and your index finger, gently hold the shape upright. Without letting it unfold, cut a ½"-inch incision into the bottom, through all layers. Gently place the rose onto a glass rim and place a bay leaf or a mint leaf into the outer layer to give it a natural touch.

LIQUID TAI CHI

This is a perfect fireplace potion. It contains so many great flavor combinations. Best of all, it's a winetail, a wine-based cocktail that can be served hot or cold.

CHAI TEA:

8 ounces water

1 chai tea bag

3 teaspoons sugar

LIQUID TAI CHI:

3 ounces apple cider

2 ounces chai tea

2 ounces Ecco Domani merlot

1 ounce Svedka Vanilla Vodka

Pinch of ground ginger

DIRECTIONS:

CHAI TEA: Boil the water in a small saucepan. Once the water boils, add the chai tea bag and sugar. Reduce heat and stir. Simmer for 10 minutes. Cool before continuing the recipe.

LIQUID TAI CHI: Combine all ingredients in a cocktail shaker filled with ice. Shake vigorously for 8 seconds and strain into a martini glass.

GARNISH: APPLE SLICE

All garnishes should reflect at least one of the ingredients present in the libation. The apple is perfect for this drink. We can either use a good old cookie cutter for a shape (such as a leaf, as I like to use), or simply cut an apple slice and place it on the rim of the glass.

ACTIVE INGREDIENT: CHAI

Chai tea is made up of several ingredients, with a base of black tea. It contains polyphenols, which are extremely beneficial for heart health and in prevention of cancers. Black tea also contains tannin, which acts like caffeine, but unlike caffeine from coffee, it calms the nervous system. Cloves, ginger, cardamom, pepper, and nutmeg are the remaining ingredients, all of which have additional healing powers and endow chai with a beautiful fragrance.

HANGOVER PREVENTION CURES & RESPONSIBLE REVELRY

What are hangovers and why do they hurt so much?

While there are products that promise relief the day after alcohol consumption, the truth is that by the time the hangover sets in, it's irreversible. The following cures jumpstart the body's natural recovery process before hangover symptoms have the chance to ruin your day. For starters, forget about the myths of burgers and other fatty comfort foods being cure-alls. They only temporarily disguise the pain.

When you drink alcohol you ingest a toxin. The body needs certain substances to fight these toxins. If they are depleted you have a real problem. Acetaldehyde, a toxic byproduct of alcohol, is one of the main culprits that makes your life a living hell. It produces pounding headaches and nausea. There are a few amazing substances that fortify your body against the damages caused by alcohol. Amino acids, vitamins, antioxidants, electrolytes, and several herbal supplements are needed to detoxify your body, boost its defenses, and replenish key nutrients. This chapter deals with natural and nutrient-packed cocktails that help prevent the aftereffects of a hangover.

ANGEL OF MERCY

This cocktail was the first designed using the hangover prevention drink I helped to develop and flavor, Mercy. Since the product has a neutral lemon flavor, it can work as the citrus component of any cocktail.

3 ounces cranberry juice
1½ ounces New Amsterdam Gin (or Svedka Vodka—any neutral grain base will work)
1 ounce grenadine
3 pinches of ground ginger
2 ounces Mercy

DIRECTIONS:

Combine the cranberry juice, gin, grenadine, and ginger in a cocktail shaker. In general, it is not recommended that you shake carbonated beverages in a cocktail shaker. The shaker will pop open and shower you with fizzy liquid. So set the Mercy aside for now and shake the mixture and strain into an ice-filled highball glass, ¼ of the way up. Float the Mercy on top and serve with a straw.

GARNISH: GINGER AND JASMINE

This cocktail can be garnished with several ingredients that are featured in the recipe. A lemon wheel, some fresh cranberries, or as featured in this shot, two slices of ginger root and a fresh jasmine flower. Simply slice off two interesting sections from a big ginger root, cut an incision into each, and place them on the rim of the cocktail glass. Wedge a fresh jasmine flower in between.

ACTIVE INGREDIENT: MERCY

Mercy launched in the spring of 2011. I was introduced to Dave Shor, the founder of the product, two years earlier. He led me into the amazing research he has conducted over ten years and asked me if I could refine the formula and flavor the product. After endless flavor experiments, hot box tests, trips to the lab, and vitamin B buzzes, we finally did it: we created a lightly carbonated, caffeine-free, nonalcoholic beverage that could fortify the body against the damages of alcohol, replenish nutrients, and alleviate the alcohol flush (the red cheeks).

Mercy is a unique proprietary blend of alpha-ketoglutaric acid; chamomile extract; milk thistle; L-carnitine; N-acetyl cystein; vitamins B1, B3, B6, B12, and C; and folic acid. It's flavored by a natural citrus accompanied by undertones of lemongrass, jasmine, and ginger. You can drink it during or after alcohol consumption. Have one can of Mercy for every five drinks containing spirits. It can be drank on its own or mixed with your favorite spirit to create a variety of delicious cocktails.

SCOTTISH MARY

This is one of my all-time favorite savory brunch drinks. Additionally, this single malt scotch Bloody Mary makes a great marinade and base for steak sauce.

    4 ounces tomato juice
    1½ ounces Ardbeg Single Malt Scotch
    1 ounce grenadine
    ½ ounce fresh lemon juice
    1 teaspoon bacon bits
    2 pinches of cayenne pepper

DIRECTIONS:

Combine all ingredients in a cocktail shaker filled with ice. Shake vigorously and strain over an ice-filled highball glass.

GARNISH: TOMATO-BASIL-LEMON SPEAR

Spear a cherry tomato, a basil leaf, and a lemon slice with a skewer. Place the skewer on top of the glass. You can also float a teaspoon of bacon bits on top for extra flavor.

ACTIVE INGREDIENTS: TOMATO, LEMON, AND CAYENNE PEPPER

As we know, we need a fair amount of antioxidants, vitamins, and nutrients to replenish our body after a night of debauchery. Some juices are perfect for this purpose, including tomato. The main organic compound found in tomatoes is lycopene, a carotene rich with antioxidants and anti-aging properties that is great for hangover prevention. When ingested, lycopene collects in the liver and in men, the prostate. Additionally, the levels of vitamins A and C in tomato juice provide the body with 72% of the daily recommended amounts. These are important in helping the immune system and destroying the toxins in our blood stream that are responsible for cell damage.

Our second fighter in this cocktail is lemon juice, which is loaded with ascorbic acid, the dose of vitamin C we need to fortify our body.

Lastly, we have cayenne pepper, which contains magnesium, an important mineral that is depleted in the body during alcohol consumption.

A DATE WITH ALEX OTT

People who consume small amounts of alcohol mixed with fresh juices over a longer period of time will not only have a better time than their friends downing vodka shots, but also a better functioning body the next day. Following is my safe "long drink" for going out on the town. It's tequila based and has a great flavor combination.

2 ounces Don Julio Blanco Tequila (or Fidencio Mezcal)
4 ounces pineapple juice
2 lime wedges

DIRECTIONS:

Fill a highball glass with ice. Pour in the tequila, then the pineapple juice, and then squeeze the juice of both lime wedges on top.

GARNISH: TRAPPED PINEAPPLE AND LIME WHEEL

For this drink, let's go a little crazy. Cut a fresh pineapple slice into four equal triangular pieces. Take one triangle and filet it right in the middle to create an open pineapple slice. Cut off a thin slice of lime and place it in the pineapple pocket. The last step is to cut an incision through both the pineapple skin and the trapped lime wheel inside. Hold the fruit in place so they don't shift and place the garnish on the rim of the glass.

ACTIVE INGREDIENT: PINEAPPLE

Pineapple juice is our main friend here. This drink is basically all pineapple. Yes, tequila is made from a pineapple. The core of the agave plant is a "piña," in which there is sugar to produce alcohol. Fruit juice, like pineapple, increases energy, replaces depleted vitamins and nutrients, and speeds up the process of ridding the body of toxins. Pineapple juice contains an enzyme called bromelain, which is a natural anti-inflammatory and encourages healing in the body. It is also rich in B vitamins and potassium that the body needs, especially after and during alcohol consumption. The B6 in pineapple juice helps regulate the blood sugar levels and the immune system. This is an easy drink to order at a bar when there is nothing else decent on the menu!

COPACABANA

This drink is a great potion to boost your body's immune system and provide it with plenty of vitamin B complexes to fight against the toxins of alcohol consumption. I designed this drink during a surfing trip in Maresias, Brazil, where I had way too much access to bananas and rum, especially cachaca. Great and affordable brands of cachaca for this drink are Beleza Pura and Pira Pora.

1 lime
Half of a banana
1½ ounces light rum (Bacardi Silver, Montecristo Platinum, or cachaca)
1½ ounces guava juice
1 teaspoon sugar

DIRECTIONS:

Get your biceps and your muddler ready for some mashing action. Cut the lime into 8 pieces and place them in the shaker glass. Muddle the lime, extracting as much juice as possible. Peel a banana and use half of it for our drink. Tear the banana piece into a few chunks and toss them on top of the limes. Muddle until the banana is fully mashed. Next, add all remaining ingredients to the glass along with ice. Shake the mixture vigorously and pour all ingredients in a rocks glass.

GARNISH: BANANA

We can use the other half of that banana for our garnish. Cut the piece in two diagonal sections. A slice of banana might look a little boring, but our elongated splinter will give the drink a more interesting dynamic.

ACTIVE INGREDIENT: BANANA

Bananas provide B6, B12, and electrolytes that replenish potassium and magnesium lost because of the diuretic effects of alcohol. Bananas also contain tryptophan, an essential amino acid. Trypophan has the effect of reducing depression after drinking. It functions as a precursor for serotonin and niacin, which lead to an improved mood.

TOKYO FIZZ

This exceptional refresher will knock your socks off. Not as potent as other cocktails, it's a replenishing elixir that will keep you going for a long time.

1 ounce simple syrup
Stems of lemongrass
Sprig of fresh mint
2 ounces Junmai sake (Otokoyama or
  Kaori are flavorful and inexpensive)
¾ ounce fresh lime juice
3 pinches of ground ginger
1½ ounce sparkling mineral water

DIRECTIONS:

Make simple syrup by dissolving 1 part sugar in 1 part hot water. Store in the refrigerator and cool before continuing the recipe. Cut the lemongrass stem into small pieces. The stem has many layers, so it will be easiest to cut it at a crooked angle. Place the pieces in a cocktail shaker glass and muddle hard, pounding down on the lemongrass 15 times. Detach about 10 leaves from the mint sprig and toss them into the glass. Muddle a few times to release the mint flavor.

Add the sake, simple syrup, lime juice, and ground ginger to the glass. Add ice and shake vigorously for about 8 seconds. Strain into an ice-filled highball glass, up to ¾ full. Float sparkling mineral water on top.

GARNISH: LIME WHEEL

Cut a lime in half and slice off a wheel from the center. Cut halfway up from the bottom and place the garnish on the rim of the glass.

ACTIVE INGREDIENT: GINGER

Ginger is a magic product. It takes up most pages in any herbal manual, health book, or homeopathic encyclopedia. It is a powerful antioxidant, anticoagulant, and benefits the liver by helping the assimilation of compounds from other herbs. The liver usually breaks down chemicals from herbs and makes them less effective; ginger prevents this process. Thus, using ginger before or during drinking keeps liver cells healthy. Ginger is also beneficial after drinking because its compound acts as an anti-diarrheal. The aforementioned "other herbs" that play with ginger in this drink are lemongrass and mint, both of which also contain powerfully beneficial chemicals.

DRINKING THE FOUNTAIN OF YOUTH: ANTI-AGING ELIXIRS

Today's beverage industry is problematic and confused by an incredibly high volume of products and marketing traps. Many beverages, like energy drinks that promise you the stamina of a six-year-old at a birthday party, are fortified with insane amounts of high-fructose corn syrup, modifiers, coloring agents, and preservatives, and then intensely loaded with artificial "tasty" flavors. Some of them become popular not because of the quality of ingredients, but because advertisers use the latest overnight role model to make the masses believe that the product will bring them something extra special: energy? style? popularity? Most of the time, all energy drinks do is give people stomach ulcers, cancer, insomnia, anxiety, premature aging, and a multitude of other side effects that are often irreversible. There has to be a better way.

Lifestyle is much more important in the aging process than herbs and botanicals, but the scrumptious concoctions in this chapter use ingredients that can hold back the aging process—at least for the time you're enjoying the cocktail.

THE FOUNTAIN OF YOUTH

This replenishing, spa-like drink acts as a liquid rejuvenator and anti-aging elixir. I first made this fifteen years ago in London, when I stayed with a friend who was obsessed with cucumbers, to which she attributed her great skin. She dared me to make a cucumber martini, which was indeed "daring" for a cocktail back then. From a cucumber combined with the following ingredients I found in her apartment, I came up with one of the best-selling drinks in Manhattan. It incorporates a favorite British liqueur, Pimm's No. 1, and white cranberry juice, which is a bit sweeter and less bitter than the standard cranberry.

3 slices of cucumber
3 ounces white cranberry juice
1½ ounces New Amsterdam Gin
Splash of fresh lime juice
Dash of Pimm's No. 1
Drop of Angostura bitters

DIRECTIONS:

Start by muddling the cucumber slices in a shaker. Add the remaining ingredients and ice, and shake vigorously for 8 seconds. Strain the mixture into a martini glass.

ACTIVE INGREDIENTS: CUCUMBER, BITTERS, LIME, AND GIN

Cucumber juice acts as one of nature's finest rejuvenators by liberally removing pockets of old waste material and chemical toxins from the body. It contains plenty of nutrients, including amounts of B-complex vitamins such as thiamine, riboflavin, and niacin, as well as magnesium. This cocktail would also fit perfectly in the hangover prevention chapter, but when it comes to aging, hangovers and the effect on the body go hand in hand.

The dash of bitters is helpful against ulcers and its compounds aid in stimulating appetite by supporting the secretion of saliva.

Fresh lime juice is thought to relieve muscle aches and cramps and provides the perfect acidity to our cocktail.

All combined with gin, which was once used to treat female troubles, this cocktail has been known to work wonders on ladies suffering from PMS symptoms.

GARNISH: CUCUMBER FLOWER

It's important to choose the right cucumber when cutting cucumber flowers. Slimmer is better, and the darker the cucumber the more nutrients it will contain. The ends should be hard and the mid-section firm and smooth. Depending on length, a whole cucumber can make 10–12 garnishes.

Use a sharp knife to cut into your cucumber. Do not cut with your right hand if you are right handed. Hold the cucumber in your left hand and place the knife in your right hand, but push the blade with your left thumb to cut. The right hand simply holds the knife and regulates the angle. Careful not to place the knife blade at a steep angle, start your incision by piercing the cucumber skin. In a peeling motion, push the blade parallel under the skin for about 1/2" and then cut a curved groove (if you cut a straight line, you will end up with a box-like shape) toward the middle of the cucumber. When you are about 30 percent in, stop cutting and pull the knife out. When making the second incision (petal #2), start the same way and connect it with the end of the first. I recommend no more than five incisions.

When you have completed the full circle, gently twist the end of the cucumber to the left and right until the end comes off. If you are not completely satisfied, or if the cucumber resembles a bulky crown, you probably cut the incisions too thick and straight. Don't get frustrated. Practice makes perfect!

ALOE MATE

Grow an aloe plant in your room. You will thank me for it. When you have a cut, slice off a piece of aloe and apply the gel directly to your skin. Whether you have dermatitis, burns, or cuts, aloe is the best catalyst for healing. This aloe drink, which I invented for my mother, is insanely healthy and one of my strongest anti-inflammatory potions. It has an effect on both your insides and the outside—as in your skin, the body's largest organ.

10 red grapes
3 ounces aloe juice
2 ounces lychee juice (or pineapple juice)
1 ounce Ecco Domani Pinot Grigio
Splash of fresh lemon juice

DIRECTIONS:

Place the grapes in a shaker glass and muddle until they are completely mashed. Add the remaining ingredients, with plenty of ice, and shake hard for about 8 seconds. Pour the entire contents into a wine glass.

> **GARNISH:** ALOE OR LYCHEE
>
> There are great garnish options for this potion. We can either take a piece of aloe and put it on the rim or try to find a rambutan, which is a type of lychee fruit. It looks like a gremlin that has been fed after midnight. It is a light, gelatinous fruit with a nut inside which is encased in a dark red shell covered with inch-long tentacle-like hairs. When you slice the shell halfway open it exposes the fruit. Squeeze the fruit on the rim of a glass.

Aloe has been used for more than three thousand years as a cosmetic and in medicine. Best known for its cooling effect, aloe makes the skin feel renewed. It heels sunburn and fights against acne. Aloe also works internally when ingested because its trace minerals, vitamin A and beta carotene give it anti-aging properties. It protects the body from inflammation, promotes bone growth, and even helps against allergies. Aloe juice contains amino acids that the body needs. Regular consumption of aloe juice helps keep the intestines healthy because of its antimicrobial and pain-killing properties. Because pure aloe juice tends to have a bitter aftertaste, I suggest you sweeten it with honey.

Grapes, of course, are a great base for alcoholic beverages and fermented juices, but they also contain a wonderful polyphenol called resveratrol. This is a substance that blueberries and grapes produce as a natural defense against cold temperatures and stress. It also has anti-aging properties but most amazing of all, resveratrol has been proven to prevent cancer.

THYME FLIES

I created this drink for a French-Mexican fusion bistro in Paris. Thyme was one of the powerful antioxidant herbs that they had in the cellar. I was never a big fan of the flavor of thyme, slightly bitter and very potent. They also had avocados in bulk. So what could I do for their house concoction? Here it is!

Sprig of thyme (dried thyme works too)
1 ripe avocado
2 ounces pineapple juice
1½ ounces Don Julio Blanco Tequila
   (or Fidencio Mezcal)
½ ounce fresh lime juice

DIRECTIONS:

Muddle the thyme sprig in a cocktail shaker, taking care not to destroy or rip the leaves. Carve out the flesh of the avocado and mash it to a soft pulp. Add all remaining ingredients and ice and shake the mixture for at least 12 seconds so the avocado can fully mix with the liquids. Strain into a martini glass.

GARNISH: AVOCADO AND THYME

Use avocado again for our garnish. The only way to test the ripeness of this amazing fruit is to squeeze it gently. If it feels similar to a ripe peach, get it. For the garnish, slice an avocado in half and carefully peel it, leaving the flesh in one piece. Spear the piece with a thyme sprig and gently squeeze the avocado onto the rim of your martini glass.

ACTIVE INGREDIENT: THYME

Thyme contains the organic compound caffeic acid, which has strong anti-inflammatory properties. Thyme is the most antioxidant herb on the planet. Its compound protects skin cells and has anti-cancer properties. Apigenin, luteolin, and thymonin are flavonoids in thyme that increase the healthy fat in our cell structure. Apigenin, a particularly powerful antioxidant, guards the skin from the harmful sun rays that lead to aging. For this reason, thyme is often used in skincare products.

INDIAN TIME MACHINE

The following drink is to be consumed in the morning. While working at a restaurant in Mumbai, the cooking ingredients were often depleted to one: turmeric. As strange as this ingredient might taste to Westerners, I had to find a way to integrate it into my homeopathic cocktails because of its unique and unmatched healing powers and anti-aging properties.

2 ounces fresh orange juice

1½ ounces Svedka Clementine Vodka

½ ounce fresh lemon juice

1 teaspoon orange marmalade

2 pinches of turmeric

DIRECTIONS:

Combine all ingredients in a cocktail shaker filled with ice. Shake vigorously and strain into an ice-filled highball glass.

GARNISH: ORANGE ZEST

Use a zester to create a flavorful orange garnish. Slightly rub the skin of the orange over the fine zester and create enough zest to loosely cover the surface of the cocktail.

ACTIVE INGREDIENT: TURMERIC

Turmeric has been a staple of Indian cooking for thousands of years. It's now widely praised for its healing powers. Chronic illness in India is much lower than in Western countries, especially the U.S. Turmeric owes its curative powers to one main ingredient: curcumin. Curcumin is a compound so rich in antioxidant and anti-inflammatory powers that it has been shown to improve the health and wellbeing of every organ in the human body. Its properties have been shown to protect against everything from cancer to heart attack, type 2 diabetes, Alzheimer's, and scores of other maladies.

LATIN LOVER

I first came across tamarind while growing up in Africa. There it's not normally applied in cooking; it is more often used as a folk remedy for respiratory illnesses and digestive problems. I first introduced this drink incorporating tamarind at a Japanese/Peruvian/Brazilian fusion restaurant in which I had the pleasure of working. I had no idea then what a powerful punch of antioxidants it packed, but the more I studied herbs, the more I learned how amazing tamarind is.

2 ounces tamarind paste or tamarind juice (Goya makes a great one)
2 ounces cranberry juice
1½ ounces Macallan 12 Year Old Scotch
½ ounce almond paste (or amaretto, for almond flavor)
½ ounce molasses
½ ounce lemon juice

DIRECTIONS:
Combine all ingredients in a cocktail shaker filled with ice. Shake vigorously for about 8 seconds and strain over an ice-filled rocks glass.

GARNISH: TAMARIND POD AND MARZIPAN
Tamarind pods make a great garnish because you can cut them open to use as a stirrer, constantly releasing more flavor into your drink.

Another nice garnish would be a marzipan marble. Take a piece of marzipan (which is simply almond paste). Create a perfect sphere by placing it between your palms and rolling it as if making a meatball. Gently cut a small incision into the sphere and place it on the rim of your elixir.

ACTIVE INGREDIENT: TAMARIND
Tamarind contains many powerful antioxidants, including tartaric acid, which gives tamarind its sour flavor. Tamarind is a great source of vitamin B, riboflavin, calcium, niacin, and thiamine. These phytonutrients give tamarind many healing powers and anti-aging properties. Tamarind reduces the inflammation in our cells that cause the development of many heart diseases.

APHRODISIACS &
MAGIC TINCTURES

While researchers, scientists, would-be magicians, and love-sick romantics have been attempting to produce aphrodisiacs, magic love potions, and libido enhancers for thousands of years, real and working romance-enhancing potions have rarely found their way to the average cocktail lover. The ingredients I pick up around the world that have been used as aphrodisiacs never cease to amaze me. In this chapter are some mind-blowing, stiff drinks designed for better performance.

THE LITTLE DEATH

I designed this shot years ago after returning from Mexico for the first time. As you have probably experienced after coming back from vacation and enjoying a special beach cocktail, it never tastes quite as good when you try to recreate it at home. Why, you ask? Well, obviously the atmosphere is more pleasant on vacation, but your palate is also more excited and stimulated when you are in a foreign country and you are more open to new things. This libation is designed to give you an experience of rare flavor combinations.

Most people take tequila in a margarita or as a shot. What's in a margarita? Tequila mixed with orange liquor and some lime juice. At most average bars, chances are the margarita is made with triple sec, an artificially orange-flavored, high-fructose corn syrup mixture with alcohol, and sour mix, which in most cases consists of artificial lemon/lime-flavored high-fructose corn syrup. No wonder people end up having some stomach problems and weight gain. Meanwhile, tequila shots are mostly served with salt and lime, which closes your palate and gives us a sour face. Neither method highlights the undertones and nuances of this wonderful spirit made from the pineapple (piña) of the blue agave plant. If you've had bad experiences with tequila in the past, the following recipe will change your mind. You can use almost any variety of tequila for this drink, but it works particularly great with aged tequilas, the so-called añejos.

1½ ounces tequila
1 orange
Pinch of ground cinnamon

DIRECTIONS:

Pour the tequila into a shot glass and set it aside while you prepare the chaser. First, cut off the end of the orange and then cut a ¾"-thick slice. Lay the slice flat on a cutting board and cut the skin off to create a perfect square with 90 degree angles. One square can provide up to 4 chasers. If there are two doing a shot, cut the square diagonally into two triangle-shaped orange chasers. Using your index finger and thumb pick up a small amount of ground cinnamon and place a mound on top of each chaser. Take your shot of tequila and follow with the chaser.

ACTIVE INGREDIENTS: TEQUILA AND CINNAMON

The potent active ingredient in this is alcohol. Yes, that's it! Now, don't go shut the book and tell your friends that you've finally found the magic potion. It is true that alcohol works as a very strong aphrodisiac since it is a central nervous depressant. It can relieve stress, muscle tension, and pain; hence, the cool cowboy drinking a swig of whiskey before removing the bullet. Its euphoric effects combined with the decrease in social inhibitions provided by alcohol works as a very effective sexual stimulant indeed.

In men, alcohol consumption accelerates testosterone production, making it a potent aphrodisiac. In women, alcohol increases their levels of the hormone estradiol, the most potent of all estrogen steroids, leading to an overall interest in sex. One might say that this would be enough and let's wrap it up, but chemistry is a wonderful thing, and the plethora of feelings that phyto chemicals evoke has to be fully experienced.

Cinnamon increases sex drive gradually. It allows more blood flow to the genitals, because it lowers blood sugar, resulting in longer and better sex.

LOVE IN A GLASS

This libido-enhancing drink was originally designed for Sushi Samba, where it was called Choco Loco. I created it to make people fall in love with each other. My regular customers called it "love in a glass!"

1½ ounces Svedka Vanilla Vodka
1½ ounces chocolate syrup (or Nutella)
1 ounce espresso (or coffee)
2½ ounces heavy whipping cream
1 teaspoon sugar

DIRECTIONS:

Combine the vodka, chocolate syrup, and espresso in a cocktail shaker filled with ice. Shake vigorously and strain into a martini glass.

Grab a second shaker (or clean out the first) and combine the cream and sugar. Shake for about 6 seconds, then check to see if it's still liquid. The cream has to be thick but still able to pour. With the cream inside the tin part of your cocktail shaker, hold it over the martini glass and rest the rim of the shaker on the rim of the glass. Let the cream slowly pour along the glass side, down into the base. The cream will distribute itself and stay layered forever. It won't sink unless you dilute it. Note this process will work with whipping cream but not any other kind of milk.

> **GARNISH:** GOLD LEAF
> To decorate this drink, I often use 23-carat gold leaf or sterling silver flakes called Argento Fino or Oro Fino from Easy Leaf Products (info@easyleaf-products.com). It is a bit pricey, but will make a seducing difference in your cocktail garnish.

ACTIVE INGREDIENT: CHOCOLATE

This wonderful product made out of cocoa beans contains two chemicals that boost sexual desire and enhance moods. Phenylalanine is an amino acid that boosts arousal. Seratonin is a strong mood enhancer. When we eat chocolate the two combine and are released into the central nervous system the same way they are when the brain releases them. This induces feelings of love and lust. Caffeine, which is also present in cocoa, energizes and improves longevity, stamina, and libido. The extra kick of espresso or coffee makes our libation a strong libido enhancer.

APHRODITE'S PUNCH

We already used damiana, in the chapter for anti-stress and anxiety drinks, but what I didn't tell you then is that damiana is also the "lover's herb," a strong aphrodisiac. This punch makes perfect sangria and works well on long, hot summer nights. One of the main reasons I chose this drink to be consumed before bedtime: it induces erotic dreams!

DAMIANA AND HIBISCUS TEA:
   2 liters spring water
   10 hibiscus tea bags
   10 damiana tea bags

APHRODITE'S PUNCH:
   ½ gallon/2 liters hibiscus and damiana tea
   1 bottle of Ecco Domani Merlot
   3 ounces lemon juice
   12 tablespoons sugar

DIRECTIONS:

DAMIANA AND HIBISCUS TEA: In a large pot, bring the water to a boil. Once boiling, reduce the heat and add the damiana and hibiscus bags. Steep for about 6 minutes, then squeeze the remaining fluid from the tea bags and allow the tea to cool before continuing the recipe.

APHRODITE'S PUNCH: Combine the tea, merlot, lemon juice, and sugar with the remaining ingredients in a punch bowl. Cover and store in the refrigerator for 2 hours.

If you want to make individual drinks right away, you can use the warm mix. Shake it up in a cocktail shaker with ice and strain into an ice-filled punch glass.

If your punch is meant for a party without a bartender, prepare a big bowl and place a large ice rock in it instead of ice cubes. The ice rock will keep the mixture cold for a long time without diluting it too much.

GARNISH: HIBISCUS

You can purchase dried hibiscus flowers at your local market. Float one or more on top of the liquid. Rose petals, from which hibiscus is derived, also provide a great floating garnish.

ACTIVE INGREDIENT: DAMIANA

Besides the anti-anxiety effects that we have already covered about damiana, it is a hormone neutralizer affecting the endocrine glands and their secretions. Damiana helps with infertility in both males and females. It increases the sperm count in the male and strengthens the egg in the female. It is also known to increase sex drive in both men and women. The leaves of our lover's herb contain sitosterol and aromatic oils that are responsible for the stimulant effect and building of the sexual reproductive systems. In women it is especially good for coping with menopausal symptoms and PMS. If all that's not enough, damiana also provides the body with essential calcium, potassium, selenium, and vitamin C.

TURISTA

I went to Brazil a long time ago, many years before a known energy drink (that makes you "fly") flooded the market. There I was introduced to an amazing extract from which sodas could be made: guarana. It affected me in a few cool ways and I decided to do some more research, which led me to use guarana in many more drinks. One of these is the Turista, which also incorporates cachaca, Brazilian rum made from fresh-pressed sugar cane juice. This cocktail is a simple, foolproof way to have fun wherever you go, be it the Amazon or in the city jungle.

Half of an orange
3 teaspoons light brown sugar
1½ ounces cachaca (or dark rum)
1 teaspoon guarana powder

DIRECTIONS:

Chop the orange half into 4 pieces and place them in a cocktail shaker. Pour the brown sugar on top and muddle until all the orange juice is extracted.

Add the cachaca, guarana, and ice, and shake vigorously. Pour all contents into a rocks glass.

ACTIVE INGREDIENT: GUARANA

Guarana is a berry of a climbing plant that grows in the Amazon basin. Its seeds are ground and used for many purposes. It contains guaranine, a crystallized compound which, at its chemical basis, is identical to caffeine. The stimulant properties of guarana increase not only sexual arousal but alertness, too. It stimulates the nerves and stays effective for a more prolonged period than caffeine from coffee beans.

GARNISH: CLEMENTINE WHEEL

You can do this with a clementine, small orange, or lemon, as pictured here.

Take a clementine and cut off the very end of the fruit so you expose the flesh. With a sharp, non-serrated fruit knife, make an incision into the fruit holding the knife blade at a 45 degree angle while you slowly push and rotate the fruit on the cutting board forward for about 1/3 of a whole rotation while you cut back and forth three times. Repeating this motion will create an endless spiral. When you turn the fruit twice you'll have about three thin layers. Cut the garnish from the fruit, pull it apart a bit, and place it over the rim of the cocktail glass, as shown on page 101.

AS THE ROMANS DO

I designed this cocktail for a well-known wine producer. No matter what wine connoisseurs say, wine can indeed be mixed into cocktails. The invention of "winetails" goes back a long time. The Egyptians, for instance, were superior to present-day naysayers when it came to "cocktail alchemy." The Druids also knew a lot about alchemy and aphrodisiacs. Inspired by our ancient ancestors, I introduced this potion as part of my collection.

Sprig of rosemary
Half of a lime
1½ teaspoons sugar
2½ ounces Ecco Domani Merlot
½ ounce fresh orange juice

GARNISH: ROSEMARY AND LIME SPEAR

We will use the other halves of the rosemary and lime for our garnish. First, cut a slice of the lime. Spear the lime wheel in the middle with the sprig of rosemary. Place the skewered lime wheel on the surface of the elixir.

DIRECTIONS:

Split the rosemary sprig in half and place one piece inside a cocktail shaker glass.

Gently muddle until the overpowering scent of rosemary hits your nose. Cut the lime half into 6 pieces. Add the lime and sugar to the cocktail shaker and muddle again. Once the lime juice has been extracted, add the wine and orange juice and fill the shaker with ice. Shake vigorously and pour all contents into a rocks glass.

ACTIVE INGREDIENTS: RED WINE AND ROSEMARY

Red wine is a powerful aphrodisiac, especially in women. (Not to worry, ladies, our second active ingredient has a stronger affect on males.) The chemical compounds in red wine increase blood flow to erogenous zones. Red wine contains resveratrol. This substance comes from the skin of grapes and increases estrogen and testosterone production, both of which heighten arousal and raise libido levels.

Rosemary is also a physical stimulant because it contains caffeic acid. This increases mental alertness and leads to increased sex drive. Rosemary's intoxicating scent is also said to evoke sensual arousal in men. So next time you cook chicken and potatoes for a date, make sure to use rosemary. You never know what the night may have in store for you.

LEFT: THE VIEW FROM THE HUNTLEY HOTEL IN SANTA MONICA. I USUALLY COME TO CALIFORNIA FOR THREE THINGS: GREAT SURF, ORANGES, AND BLUEBERRIES.

RIGHT: THE VIEW FROM THE PALACE OF MY FRIEND PRINCESS PADMAJA, LOOKING OUT TO THE LAKE IN UDAIPUR, INDIA. IT WAS HERE I WAS INTRODUCED TO LIFE-CHANGING FLAVORS SUCH AS SANDALWOOD, JASMINE, AND ROSE.

UPPERS, DISCO DRINKS, & LIFE SAVERS

Forget about "The Vesper," ulcer-causing energy drinks, or illegal drugs. These cocktails will stimulate every synapse, keep you going without crashing, and make you look like nothing can bring you down.

TOBACCO VANILLA

A few years ago I was hired to consult on a fragrance for one of my favorite clothing designers. I was happy to see it become a best seller in select stores across Manhattan. Women love it. I decided to design a drinkable version to achieve a similar olfactory experience with a stimulating effect. The result was one of my all-time most popular concoctions. I feature this cocktail in some of the most high-end events around the world, and now share the recipe with you.

½ ounce liquefied honey
2½ ounces pear juice
1½ ounces spiced rum (Montecristo or
   Captain Morgan)
½ ounce fresh lime juice
1 teaspoon fig jam
Pinch of sandalwood powder (available in
   Indian spice stores)

DIRECTIONS:

Make liquefied honey by dissolving 1 part honey in 1 part hot water. Cool in the refrigerator before continuing the recipe. Next, combine all ingredients in a cocktail shaker filled with ice. Shake vigorously for about 10 seconds and strain over ice in a tumbler.

GARNISH: FIG OR LIME
Fresh figs are a perfect garnish for this drink. Cut a fresh or dried fig in half and place it on the rim of the glass, as pictured. We can also use a square citrus garnish for this drink. Cut a lime in half and slice a thick lime wheel. Using 90-degree angled cuts, create a square lime garnish. The lime garnish also provides some extra citrus to the elixir in case it is too sweet for you.

ACTIVE INGREDIENT: PEAR
Pears contain high levels of glucose and fructose, and keep you going for the whole day—or your night out on the town.

GAS PANIC

Energy drinks nowadays are designed to give you energy, but they come with a ton of side effects, too. Among the multitude of problems you risk unleashing on your body when you consume some of those curiously flavored 2–10-hour energy drinks are insomnia, sweats, and jitters. I have to wonder if the creators of these products actually enjoy drinking them. While working in Tokyo, I consulted for a nightclub whose employees were hooked on energy drinks. Within a week I converted them all to the local gold people have consumed for a thousand years: green tea! If you plan on staying up and partying while drinking, this elixir is perfect for you.

2½ ounces mango nectar
1½ ounces Svedka Vodka (or New Amsterdam Gin)
½ ounce fresh lemon juice
2 pinches of powdered green tea

DIRECTIONS:

Combine all ingredients in an ice-filled cocktail shaker. Shake vigorously and strain into a martini glass.

GARNISH: LEMON WHEEL AND ZEST

To increase the citrus in our potion, use a zester on the outside of a lemon and sprinkle a dusting of zest on the surface of the cocktail. Next, cut a slice of lemon and place the wheel on the glass rim.

ACTIVE INGREDIENT: GREEN TEA

Green tea contains the alkaloids caffeine, theobromine, and theophylline. Theobromine widens your heart vessels. This substance stimulates your heart to a greater degree than caffeine or taurine, with less of an impact on the central nervous system. The caffeine and polyphenols in green tea also stimulate fat oxidation and are a big metabolism booster.

My friends Jorge Vergara and Angelica Fuentes had an amazing wedding celebration in India and Mexico a few years ago and they hired me to concoct some special drinks for the beach party. After consuming all the champagne at the beginning of the soiree, people started to crash a bit even though the night was still young. I prepared a special drink that could satisfy people's food craving and pick them up to get the party going again. It did the trick! When I go out in New York (or any other city), I choose this drink, the ingredients of which are stocked in the kitchens of most restaurants.

Sprig of cilantro
1½ ounces Fidencio Mezcal (or Don Julio Blanco Rum)
3 ounces pineapple juice
2 teaspoons fresh lime juice
1 Thai chili pepper (or jalapeno)
2 pinches of cayenne pepper
Pinch of ground ginger

DIRECTIONS:

Place the cilantro sprig in a cocktail shaker. Muddle until you detect the cilantro scent and see a few green drops of cilantro juice. This will give the cocktail a light green color.

Add all remaining ingredients, plus ice, to the shaker. Shake vigorously for about 8 seconds and strain the mix over ice in a rocks glass. You will notice a white froth on top of your potion. If there's no froth, put it back in the shaker and shake longer.

Pineapple juice is responsible for the froth. When shaken hard it gives cocktails great texture.

ACTIVE INGREDIENT: CAYENNE PEPPER

Cayenne pepper is our upper. It contains a powerful phytochemical called capsaicin. Capsaicin stimulates the body without the threatening side effects of increased heart rate and high blood pressure caused by most "upper" drugs. Capsaicin enhances cardiovascular function and boosts circulation, making it a very strong stimulant. Cayenne pepper also contains magnesium, one of the body's nutrients that is lost during alcohol consumption.

GARNISH: CHILI PEPPER RIM

In the middle of a saucer pour ½ teaspoon of honey. Around it, pour a handful of crushed chili pepper in a circular motion so it resembles a ¼"-inch high ring. Next, dip the rim of the glass into the honey and rotate it to cover the entire rim. After an even honey rim is achieved, dip the glass rim into the crushed pepper ring and gently shake off the loose pieces.

BARDOT

For those who work or study a lot and need to stay up, grapefruit juice is the way to go. I drank it quite a bit when I went to art school. To me it had the same effect as coffee, only without the nervousness and sweats. This elixir is pretty much this incredible juice itself, but of course I want to mix it up with a great flavor combo for you. The next drink is a very sexy martini that I designed for the Buddha Bar and Brigitte Bardot in Paris.

This recipe calls for lychee juice. Look for canned lychees. You can put the contents of the can (including syrup) in a blender and liquefy. Strain the mix through a fine kitchen strainer and store it in the refrigerator. You can even freeze it in a freezer bag. Same goes for the strained pulp, which makes a tasty snack.

2 ounces Ruby Red Grapefruit Juice
1½ ounces Svedka Citron Vodka
1 ounce lychee juice (or pineapple juice)
2 teaspoons fresh lemon juice

DIRECTIONS:

Combine all ingredients in a cocktail shaker filled with ice. Shake for about 8 seconds and strain over ice into a martini glass.

GARNISH: LYCHEE

If you can get your hands on some lychees, or their fuzzy friend the rambutan, cut an incision into the fruit and place it on the rim of the glass.

ACTIVE INGREDIENT: GRAPEFRUIT

One cup of grapefruit juice is packed with energy-boosting vitamins, carbohydrates, and phytonutrients. Its B vitamins keep you energized and the calcium and potassium replenish electrolytes lost during your partying. Grapefruit juice contains thiamine, which converts food into energy. Then the compound nootkatone in grapefruit activates proteins to increase energy.

A warning to those taking prescription drugs (especially anti-anxiety): Grapefruit blocks enzymes that are responsible for breaking down medications and proper absorption by the body. Please consult your physician because when these enzymes are blocked while you're on medications, it is possible that an excess of the drugs could leak into the bloodstream and cause serious side effects or overdose. Be aware that just one glass of grapefruit juice is powerful enough to cause this.

STUDIO 54

If you want "fruity" cordials when you go out and party, do it the right way and ask your server or bartender if they have naturally flavored products. They simply have to check the label on the bottle. Using natural flavors plays a big role in your ability to stay awake and enjoy your night without getting sick quickly. If you decide to have a sweet libation, go with honey instead of sugar. Every nightclub, bar, or restaurant is stocked with honey, and boy, does this underestimated syrup lend a beautiful flavor to an elixir. It pairs well with dark alcohols, such as rum, scotch, bourbon, and brandies.

¾ ounce liquefied honey

2 ounces light rum

½ ounce fresh lime juice

DIRECTIONS:

Make liquefied honey by dissolving 1 part honey in 1 part hot water. Cool in the refrigerator before continuing the recipe. Next, combine all ingredients in a cocktail shaker filled with ice. Shake vigorously and strain over an ice-filled rocks glass.

GARNISH: LIME

I prefer this elixir to be very citrusy, so I recommend a slice of lime. If your drink is not sour enough, you can squeeze some extra juice from the garnish.

ACTIVE INGREDIENT: HONEY

Honey contains equal parts fructose and glucose, but it is overall better for you because it contains antioxidants, minerals, and vitamins that regular sugar doesn't. Niacin, riboflavin, and pantothenic acid are the main players in honey. They provide a natural boost of energy that will help you get through the night while also replenishing some of the nutrients lost during drinking. As a carbohydrate, honey supplies the body with energy, too.

Left: This is on set of the movie THE BEACH in Phi Phi Leh Island, near Thailand, where I lived for a while. It's a prime place for young, cold, and sweet coconuts.

Right: Me on the outside wall of Fateh Prakash Palace. In the background are ancient paintings and flowerpots with exotic spices.

LIQUID BEDTIME STORIES & RELAXING ELIXIRS

If you don't have pretty poppies growing in between your backyard tulips that would be perfect for producing opium (the world's oldest medicine), try some of these sleep-inducing drinks, calming concoctions, and jazz bar favorites. This chapter is all about liquids that help you fall asleep, calm or relax you, and decrease your brain activity.

Before we begin, I'll name some things you should stay away from in general before bedtime: nicotine, alcohol, caffeine, and spices. From cinnamon to peppers, spices increase your blood flow and will seriously screw up your sleep patterns. And yes, I did say alcohol! Sorry, but even one ounce too close to bedtime can wake you up again in no time. For that reason, the relaxing libations featured in this chapter contain less than an ounce of alcohol or are entirely spirits-free.

This chapter is not as complex as the others in terms of ingredients, garnishes, and preparation. Traditionally, a cocktail consists of at least three ingredients: the spirit, the modifier, and the flavoring agent. Many spirits companies claim that rum and coke is the most sold cocktail on the planet, but it's actually a long drink. If you add lime juice, you have a Cuba Libre. That's a cocktail. Having said that, I admit the next group of potions are not really cocktails either. Most of the libations will consist of only two ingredients.

Here we will see the simplicity of using the barest minimum of everyday household ingredients that are rich in tryptophan, an amino acid the body uses to create serotonin and other phytochemicals that give us a sense of wellbeing. Look into your pantry, spice rack, and refrigerator and memorize what you have. It comes in handy in this chapter.

KIBA

The KiBa is a popular mix at clubs in Germany. The name is short for *kirsch* and *banane*, meaning cherry banana, and that's exactly what it is: equal parts cherry and banana juice on ice. During my teenage years in Germany I noticed a lot of people drinking it. Soon enough I understood why. Try this and decide for yourself.

3 ounces banana juice (blend a banana with a bit of water to make your own)

3 ounces cherry juice

DIRECTIONS:

Fill a highball glass completely with ice. Pour the banana juice. Wait until it settles to the bottom. Next, slowly pour the cherry juice on top. You will get two layers of juice to enjoy.

GARNISH: CHERRY

The perfect garnish for this potion would be, of course, a fresh cherry on top.

ACTIVE INGREDIENTS: CHERRY AND BANANA

Cherries in general start a pretty amazing habit. They contain high levels of melatonin, a hormone produced by the pineal gland to regulate sleep patterns. If cherries are consumed regularly they will control and regulate your everyday sleep cycle. Researchers recommend eating tart cherries an hour before bedtime or before a trip when you want to sleep on the plane.

Bananas contain potassium and magnesium, which are great for muscle relaxation. They also contain the amino acid L-tryptophan, which gets converted to 5-HTP in the brain. The 5-HTP in turn is converted to the relaxing neurotransmitters serotonin and melatonin.

Historians believe that my favorite summer elixir, Radler's Alster, was invented at the end of the nineteenth century. There are many stories about the origin and the person who supposedly invented this thirst-quenching beverage. I was mixed up about the story for most of my life, until the "Commission of the Radler Research" found new evidence. The latest story is that it was invented by bicycle clubs whose sporting members would visit a biergarten, have some fun, and as a to-go cup, take a container filled half with beer and half with lemon-flavored soda, to dilute the alcohol for the ride home.

I personally use this drink to accompany a burger or steak. The taste and smell of beer with more carbonation and a zesty aftertaste of fresh lemon is divine. Great for serving at barbeques, what I like best is the relaxing effect Alster has on the mind and body.

1 bottle of beer (hoppy, like an India Pale Ale)
1 can or bottle of lemon-flavored soda (Pellegrino's Limonata is the best, but regular Sprite or 7Up work too)

DIRECTIONS:

If both ingredients are ice cold you can pour them together in a pint glass. If not, fill the glass with ice, and pour a 50/50 mix of beer and soda.

GARNISH: LEMON WHEEL

Cut a slice of lemon and place it on the surface of the drink.

ACTIVE INGREDIENT: BEER

The bitterness of beer comes from the hops. It is used as a preservative and to balance the sweet malts. To put it simply, it makes beer delicious. It is also very useful as a sleep inducer. It has antioxidant, anti-inflammatory, and estrogen-like properties. Hops also contain melatonin, something we already know a lot about in this chapter, along with the tryptophan amino acid.

The scent of the hop plant is used in aromatherapy to calm nerves. That's why it's so important to have a lot of foam on top of your freshly poured beer. That's something I don't see very often in the U.S. In Germany, if you don't have at least 2" inches of foam ("die blume," German for flower) on top of your beer, you may give it back to your server or bartender!

HELLO SPENCER

Don't ask me what year *Hello Spencer* was playing or if it was just on European television, but this show made me want to eat marzipan balls like crazy. The Muppet-like star of the show would receive his mail and candy in a vacuum Plexiglas shoot. Influenced by the show, marzipan balls became one of my favorite candies, especially on Christmas. I always fell asleep a bit quicker after eating them—that and the fact that I would steal little sips of my dad's holiday cheer: his single malt scotch.

½ ounce Macallan 12 Year Single Malt
   Scotch (optional)
1 tablespoon oatmeal
2 teaspoons plain yogurt
Handful of almonds (almond paste or
   marzipan work too)
Juice of half a lemon

DIRECTIONS:

Combine all ingredients in a blender on high. Pour the blended ingredients into a cocktail shaker with ice. Shake vigorously for about 15 seconds, then strain the mixture into an ice-filled rocks glass.

Extra tip: If you want to make a shake out of this recipe, add a few ice cubes and blend on high. The smaller the cubes of ice the more perfectly the mixture will freeze.

ACTIVE INGREDIENTS: YOGURT, OATMEAL, AND ALMONDS

We have a lot going on here. This recipe is a perfect example of how many everyday ingredients can fulfill our desires.

Yogurt is a fermented dairy product made by adding bacterial cultures to milk, which transforms the milk's sugar, lactose, into lactic acid. This process gives yogurt its refreshingly tart flavor and unique texture. The quality is reflected in its original Turkish name, yoghurmak, which means "to thicken." As with milk, yogurt contains tryptophan.

Our second ingredient is oatmeal. Nope, it's not just for breakfast. It's a filling and delicious snack loaded with melatonin, which helps to promote sleep.

This shake-like potion will have crunch because of the almonds. They, too, contain plenty of tryptophan and magnesium, a muscle relaxer.

Another ingredient to mention is alcohol. Generally, stay away from alcohol before bedtime. Alcohol will make us sleep soundly without REM sleep for the first half of the night, but it will spoil the second half. If you keep the alcohol content below one ounce, as with this recipe, you'll be fine.

GARNISH: ALMONDS AND OATMEAL

Using a wide flat blade of a kitchen knife, crush four almonds into tiny pieces and sprinkle them on top of your potion along with some rolled oats.

SEABISCUIT

This is another elixir I invented while rummaging through a friend's kitchen. The friend was a hyperactive owner of a well-known restaurant chain in New York. He ate a lot and had constant digestive issues that he dared me to fix with a drink. He was a big horseracing fan and obsessed with mint juleps. Of course I found a bottle of bourbon and some other helpful ingredients to calm the man down. I did make his drink a bit stronger than this recipe. As I've said before, go easy on the alcohol if you want a good night's sleep.

MINT TEA:

- 8 ounces hot water
- 2 sprigs of fresh mint leaves (or 2 teaspoons dried mint leaves)
- 2 teaspoons sugar

SEABISCUIT:

- 2 ounces mint tea
- ¾ ounce bourbon (Woodford Reserve, Maker's Mark, or Bulleit)
- 1 teaspoon apricot jam (any jam or preserves work)
- 2 teaspoons fresh lemon juice
- Pinch of dried marjoram

DIRECTIONS:

MINT TEA: Place mint leaves in hot water for about 5 minutes. Finish by adding the sugar.

SEABISCUIT: You can serve the drink warm by just adding all the ingredients to the tea and pouring the mix into a tea cup. To serve cold, allow the tea to cool, then pour it into a cocktail shaker with all remaining ingredients and shake with ice for about 8 seconds. Strain over ice in a rocks glass.

GARNISH: FRUIT

Use any fresh fruit that you used to flavor your tea. For instance, if you used peach jam, garnish with a peach slice; if you used raspberry jam, toss a few raspberries on top of your libation.

ACTIVE INGREDIENTS: MINT AND MAJORAM

Mint is an excellent source of the minerals calcium, iron, manganese, magnesium, and potassium. It's also rich in antioxidants, including beta carotene and vitamins A, C, E, and K. The B-complex vitamins riboflavin and pyridoxine are present, too. Mint is also loaded with dietary fiber that helps control cholesterol and blood pressure levels. It's used as a natural painkiller. Its essential oil, menthol, relaxes muscles in the intestinal wall, and is therefore often used to treat "Irritable Bowel Syndrome."

Though marjoram resides on most American spice racks, I call it the "forgotten herb" because I haven't met many people who still use it in cooking. Marjoram relieves stomach pains, detoxifies the body, and can aid in cases of nausea. Its essential oil is one of the most relaxing and sedative and helps to calm digestive ailments.

HEALING JUICES

Our everyday life in the city, the office routine, and junk food habits slowly destroy our bodies. If you don't take charge and feed your body something useful, it will give you nothing but trouble. Most doctors are trained into the concept of prescribing one specific drug to treat one specific symptom. Mother Nature works in more mysterious ways. Most fruit, herbs, and vegetables have bi-directional abilities. The exciting use of nature's bounty is revealed in the drinks featured in this chapter. I call them healing juices, because they're made from natural ingredients that are good for us. Here are some amazing elixirs to protect your body, mind, and soul.

BEETS ME

You may say you don't like beets but please trust me on this and give it a try! I created this drink as an everyday healing supplement on the run. Take it to go or make it for your friends at night. It will make a great impression. Not only will you convert a friend to beets; you will also give them the gift of blood detox-ification.

1 beet
16 ounces spring water
6 fresh raspberries
½ teaspoon ground ginger
½ teaspoon honey

GARNISH: BEETS

Slice three very thin slices of a fresh beet. Hold the discs in between your left index finger, thumb, and middle finger to hold them in place while you arrange them as if creating a color swatch to make a triangle. Next, slice an incision that cuts through all three discs (be careful not to cut too deep). Still holding the three-disc garnish between your fingers, slowly place the incision on top of the glass rim and enjoy as the light gives you a beautiful color display.

DIRECTIONS:

Cut the beet into little cubes and place them in a blender. Add water and blend the cubes into a puree. Combine the puree with all remaining ingredients in a cocktail shaker and shake hard for about 8 seconds. Strain the mix into a high-ball glass filled with ice. For a smoothie, blend the entire mix with ice.

ACTIVE INGREDIENTS: BEET AND RASPBERRY

Of course, alcohol abuse is harmful to your health. It can lead to diseases of the pancreas, heart, and liver. Beet juice is very helpful in restoring the health of these organs. The organic mineral salts in beets rebuild damaged tissue cells. Because beet root is a blood-building herb, it detoxifies the blood and then renews it with natural sugars and minerals.

Berries are high in potassium, which controls high blood pressure. Besides vitamins A and C, calcium, and phos-phorus, berries are rich in iron, which is great for the production of red blood cells. Scientists have found that indigenous people who eat a lot of berries and nuts are vir-tually free of cancer. Raspberries, like many other berries, contain a natural plant phenol known as ellagic acid. Many cancer researchers are currently working with this acid and found that it competes for DNA receptors that are also used for chemically induced carcinogens. Pretty amazing to fight cancer with raspberries, isn't it?

ELECTROLYTE

At a convention I met a geochemist with extensive experience in the field of nutritional medicine. To prevent allergies, he recommended taking 1,000 mg of vitamin C with bio-flavonoids three times a day. The thought behind it is sound, but I came up with a drink that provides you with the needed vitamin C, only without getting the runs in the process. This is an elixir that I feature a lot in the summer, because of the seasonal availability of watermelon in the U.S. It's extremely refreshing and healthy.

Half of a small watermelon
1 ounce Svedka Vodka
½ ounce pineapple juice
2 teaspoons fresh lemon juice
1 teaspoon sugar

DIRECTIONS:

Cut the watermelon into pieces and muddle them in a cocktail shaker glass. (Or liquefy them in a blender.) Add all remaining ingredients to the glass and shake very hard. Pour all contents of the shaker into a highball glass.

GARNISH: WATERMELON

Cut a triangular slice from your watermelon wedge and simply squeeze it on the rim of the glass for a colorful garnish.

ACTIVE INGREDIENTS: LEMON AND WATERMELON

Lemon is a magic fruit. It contains great quantities of vitamin C, a natural antihistamine. Vitamin C prevents the immune system from producing histamines and helps remove them from the bloodstream. Studies have shown that a daily dose of vitamin C can prevent allergies and asthma symptoms.

Watermelon, which is also loaded with vitamin C, helps in preventing skin problems. The acidic condition of our blood after eating junk food, fries, sweets, coffee, and soft drinks is resolved by vitamin C. It flushes the acid from the system and renews the blood at the same time.

SEXUAL HEALING

If you are an "American Gigolo," this is your drink. After reading about all the beneficial properties of the delicious fruit in our next cocktail it dawned on me: That's why the Romans ate so many grapes! Besides stress, allergies, and gastrointestinal problems, our intimate life needs attention sometimes as well. Drinking this elixir may help.

3 ounces organic grape juice (or 8 red grapes)
1 ounce Ecco Domani Merlot
2 teaspoons fresh lemon juice
2 pinches of ground ginger
Pinch of green tea powder (or 2 tea bags)

DIRECTIONS:

Combine all ingredients in a cocktail shaker filled with ice. Shake vigorously and strain into a wine glass.

GARNISH: LEMON WHEEL

Slice a wheel from the center of a lemon. Make a small incision halfway into the wheel and then place it on the rim of the glass.

ACTIVE INGREDIENT: GRAPE

Fresh grapes and grape juice contain a powerful compound called resveratrol. Resveratrol is a powerful anti-viral that fights cold sores and herpes. Consuming grapes, grape juice, raisins, and even red wine can have a strong anti-viral effect. Resveratrol also inhibits all three stages of development of cancerous tumors. Grapes are also high in antioxidants and polyphenols, which help fight infection. Meanwhile, the tannins in grapes help fight viruses before they can manifest in the body.

MEMORY-EVOKING ELIXIRS

Each of us is influenced by flavors and scents and the incredible, horrible, happy, sad, life-changing, and/or everlasting memories that are attached to them. Any given taste or scent can be stored in the mind as a crystal-clear memory for a long time. Most interestingly, upon experiencing the flavor and scent again, it can stir up passionate feelings. The following shots will remind you of your diaper days, first lollipop, or maybe your very first kiss.

I can't promise you that all of these libations will take you back in time, but the chances are good. I concentrated on ingredients and products that most Americans grew up with, but may not expect to be used in drinks. After living in the U.S. for over thirteen years, I think my palette has been "Americanized." Products like peanut butter, cranberry juice, Dr. Pepper, pancakes, and chocolate chip cookies are not known in the countries in which I previously lived. For me, a vivid example of differences in food preparation in America is popcorn. I first arrived in the U.S. as an exchange student in 1990. O'Hare airport in Chicago was my first stop. I had a layover and decided to grab a snack. I walked over to a popcorn stand and purchased a box. I ended up spitting out the first bite. Did the guy grab the wrong spice jar? Why in the world would someone put salt on popcorn? In Europe popcorn is caramelized and very sweet.

What we consume defines our mood, our habits, and our social life. Take a minute and think about our favorite restaurants, our beloved beer, the snacks we eat, and of course our drinks—all of these choices are influenced by scent and flavor. Here are a few flavored memories that should evoke some long-lost feelings.

ARACHIBUTYROPHOBIA

During World War II, peanut butter and jelly sandwiches were eaten by American soldiers. Today kids eat it—and grownups, too. The average American kid eats 1,500 PB&J sandwiches by the time they graduate high school. Suitable in the morning, during the day, or at night, this American staple is impossible to forget. Combining sweet jelly with a thick, rich peanut butter is a trend that will likely never die. By the way, arachibutyrophobia is the fear of getting peanut butter stuck to the roof of your mouth!

3 ounces organic grape juice (or fresh grapes, liquefied)
1½ ounces Svedka Vodka
2 teaspoons fresh lemon juice
1 teaspoon organic peanut butter

DIRECTIONS:

Combine all ingredients in a cocktail shaker with ice. Shake vigorously for about 8 seconds and strain into a martini glass.

GARNISH: GRAPE SLICES

Cut white and red grapes into thick slices (about 3 slices per grape). Arrange them on a skewer in alternating colors of red/white/red/white.

XMAS

I fell in love with gingerbread cookies at first taste. I ate so many that my grandmother had to hide them and give me daily rations. I found the secret hiding place without telling anyone, so my "gingerbread allowance" was short-lived. When I think of Christmas, I think of a Christmas tree, gingerbread, cinnamon, and clementines. After peeling sweet clementines, I would experiment with the skin and squeeze their flammable oils on the candle we had on the dining-room table. Of course, our variety of beliefs makes us all experience Christmas a little different from others—but fruit and spices are universal.

2 whole clementines, peeled
1½ ounces Svedka Clementine Vodka
½ ounce grenadine
2 teaspoons fresh lemon juice
2 pinches of gingerbread spice

DIRECTIONS:

Separate the segments of your clementines and place them in a cocktail shaker glass. Muddle the fruit until all of the juice is extracted. Add ice and the remaining ingredients to the cocktail shaker and shake vigorously. Strain the mixture into a martini glass.

GARNISH: ROSEMARY

Use a rosemary sprig to give the potion a (Christmas) tree-like character. You can release the essential oils of the rosemary by burning the needles. Use your fingers (or kitchen tongs) to hold the sprig over a flame and carefully burn it until you see a few sparks. This will create a strong scent that when combined with your drink will act as a flavoring agent as well. Simply place the sprig on top of the drink in your martini glass.

ADAM WANTS EVE

Everybody loves apples from childhood on up. Just don't be fooled by the liquids we get in most nightclubs or bars. Artificially flavored, glow-in-the-dark-neon-green libations don't deserve to have the word apple in them. A great emergency martini á la MacGyver is the Adam Wants Eve. It's designed to evoke childhood memories and made with only three all-natural ingredients everybody should have in their kitchen. It never disappoints, especially if you travel a lot and generally only stock your refrigerator with condiments and sugar-fortified products.

Apple is a universal ingredient that goes with every spirit. Hence, you'll see this recipe calls for any spirit you have available. Here are a few tips: Vodka is flavorless, so it won't affect the apple flavor much. Brandy, such as cognac or fruit brandies, would be perfect for this drink. Sake and gin work too and will underline the apple flavor beautifully. Rum will give apple a maple and sugarcane flavor.

1½ ounces of any spirit
1 tablespoon fresh lemon juice
5 teaspoons apple sauce

DIRECTIONS:

Combine all ingredients in a cocktail shaker with ice. Shake vigorously and strain into a martini glass.

GARNISH: NUTMEG

A pinch of nutmeg will add a great scent and cut the sweetness of the apple sauce. Use ground nutmeg or pieces of a freshly shaved nut for the surface of your drink.

FLYING DUTCHMAN

The memory of smoke is a powerful thing. Different smoke scents evoke different moods and events. There's smoke from homecoming bonfires, burned marshmallows, or even a burning tobacco leaf. At some point we all have a special relationship with the fumes. As for myself, my dad used to smoke a pipe. The untouched tobacco he stuffed it with smelled sweet and appetizing. The smoke that came out of the pipe didn't. The following libation contains several flavor profiles that may remind you of a great vacation, making love on the beach, or a family camping trip.

½ ounce liquefied honey

2½ ounces pear juice (or apple juice)

1½ ounces spiced rum

2 teaspoons fresh lime juice

1 piece of wood (you can use a chopstick
or a dry twig picked up outside)

DIRECTIONS:

Make liquefied honey by dissolving 1 part honey in 1 part hot water. Cool in the refrigerator before continuing the recipe. Next, combine the pear juice, spiced rum, and lime juice in the tin part of a Boston cocktail shaker. Set the tin aside while you create the smoke.

Use a lighter or match to light the end of your piece of wood with a steady flame. Once the wood is lit, place your shaker glass upside down over the flame as you blow it out to create smoke. Capture smoke until you see the glass filled. Cover the glass and place it upside down on a fireproof surface, like a baking sheet.

Leave the smoke-filled glass shut while you add ice to the mixture in the tin. Now slowly lift the smoke-filled glass and connect it with the tin. Shake for about 8 seconds and strain the mixture over ice in a rocks glass.

GARNISH: MARSHMALLOWS

Tear one (or more) apart halfway and place them on the rim of the glass.

THE BRAIN (PLASTIC VERSION FROM MY LAB) WORKS
IN NOT-SO-MYSTERIOUS WAYS SOMETIMES. FLAVOR
AND SMELL, MORE THAN ANY OTHER HUMAN
SENSES, HAVE THE ABILITY TO EVOKE MEMORIES,
CHANGE MOODS, OR STIMULATE THE BODY AND MIND.

The lower left arrow points to the olfactory epithelium,
which contains more than twenty million nerve endings and
is also the first stop for odor that is inhaled. The upper left
arrow points to the olfactory bulb, which amplifies a nerve
message. The message then travels along the olfactory
tract, enters the limbic system, and is analyzed by the amyg-
dale and the hippocampus, which are our memory centers
(upper right arrow). After being relayed a few times to
determine what memory or emotion is being evoked by a
certain family of scent (perhaps euphoric, such as grapefruit,
ylang ylang, or jasmine), the final message is sent from the
thalamus to the pituitary gland (lower right arrow), which
produces the endorphins that are our "feel good hor-
mones."

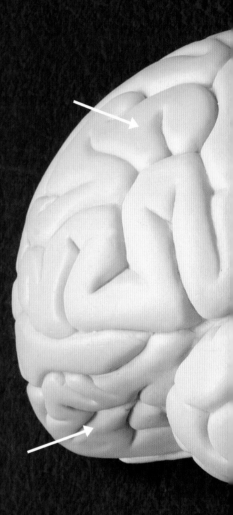

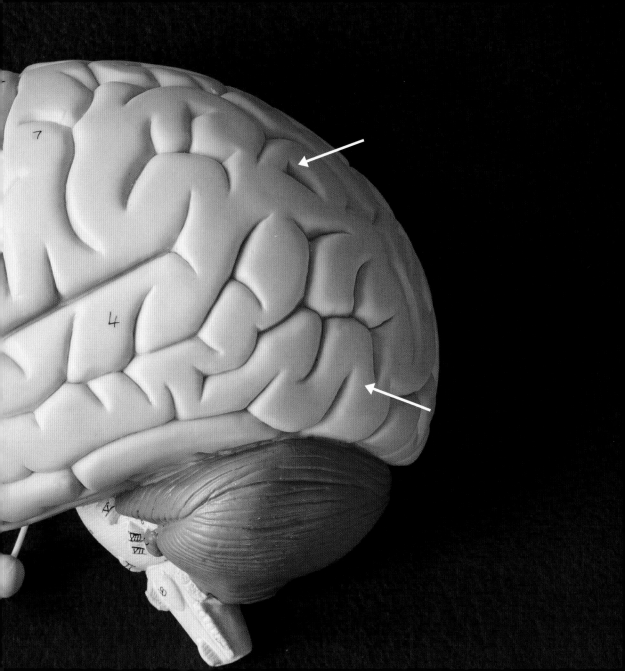

FOR THOSE WHO HAVEN'T HAD ENOUGH YET

Many conditions and diseases for which we turn to modern medicine can be treated naturally. Did you ever asked yourself why your granny had all the answers? Here are some of my own grandmother's revamped remedies that saved not only my butt but also helped a lot of my close friends. Thank you, Elfriede!

A FENUGREEK WEDDING

Ladies, did you know that you can naturally enlarge your breasts? No, I don't work for a scam telemarketing company. It's true, before *Nip/Tuck* there was fenugreek!

FENUGREEK TEA:
  16 ounces water
  8 ounces fenugreek sprouts
  2 teaspoons honey

A FENUGREEK WEDDING:
  4 ounces fenugreek tea
  1½ ounces New Amsterdam Gin
  1 teaspoon strawberry jam
  ½ ounce fresh lime juice
  1 ounce ginger ale

DIRECTIONS:

FENUGREEK TEA: Bring the water to a boil in a saucepan. Once the water boils, add the fenugreek sprouts and reduce the heat. Allow the sprouts to steep for 10 minutes. Sweeten with the honey. Strain the tea and allow it to cool before continuing the recipe.

A FENUGREEK WEDDING: Combine the fenugreek tea, gin, strawberry jam, and lime juice in a cocktail shaker filled with ice. Shake vigorously and strain into an ice-filled highball glass. Float ginger ale on top.

ACTIVE INGREDIENT: FENUGREEK

Fenugreek is the best way to naturally enhance the growth of a woman's breasts. It is an annual plant found in Europe, Southeast Asia, and the Middle East. The seeds are used as a spice. It is very potent. Fenugreek contains diosgenin, a chemical compound used in oral contraceptive pills to mimic the female sex hormone estrogen. One of many side effects of estrogen is uncomfortable tightness and swelling of the breasts. Fenugreek, on the other hand, can safely enhance breast size. Besides consuming it, liquefied fenugreek can be massaged directly into the skin. Our elixir can be used in a similar way too—feel free to get naughty and involve your partner as well!

THE GUAVA DOESN'T FALL FAR FROM THE TREE!

When I first moved to New York City, I lived with John Leguizamo's relatives in the Bronx. I was a minority in the neighborhood and absolutely inexperienced with Latin food. I lived with a family of three: a kid obsessed with video games, a beautiful mother who had *Iron Chef* talent in the kitchen, and a father, Carlos, who was the godfather of the entire neighborhood. He ate guava paste like there was no tomorrow. A few years later I found out why. Let's just say this elixir is meant for the men. We are even now, ladies and gentlemen!

2 ounces guava juice
1½ ounces Don Julio Blanco Tequila
1 ounce fresh lemon juice
½ ounce agave nectar
½ ounce fresh lime juice
Pinch of cinnamon
Pinch of sea salt

DIRECTIONS:

Combine all ingredients in a cocktail shaker with ice. Shake vigorously and strain the mixture into an ice-filled margarita glass.

GARNISH: LIME WHEEL

A simple lime wheel will do for this elixir. Cut a slice from the center of a lime. Cut through the skin and position the wheel on the rim of the glass.

ACTIVE INGREDIENT: GUAVA

I can tell you now why Carlos may have ingested large amounts of guava: he wanted to increase his fertility and sperm count. Guava is rich in vitamin C, which is used in many fertility-enhancing drugs. It's most effective at treating male infertility problems such as adhesion or sperm clumping. A steady diet of guava will also boost a man's sperm count. Guava also contains lycopene, a compound that boosts sperm concentration in infertile men. Lycopene is one of the carotenoids found in male testicles.

My favorite place to eat Halal food in Manhattan is in front of the Venus De Milo sculptures on the northwest corner of 53rd Street and Sixth Avenue. One of their main ingredients is garlic—lots of garlic. Sometimes when we are on a mission to satisfy our food craving, we don't think about the aftermath or about our later appointments the same day. Have you ever been forced to endure bad breath from a colleague that just couldn't shut up after he had smelly food? The following tasty elixir will help hide the smelly ghost of lunch past.

Sprig of dill
Sprig of cilantro
3 cucumber slices
2½ ounces pineapple juice
1½ ounces Fidencio Mezcal
2 teaspoons fresh lime juice

DIRECTIONS:

Muddle the dill in a cocktail shaker glass. Next, add the cilantro and muddle again. Add the cucumber slices and muddle once more. Finally, add the remaining ingredients plus ice, and shake vigorously for about 10 seconds. Strain into an ice-filled rocks glass.

GARNISH: DILL, CILANTRO, AND CUCUMBER

Pack this cocktail with a small rainforest of herbs by using dill and cilantro sprigs to top the liquid. In addition, you may cut a cucumber flower (see page 78. Or, fan out three cucumber slices, stack them, cut an incision through all slices, and position it carefully on the rim.

ACTIVE INGREDIENTS: DILL AND CILANTRO

A main component in dill is carvone. This natural breath freshener is the same compound found in spearmint. Chewing and ingesting dill leaves freshens the breath. You can also boil the leaves and use it as a rinse instead of commercial mouthwash.

Like dill, cilantro is very rich in chlorophyll (that's the green stuff that makes all green things in nature green). It, too, has breath-sweetening powers.

BITE ME

If there's someone who can tell you what a major pain mosquitoes are, it's yours truly. I have encountered a gazillion of these bloodsucking vampires on my trips to the tropics. One of them even gave me a very unpleasant bout of malaria! There are some hardcore sprays and topics for the skin, but many of them have a nauseating odor and don't even work. When I was in Borneo, I came across a natural spray containing lemongrass that worked. The pleasing scent of lemongrass seems to be like deadly stink to mosquitoes.

Stem of lemongrass
1 garlic clove
1½ ounces Svedka Vodka
2 pinches of ground ginger
2 ounces lemonade
1 ounce tonic water

DIRECTIONS:

Cut the lemongrass and garlic into small pieces and muddle them in a cocktail shaker. Next, add ice, the vodka, ginger, and lemonade to the shaker and shake vigorously.

Strain into an ice-filled highball glass. Top with the tonic water.

GARNISH TIP: LEMONGRASS, LIME, AND MINT

Slice a perfect wheel off from a lime. In the middle of the wheel slice a little cross with your fruit knife that will fit the diameter of a drinking straw. Take a stem of lemongrass and cut it to the size of a regular straw. Peel off the outer layer of this stem and let it snap back into a lemongrass straw. Push your homemade lemongrass straw through the lime wheel and hang it off the rim of your highball glass. Take a mint sprig and snap off the top leaves. Push them into the middle of the lime to complete your garnish.

ACTIVE INGREDIENTS: GARLIC AND LEMONGRASS

Garlic has been proven to release a powerful compound called allicin, which after being consumed is partly excreted through skin as waste. The ability of garlic to repel mosquitoes has been proven scientifically.

Lemongrass can be applied directly to the skin to treat insect bites as well as to repel them. The citronella oils in lemongrass are used to make mosquito-repelling candles.

ESSENTIAL PARTY TIPS AND BATCH RECIPES

Hosting the perfect party and making sure that everybody is happy is not easy to pull off. Do you ever get invited to a party where the host arrives five minutes after you, because he forgot the dip/she had to get a mani/pedi? Or, you show up and discover you're one of twelve people who brought a bottle of booze, but there are no mixers whatsoever? I don't know about you, but I'm tired of poorly organized parties. That's why I included this list of foolproof tips and tricks for your party planning.

1. Choose the right date. Make sure your date falls after major holidays, government deadlines, etc. Also, don't be afraid to be spontaneous now and then. A party can be pulled together the same day if the mood really strikes you.

2. Choose a fun theme. That doesn't mean that all of your guests have to dress up like Queen Mary. Even a certain flavor or color can be a theme. Look at your inventory of dishes, glassware, napkins, glasses, etc., and see what fits.

3. Invitations should be sent out three weeks prior to the party. Notice should be sent as soon as possible in the case of a spontaneous soiree, though of course don't expect it to fit everyone's schedule.

4. Invite new people! It will almost always make a party more interesting and helps create conversations. Speaking of which, for parties bringing in new people, it's a good idea to steer the conversation away from sports, religion, and politics to keep your party from potentially ending in a brawl!

5. Before shopping for glassware, plates, and accessories, go online and gather a list of local thrift stores, flea markets, and antique shops. You will find amazing deals on old crystal glassware, sterling silver trays, punch bowls, etc.

6. Decorations such as flowers go a long way in creating a festive mood. Fruit used as decorations are a feast for the eyes and can be used for making spontaneous drinks. I use large vases and baskets filled with fresh fruit.

7. Music is probably the most important of all party components. Of course you know your audience better than I do, but I've found for mixed groups, Nina Simone, Billy Holiday, Sarah Vaughan, and classic jazz set great moods. If you want to be a bit hipper, alternative rock and ambient compilations are perfect and sexy party music.

8. For lighting, regardless of the party's theme, always choose candles—a lot of them, the thicker the better. People feel more comfortable with their looks when not confronted with bright overhead lights or kitchen neon.

9. When choosing your ingredients for hors d'oeuvres and cock-tails, go seasonal for the freshest product. Store enough back-up foods such as cheese assortments, hummus, olives, bread, and mixed fruit. Inexpensive caviar can be purchased to instantly make a party look high end.

10. If possible, always premix your cocktails to avoid excessive work and exhaustion. I recommend choosing three main cocktails to serve throughout the night. I usually go with a tequila-based drink, a gin-based drink, and a rum-based drink. From this book, I recommend a few great bio-rhythm stimulants: The Fountain Of Youth (page 77), Tobacco Vanilla (page 110), and The Little Death (page 91).

11. Practice responsible revelry. If you're hosting a smaller gathering of family and close friends, it's generally fine to have your guests serve themselves. However, if there are newcomers to your circle or you know someone in the group tends to overdue it on the alcohol, I recommend having someone bartend or take shifts shaking and pouring cocktails. That way you have an idea how many cocktails your guests have consumed.

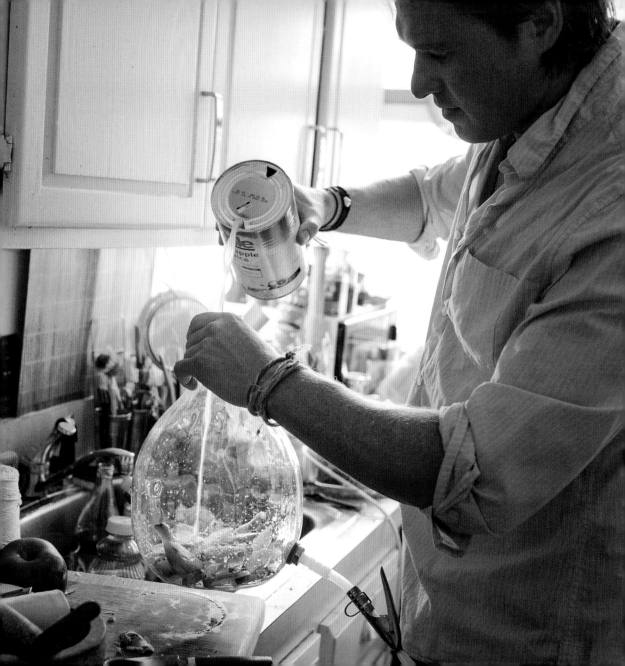

PREMIXES AND TAILGATE COCKTAILS

I used to premix cocktails almost every day when doing consulting for spirits companies, special events, movie premieres, and weddings all over the world. Now I only premix for three large-scale parties: Charity Water, Petra Nemcova's Happy Hearts Fund, and biggest of all, the Oscars. The last involves premixing some 280 gallons of cocktails that it takes Tinseltown's finest only an hour and a half to finish.

When determining quantities of premix for your guests, ask yourself what kind of crowd you're hosting. At a private party your average guest will consume two or three cocktails per hour. You will probably run out earlier than you think. Take it as a compliment. If, on the other hand, you happen to have leftovers at the end of the night, instead of pouring it down the toilet send guests home with a to-go bottle. Just keep in mind that the elixirs and potions featured in this book contain a fair amount of spices, herbs, and bits of pulp that should be stripped of the drinks with a superfine strainer before storing away. If not, the herbs will continue to flavor the drink and the cocktail that was medium spicy in the beginning of the night will be mega spicy by the end! Strain properly and these pre-mixes will hold up for a few days.

Batch recipes for 2 gallons/8 liters provides 256 ounces for 40 people.

Batch recipes for 5 gallons/20 liters provides 640 ounces for 110 people.

NEW AMSTERDAM SLING

1 gallon/4 liters orange juice

½ gallon/2 liters pineapple juice

1¼ liters/1½ bottles New Amsterdam Gin

8 ounces fresh lemon juice

2 teaspoons ground ginger

DIRECTIONS:

Combine the ingredients in a 2-gallon/8-liter container and stir for 30 seconds. Seal the container and refrigerate.

MAN'S BEST FRIEND

1½ gallons/6 liters Ruby Red Grapefruit
   Juice
1 liter/1¼ bottles New Amsterdam Gin
¼ gallon/1 liter pineapple juice
2 teaspoons sea salt

DIRECTIONS:
Combine the ingredients in a 2-gallon/8-liter
container and stir for 30 seconds. Seal the container and refrigerate. Shake before serving.
   This drink expires 3 days after mixing.

BRONX TO BATTERY

1½ gallons/6 liters tomato juice
1½ liters/2 bottles Ardbeg 10 Year Old
   Single Malt Scotch
16 ounces fresh lemon juice
16 ounces bacon bits
8 ounces balsamic vinegar
1 teaspoon cayenne pepper
1 teaspoon ground pepper

DIRECTIONS:
Combine the ingredients in a 2-gallon/8-liter
container and stir for 30 seconds. Seal the container and refrigerate.

THE LONG STITCH

CHAMOMILE TEA:

    1½ gallons/6 liters hot water

    20 chamomile tea bags

    16 ounces sugar

THE LONG STITCH:

    1½ gallons/6 liters chamomile tea

    1¼ liters/1½ bottles bourbon

    ¼ gallon/1 liter raspberry jam (or strawberry)

    16 ounces fresh lemon juice

DIRECTIONS:

CHAMOMILE TEA: Bring the water to boil. Then, place the tea bags in the hot water. Dissolve the sugar into the tea. Steep for fifteen minutes, then remove the tea bags and stir.

THE LONG STITCH: Pour the chamomile tea into a 2-gallon/8-liter container. Add bourbon and raspberry syrup and stir. Add lemon juice. Stir again for 30 seconds. Seal the container and refrigerate.

REMBRANDT SANGRIA

HIBISCUS TEA:

1½ gallons/6 liters hot water

12 hibicus teabags

12 tablespoons sugar

REMBRANDT SANGRIA

½ gallon/2 liters hibiscus tea

½ gallon/2 liters Ecco Domani Pinot Grigio (for a red sangria use Ecco Domani Merlot)

½ gallon/1½ liters Don Julio Blanco Tequila

½ gallon/1½ liters white cranberry juice (for red sangria use red cranberry juice, plus 8 ounces sugar)

8 ounces fresh lemon juice

DIRECTIONS:

HIBISCUS TEA: Bring the water to boil. Then, place the tea bags in the hot water. Dissolve the sugar into the tea. Steep for fifteen minutes, then remove the tea bags and stir.

REMBRANDT SANGRIA: Combine the ingredients in a 2-gallon/8-liter container and stir for 30 seconds. Seal the container and refrigerate.

Before serving, place 2 teaspoons of fruit cocktail medley into the bottom of each glass. This medley can be decorated with dried hibiscus flowers, red grapes, fresh cherries, or cut watermelon pieces.

FORMULAS FOR METRIC CONVERSIONS

Ounces to grams	multiply ounces by 28.35
Cups to liters	multiply cups by .24

METRIC EQUIVALENTS FOR WEIGHT

U.S. Metric

1 ounce	28 grams
2 ounces	57 grams
3 ounces	85 grams
4 ounces	113 grams
5 ounces	142 grams
6 ounces	170 grams
7 ounces	198 grams
8 ounces	227 grams
16 ounces (1 lb.)	454 grams

METRIC EQUIVALENTS FOR VOLUME

U.S. Metric

J teaspoon	0.6 milliliters	—
¼ teaspoon	1.2 milliliters	—
½ teaspoon	2.5 milliliters	—
¾ teaspoon	3.7 milliliters	—
1 teaspoon	5 milliliters	—
1½ teaspoon	7.4 milliliters	—
2 teaspoon	10 milliliters	—
1 tablespoon	15 milliliters	—
1½ tablespoon	22 milliliters	—
2 tablespoon (⅛ cup)	30 milliliters	1 ounce
3 tablespoons	45 milliliters	—
¼ cup	59 milliliters	2 ounces
⅓ cup	79 milliliters	—
½ cup	118 milliliters	4 ounces
⅔ cup	158 milliliters	—
¾ cup	178 milliliters	6 ounces
1 cup	237 milliliters	8 ounces
1¼ cups	300 milliliters	—
1½ cups	355 milliliters	—
1¾ cups	425 milliliters	—
2 cups (1 pint)	500 milliliters	16 ounces
3 cups	725 milliliters	—
4 cups (1 quart)	.95 liters	32 ounces
16 cups (1 gallon)	3.8 liters	128 ounces

SOURCE: Herbst, Sharon Tyler. *The Food Lover's Companion*. 3rd ed. Hauppauge: Barron's, 2001.

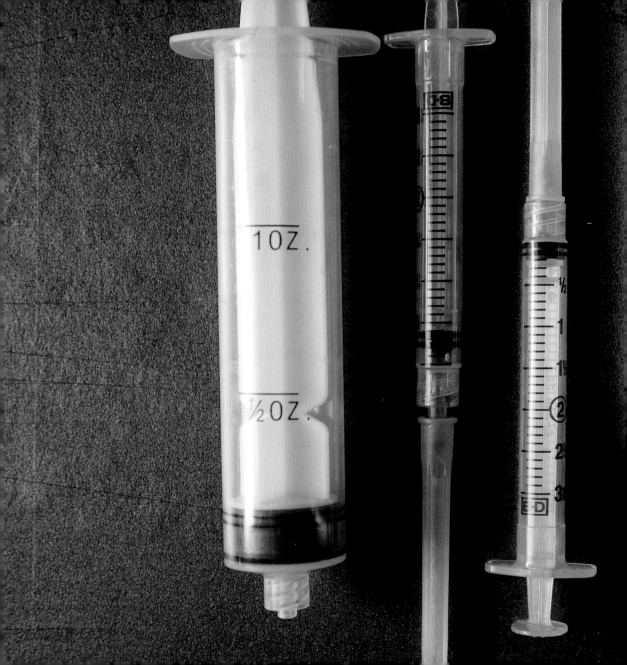

AUTHOR'S POSTSCRIPT

A lifetime being surrounded by plants, animals, scents, and jungles made this book happen. Again, this wouldn't be possible without my parents who made me travel all over this beautiful planet and introduced me to their wisdom of loving nature and respecting all living things. I developed my green thumb by watching my dad work in our garden, which hosted so many different spices, veggies, fruit, and flowers. My mother and grandmother taught me how to cook and bake. Back then my friends made fun of me for it!

I decided to study organic chemistry and biology by tenth grade. Years later, after I began working at Sushi Samba in New York City, I witnessed how my knowledge of chemistry and spirits seemed to blend together to the benefit of my customers. That's what sparked the idea of fusing health, nature, gin, tequila, and other fine spirits to create unique potions and elixirs that can enhance the mood, be it for personal use, private parties, or at people's favorite establishments.

If anyone had told me twenty years ago that this would be my calling, I would have laughed at them. I understand that this "gift" of having a great nose or palate poses a lot of questions, including whether anyone would listen to me and understand how important it is to know their own body like a physician. I urge everyone to take care of their body and not to take their health for granted. Being prone to accidents, I had a few near-death experiences that prompted epiphanies that have influenced my outlook. My passion and devotion for the miracle of nature and the urge to educate and enlighten my friends led me to write this book for you. I leave you with the wise words of an amazing human being:

"All that man needs for good health and healing can be found in nature, it is the job of science to find it."

—Paracelsus, Father of Pharmacology, 1493–1541

REFERENCES

Over my many years of research, studying botanicals, working with the most brilliant minds in medicine, flavor chemistry, and food science, I acquired a vast library of books and journals. The following list is by no means complete, but it underlines some of my favorite, essential references on herbal medicine, flavor chemistry, and alternative medicine.

Kaiser, Roman. *Meaningful Scents around the World*. Verlag Helvetica Chimica Acta: Zurich, Switzerland, 2006.

Kaiser, Roman. *Scent of the Vanishing Flora*. Verlag Helvetica Chimica Acta, Zurich, Switzerland, 2011.

Balch, Phyllis A. *Prescription for Nutritional Healing*. Penguin, New York, 2010.

Heinerman, John. Heinerman's. *Encyclopedia of Healing Juices*. Parker Publishing, Paramus, New Jersey, 1994.

Duke, James A. *Anti-Aging Prescriptions*. Rodale, New York, 2001.

Aggarwal, Bharat B. *Healing Spices*. Sterling, New York, 2011.

Duke, James A. *The Green Pharmacy*. Rodale, New York, 1997.

Li Shi Zhen, Ben Cao Gang Mu. *The Book of Healing Herbs*, Bejing, China, c. 1590.

Arrowsmith Allegria Nancy. *Herbarium Magicum: The Book of Healing Herbs*. Llewellyn Publications, Woodbury, Minnesota, 2009.

INDEX

ACKNOWLEDGMENTS

I extend my gratitude to those individuals of endless wisdom who helped me create this important book. The initial push into the world of cocktails was provided by my mentors, Heiko Beck and Thomas Kothe, both masterminds of mixology and garnish art. Thank you for your daily abuse and tough love behind the bar.

I thank my family, especially my grandmother Elfriede, who taught me everything there is to know about gardening, baking, cooking, and eating everything precious our planet has to offer. Thanks to my agent, Megan Thompson, and my editor, Cindy De La Hoz, who contributed to the conception, development, and promotion of this book.

Most importantly, thanks to all my friends, my doctor, consulting molecular biologists, astronauts, food scientists, and my clients who believed in my loved profession and never-ending research in giving the gift of flavor.

SOUTHERN
SANCTUARY

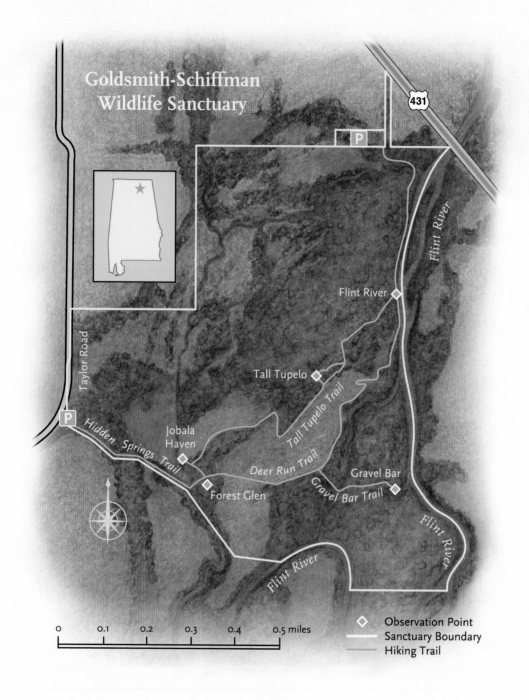

Goldsmith-Schiffman
Wildlife Sanctuary

431

Taylor Road

Flint River

Flint River

Tall Tupelo

Hidden Springs Trail

Jobala
Haven

Tall Tupelo Trail

Deer Run Trail

Forest Glen

Gravel Bar

Gravel Bar Trail

Flint River

Flint River

0 0.1 0.2 0.3 0.4 0.5 miles	

◇ Observation Point
    Sanctuary Boundary
    Hiking Trail

SOUTHERN SANCTUARY

A Naturalist's Walk
through the Seasons

MARIAN MOORE LEWIS

The University of Alabama Press Tuscaloosa

The University of Alabama Press
Tuscaloosa, Alabama 35487-0380
uapress.ua.edu

Inquiries about reproducing material from this work should be
addressed to the University of Alabama Press.

Typeface: Scala Pro and Scala Sans Pro

Manufactured in Korea
Cover photographs: A golden spring meadow (top left),
a passion flower (top right), a red maple tree in the fall (bottom
left), and the tupelo swamp in snow (bottom right)
Frontispiece map: Deborah Reade
Design: Michele Myatt Quinn

∞

The paper on which this book is printed meets the minimum
requirements of American National Standard for Information
Sciences—Permanence of Paper for Printed Library Materials,
ANSI Z39.48-1984.

Library of Congress Cataloging-in-Publication Data

Lewis, Marian Moore, 1937–
  Southern sanctuary: a naturalist's walk through the seasons /
Marian Moore Lewis.
      pages   cm
  Includes bibliographical references and index.
  ISBN 978-0-8173-5783-2 (pbk.: alk. paper) — ISBN 978-0-8173-
8773-0 (e book)
  1. Natural history—Alabama. 2. Natural areas—Alabama. 3. Flint
River Watershed (Tenn. and Ala.) I. Title.
  QH76.5.A2L49 2015
  508.761'94—dc23   2014009839

This publication was made possible in part by generous contribu-
tions by The Friends of the Preserve and Sanctuary, the Tennessee
Valley Audubon Society, and the Land Trust of North Alabama.

To MARGARET ANNE GOLDSMITH, who, through her vision, sense of stewardship, philanthropy, and love of nature, donated the land for the Goldsmith Schiffman Wildlife Sanctuary to the City of Huntsville, Alabama. In her own words: "It is my wish that this land will be preserved as a haven for wildlife and for education and enjoyment of our children and future generations; that it will always be a place that lives, suspended in time, yet ever-changing, where all can experience a kind of peace and solace like that found in sacred places."

When wonder matures, it peels back experience to seek deeper layers of marvel below. This is science's highest purpose. . . . When laughing children chase after fireflies, they are not pursuing beetles but catching wonder.

—David George Haskell
from *The Forest Unseen: A Year's Watch in Nature*

Contents

Illustrations

Tables

Preface

My fascination with the wild land bordered on the east by the Flint River and located about 10 mi (16 km) southeast of Huntsville, Alabama, began on a cool day in mid-March 2009, when I first walked through the red metal gates and hiked the rudimentary trails of what would become the Goldsmith Schiffman Wildlife Sanctuary. The land was donated to the city of Huntsville in 2003 by entrepreneur and naturalist Margaret Anne Goldsmith. She envisioned it becoming a sanctuary for wildlife and a place for learning about nature and restoring the spirit. The sanctuary encompasses approximately four hundred acres of open bottomland meadows, marshes, sloughs, streams, vernal pools, and forests.

On that day in March when I first visited the Sanctuary, I discovered numerous wildflowers—spring beauties, violets, early saxifrage, spring cress—all beginning to bloom. Great blue herons circled a rookery across the river. In the woods, burgeoning red buckeye buds added a splash of color. Three-inch-tall dwarf wakerobins bloomed lavender or white near the base of a large oak tree in the tupelo swamp. And in the meadow, deer, raccoon, rabbit, canid, and bobcat tracks provided evidence of abundant animal species.

Always a watcher of nature, I was thrilled by the discovery of this new wildlife sanctuary. My outdoor adventuring began when I was a young child running wild and barefoot through the woods and exploring aquatic life in the streams on my family's farm in the Piedmont region of Georgia. I collected bugs and insects and dreamed of becoming a naturalist. Instead, I became a research scientist, an explorer of cellular life and molecular associations. Nature, field exploration, and photography have nevertheless survived the years as my lifelong avocations. During my many excursions, I learned about endemic flora and fauna of the Georgia Piedmont region, Arizona deserts, Maine woods, Texas coast, Costa Rican cloud forests, African savannas, and Belizean jungles and coral reefs. The Goldsmith Schiffman Wildlife Sanctuary, populated with such abundant and diverse plant and animal species, allowed me the opportunity, closer to home, to indulge my enduring desire to explore and write.

I returned to the Sanctuary often to photograph and document each wildflower, insect, reptile, mammal, bird, and scene that caught my attention, or about which my fellow hikers asked questions. The habits of keen observation and meticulous record keeping, which I learned as a research scientist, were applicable in the field as well. Over the course of four years, as my journals filled notebooks, the idea materialized for a book that would document the natural history of this wild riparian habitat and serve as a guide to the diverse species one may find there. It has been a joyful experience to explore the Sanctuary, document its life forms, and write about them.

In *Southern Sanctuary: A Naturalist's Walk through the Seasons*, I hope to promote awareness of the unique, diverse, and rich natural history of Alabama, to encourage its protection, and to inspire others to explore and connect with nature and the outdoors. The Sanctuary can be a mecca for students, something that I hope the book will convey to its readers. I have walked the Sanctuary trails many times since that first day in March, and each time I have discovered something new as I watched the land, and its inhabitants, change with the seasons. I wrote the book to share this excitement of discovery.

I am inspired by the philosophy of Philip Henry Gosse, the English naturalist who visited Alabama in 1838 and described the bountiful populations of plants and animals he found. Just as his book *Letters from Alabama* created an environmental history of a region of Alabama in 1838, the photography and descriptions I have included here freeze in time the environmental history of a wild North Alabama riparian habitat from the years 2009 through 2012 and make it available for future generations.

Both the book and the Sanctuary offer an opportunity to learn about—and really "see"—the myriad existences in nature. To quote Gosse, "Such a morning walk in such a clime, at such a season, you may easily imagine is not performed without multitudes of objects to catch the eye and delight the mind of an observant naturalist."[1] I take the liberty of expanding "observant naturalist" to include each of us as we hike the Sanctuary's trails.

In the beginning of any endeavor, we cannot know to what magnitude a single idea or action may grow. It is just so with the Sanctuary and the Sanctuary Artists—and with this book. The seed for all was planted when Margaret Anne Goldsmith donated the first three hundred wild, bottomland acres along the Flint River in North Alabama to the city of Huntsville as a wildlife sanctuary. I hope this book will inspire others to explore the richly diverse habitat of this Sanctuary, to learn about it, to see its beauty, and to appreciate the physical and psychological benefits that can be gained from spending time with nature. It is also my hope that the book will engender a spirit of stewardship for the land and wildlife living there.

1. Philip Henry Gosse, *Letters from Alabama; Chiefly Relating to Natural History* (1838), Authoritative edition edited by Gary R. Mullen and Taylor D. Littleton (1838; 2nd ed. Tuscaloosa: University of Alabama Press, 2008), 45.

Acknowledgments

This book includes information about a broad spectrum of flora and fauna, and without the help of many individuals whose guidance was generously given I could not have tackled a project of this scope. I am deeply grateful for their support.

Dr. Kenneth Ward, professor of entomology and forestry at Alabama A&M University and president of the North Alabama Birdwatcher's Society, read the manuscript and provided counsel on entomology and ornithology. He also contributed to the list of trees in Appendix 1.

Horticulturist Drucilla Esslinger provided information about wildflowers and native plant species. Margaret Vann, Stephanie Hanna, George Hanna, Jerry Green, and Brian Finzel read sections of the manuscript and also contributed valuable information about wildflowers.

Dr. Ronald H. Petersen, Mycology Lab supervisor, University of Tennessee at Knoxville, helped me to identify fungi and introduced me to witches' butter. Nannette Schwartz also shared information on mushrooms and fungi of the area.

Jud Easterwood, supervising wildlife biologist at the Alabama Division of Wildlife and Freshwater Fisheries, verified the identification of the midland water snake and tracks of a river otter.

Nicholas W. Sharp, Alabama Nongame Wildlife Program, Division of Wildlife & Freshwater Fisheries, showed me the fine points of track identification and confirmed tracks of the river otters. I am sincerely grateful to Nick for providing the definitive photograph of bobcat tracks.

I thank Brad Scott, former principal of Goldsmith Schiffman Elementary School; Jane Russell of the Huntsville public schools' Earthscope Program; Hallie Porter and Cynthia Potts of the Land Trust of North Alabama; and Stephanie Quallis, curator of exhibitions at the Tennessee Valley Art Association in Tuscumbia, Alabama, for their encouragement and enthusiasm in support of this project.

My appreciation is extended to the City of Huntsville's Operation Green Team director Joy McKee for her enthusiastic interest in the project, and especially to Jim Poff for mounting the night vision, motion-activated cameras that photographed deer, bobcats, and turkeys up close and gave us insights into their lives in the Sanctuary.

I am grateful to OMI Engineering, Inc., a Huntsville geotechnical and environmental engineering company, for providing information about the types of soils and other physical characteristics of the Goldsmith Schiffman Wildlife Sanctuary.

Rusty Bynum, Sara McDaris, Bill Case, Bill Goodson, and Richard Modlin, members of my writer's group, provided invaluable editorial suggestions and encouragement. My special appreciation goes to Rusty Bynum, who read the manuscript with a writer's keen eye and kept sneaky writing gremlins at bay. I also thank my brother, Joseph H. H. Moore, for his continued encouragement and belief in this project, and for convincing me that reading the *Chicago Manual of Style* can be fun.

I express my sincere appreciation to the Sanctuary Artists (www.sanctuaryartists.net), a unique group of individuals who walked the trails with me many times, and whose artistic works memorialize the beauty and diversity of the Sanctuary. Members include Margaret Anne Goldsmith, philanthropist and naturalist; Clayton Bass, Maggie Little, Katrina Webber, Mary Ann Pope, Jim Jobe, and Jerry Brown, painters; Dee Burt Holmes, painter and printmaker; Sam Tumminello, photographer; Drucilla Esslinger, archivist and photographer; Jimmy Robinson, poet; Sara McDaris, storyteller and writer; Jack Rogers, wood sculptor;

Guadalupe Robinson, ceramic artist; Susan Knecht, glass blower; Larry Long, archivist and trail guide; and Chuck Weber, webmaster and musician. The idea for the Sanctuary Artists was conceived in February 2009 by Margaret Anne Goldsmith and Clayton Bass, former director and CEO of the Huntsville Museum of Art. They assembled this diverse group of individuals for the purpose of publicizing the Sanctuary through the creative arts, and the varied works of the Sanctuary Artists have been presented as a group in exhibitions throughout North Alabama and beyond. Their first names (and those of other individuals who hiked the trails with me) appear throughout the book, and I thank them for their enduring enthusiasm and help with this project. They opened the door into the world of art by inviting me to become a member of the Sanctuary Artists. As a naturalist, photographer, and writer, I am honored to be a member of this group.

I express sincere and special gratitude to my husband, Dr. Richard F. Modlin, professor emeritus of biological sciences at the University of Alabama in Huntsville, for his patience and sacrifices during the writing of this book. He provided invaluable expertise and counsel in areas of biology in general, and specifically in identification of fish and aquatic vegetation. I thank him, too, for reading the manuscript many more times than once.

My sincere thanks to the Friends of the Preserve and Sanctuary, whose generous support helped make this book a reality. Appreciation also goes to the Land Trust of North Alabama and the Tennessee Valley Audubon Society.

I am especially and deeply grateful to the staff at UA Press. To my acquisitions editor, Elizabeth Motherwell, for her continued encouragement and unending belief in *Southern Sanctuary*. Without her, this book would have never existed. To my designer, Michele Quinn, for her dedication and effort in creating the book's beautiful design. And to the managing editor, Vanessa Rusch, for her assistance, patience, and encouragement, and for guiding this book to its final publication.

SOUTHERN
SANCTUARY

INTRODUCTION

COME WITH ME ON A HIKE through a wild riparian habitat. It's a humid, hazy, 75-degree September day in North Alabama. We begin at a swamp overlook, accompanied by the music of a Carolina wren. The swamp is peaceful. Mountains in the distance stand as a backdrop, emphasizing the swamp's flatness. Clumps of arrow arum growing in the dark water point their arrow-shaped leaves upward toward the shade of a swamp-loving red maple. We leave the overlook to walk along a trail that wanders beside a stream. At the stream's marshy edge, cattails tower above patches of frilly aquatic plants. The air is heavy with the scent of marsh vegetation and fall wildflowers. Goldenrod, daisy fleabane, Asiatic dayflower, woodland lettuce, and giant ironweed bloom nearby. A breeze rustles the alders and pink-blooming smartweed at the marsh edge.

This book is about exploration, observation, discovery, and engaging the senses. Written in an informal style, *Southern Sanctuary* is a guide to the diverse species along the trails in lands bordering the Flint River in North Alabama, and characteristic of riparian habitats in the Southern Appalachian Mountain region. In each of the twelve chapters, the reader is invited on a virtual hike to walk the trails of the Goldsmith Schiffman Wildlife Sanctuary via prose descriptions and photographs. The book begins in the spring with the newness of life and progresses month by month through the seasons.

Although the species depicted here are found in the Goldsmith Schiffman Wildlife Sanctuary in North Alabama, they also occur in Tennessee and North Georgia as well as other areas of the country and, indeed, the world. For instance, the Caesar's mushroom, an *Amanita* species I found near the Flint River, has been known in Italy for 2,000 years. Birds that sing in the woods beside Jobala Pond also sing in Ohio, Canada, and Central America. *Southern Sanctuary* is basically about noticing, questioning, and enjoying nature. As such, it has universal appeal. The book can be read as a treatise on natural history as well as for the wealth of information included in its pages. Organization of chapters as a series of monthly hikes is intended to engage nature enthusiasts and armchair nature adventurers no matter where they live. Both the Sanctuary and this book provide information and an invitation to teachers, students, birdwatchers, hikers, botanists, newcomers to the area, researchers of riparian habitats, and ecologists to investigate the beauty, diversity, and processes that occur in nature.

Each chapter describes a hike along the Sanctuary's trails. However, information derived from numerous hikes and observations over more than three-and-a-half years is also included. A list at the end of each chapter names the various species observed in the Sanctuary for each month during these years. These lists do not include all species living in the Sanctuary. Rather, they serve as a guide to species one might expect to find in each of the months represented in chapters 1–12. The most common trees are mentioned throughout the book, and a list of trees typically found in riparian habitats is included in Appendix 1. Identification, current nomenclature, and range and distribution information for plant and wildflower species are based on information obtained from the *Alabama Plant Atlas* of the Alabama Herbarium Consortium and the University of West Alabama (http://www.floraofal abama.org) and from The United States Department of Agriculture's Natural Resources Conservation Service (http://plants.usda.gov). Atlas volumes are compiled from herbarium specimens; not all the plants found in the Goldsmith Schiffman Wildlife Sanctuary are shown on Alabama maps (from either source) as occurring in Madison County.

Also, not all the species listed will be present each month or every year. In nature, populations vary depending on environmental and other factors. Variations in temperatures, rainfall, snow, ground freezing, and the severity and duration of seasonal flooding influence populations of plants, insects, and animals in the Sanctuary. The genetic makeup of a species also affects its population density at any given time. Species of periodical cicadas emerge at thirteen- or seventeen-year intervals and are not present in other years. In the late spring of 2011, thirteen-year cicadas emerged in large numbers in the Sanctuary. Such abundance will not occur again until 2024, during the next cycle characteristic of these cicadas. The effects of human intervention, such as channeling stream flow and clearing vegetation, will also influence species population statistics.

Though not a standard reference guide, this book describes species endemic to riparian habitats in North Alabama and the Southern Appalachian Cumberland Plateau physiographic section. Basic descriptions of flora and fauna include genus and species names, ecological niche, food sources, and predation. Anecdotes and personal impressions are given, as well as the occasional bit of folklore relating to the use of plants as medicinals, dyes, and food sources by early Colonial Americans and American Indians. The Sanctuary's environment is dynamic, and the plants and animals that live there must constantly adapt to changing conditions. The entire area encompassed by the Sanctuary is a wetland floodway. Its wetland hydrology is characterized by periods of complete inundation to a depth of 5' (1.5 m) or more several times a year. Minor flooding episodes also occur during the winter and early spring months. The water usually recedes within two to four days, and there is little damage to plants from these occurrences. Major winter flooding episodes scour ponds and cause noticeable changes in vegetation around the ponds, in wooded areas, and in the surrounding fields.

The land that is now the Sanctuary was acquired by the Goldsmith family in the 1930s. At the time of purchase, some portions were already cleared for farming, and those areas continued to be farmed or mowed during the seventy-five years that the family owned the land.

Forests were left uncut except for one selective logging in the early years of the family's ownership. Many of the remaining trees, particularly in the tupelo swamps, are now over one hundred years old. Since 2003, when Margaret Anne Goldsmith donated the land for the wildlife sanctuary to the city of Huntsville, the city has acquired an additional one hundred and seventy-five acres. Farming of selected fields has continued to keep these fields clear in anticipation of eventually restoring them as wetlands.

In addition to the Sanctuary, the city of Huntsville owns the 552-acre Hays Nature Preserve located across Highway 431 from the Sanctuary. The two properties share a similar ecology, and many of the species found in the Sanctuary are also found in the Hays Preserve. The city of Huntsville is proud of its record for preserving natural beauty and biodiversity and is committed to providing a quality nature experience to a large number of people. By connecting the Sanctuary with the Hays Nature Preserve via a paved bicycle path, the two city greenspace properties expand destinations and increase access to trails to accommodate a large number of hikers and nature enthusiasts.

Knowledge and understanding of nature come from careful observation, paying attention to subtleties and noticing inconsistencies. From the time my mother turned over a log and showed me a beetle and the red hourglass shape on a black widow spider's ventral side, my fascination with nature has never faltered. Tuning in to bird songs, twitters, and alarm calls can tell us much about what is going on in the woods. In the technologies of our fast-moving world, we have lost much of the perceptive powers our ancestors used to survive in this diverse and wonderful land. But with practice in listening, noticing, and absorbing, we can reawaken the ability. Nature teaches us this, and the lessons carry over into our human relationships and foster peace of mind and spirit.

Becoming attuned to sounds—the songs of birds, water flowing, wind, animal vocalizations, and insect noises—provides us a key to their world. It also opens a new world for us to explore. In his book

What the Robin Knows, Jon Young suggests that if parents listen to the language of birds with their children, it will help children to connect with their "deepest instincts and selves." I hope this book will inspire us to tune in to what the robin can tell us; to be in communication with nature.

APRIL

Bird Songs and Bobcat Tracks

Boredom cannot exist in the company of Nature.
—M. M. Lewis, 2012

Date: April 9
Begin: 9:00 A.M.
End: 12:30 P.M.
Weather: 9:00 A.M., 48°F (9°C), clear, sunny, low wind
  12:30 P.M., 70°F (21°C)
Participants: Drucilla and Marian
Purpose: To discover, photograph, and document spring in the
  Sanctuary

TODAY I BEGIN MY FIRST exploratory excursion into the bottomland habitat that is to become my project and passion for the foreseeable future. When I came here the first time two weeks ago with the Sanctuary Artists, a group with a strong affinity for creating nature art, I found a place of boundless natural beauty with an abundance of birds, wildflowers, and wild areas to discover and explore. I made the decision to come back often to photograph and document this Sanctuary honoring and protecting wildness.

So today, Drucilla, a like-minded nature enthusiast, and I meet at the Sanctuary entrance. We park our cars on the gravel driveway in front of the gate. The Sanctuary is not officially open, so we climb over the gate and proceed along Hidden Springs Trail. Our backpacks are stuffed with rudimentary trail maps; several bird, animal track, and wildflower identification books; and our notes on the location of the dwarf wakerobin we discovered two weeks ago on our introductory hike. The official opening of the Sanctuary is about a year away, so I have an excellent opportunity to photograph and document the plants, animals, and wildness before the Sanctuary's trails, streams, and meadows are modified, which will surely happen as more trails are developed.

We pause near the entrance to view Hidden Springs Swamp. Arrow arum, watermilfoil, alligator weed, and several species of smartweed provide various shades of green. A few yellow wildflowers in the foreground add contrast. Continuing on Hidden Springs Trail, we note numerous red buckeye bushes in bloom and showy cascades of white drape from the black locust trees that line the left side of the trail.

Red buckeye (*Aesculus pavia*)

Black locust (*Robinia pseudoacacia*)

The Red Gates—portals to the Sanctuary

Following the path past the red gates, our portal into the Sanctuary, we come to the marsh at the head of Jobala Pond. Here we notice ragged cattails, evidence of recent spring flooding. Several song sparrows search for seeds near the water's edge, and a towhee trills "drink your teeee" in the woods across the marsh. A northern cardinal flies by overhead. Farther along the trail, we pause to watch a pair of Canada geese land at the far end of Jobala Pond. When they see us they take off, splashing water with their feet as they release themselves from the pond's surface. Drucilla tells me that her husband, Larry, spent happy hours swimming in this pond when he was a boy. It was known then as "the fishing hole."

Continuing on Hidden Springs Trail, we cross the footbridge at the south end of Jobala Pond, turn right, and follow Deer Run Trail to the small pond at Forest Glen Observation Point. Here we find a patch of sensitive fern (*Onoclea sensibilis*) flourishing on the bank of the ditch that drains into this pond. A Carolina wren sings in the woods, and a goldfinch lands in a thicket not far from us. Carolina chickadees and tufted titmice scold. This is an excellent birding area.

We leave Forest Glen and follow Deer Run Trail to the edge of the woods where the trail enters a large, open meadow. Here we stare in wonder at the magnificent, terrestrial sunburst of yellow wildflowers covering this field. There are buttercup species, but the dominant, taller, yellow-blooming plant is butterweed (*Packera glabella*). This annual wildflower belongs to the aster family (Asteraceae). Native in the central and southeastern United States, butterweed grows to a height of about 3' (0.91 m) when mature. Its daisy-like blooms often cover open meadows, as we see here in the Sanctuary today.

Above: **Sensitive fern** (*Onoclea sensibilis*)

Right: **Butterweed** (*Packera glabella*)

A golden spring meadow

Butterweed, also called smooth ragwort and cressleaf groundsel, can be easily confused with golden ragwort (*Packera aurea*), which looks similar but grows in wet areas along stream banks and in mesic woods (woods with a wet or well-balanced moisture supply). Golden ragwort also differs from butterweed in that it has few undivided leaves near the base of the stem, whereas butterweed has numerous divided leaves along the entire stem.

We notice that bright yellow buttercups fill in the lower story of this yellow meadow. Small white flowers are blooming here, too. These are beaked cornsalad (*Valerianella radiata*). Cornsalad sounds more

Beaked cornsalad (*Valerianella radiata*)

appropriate for a luncheon than for a wildflower. This plant grows 6" to 18" (15 cm to 46 cm) tall. It has a four-sided central stem that branches into two parts at the upper half. Each of the stem branches produces a flat-topped cluster of four to twelve individual small white flowers. Bees, wasps, and several types of flies sip nectar from the blooms.

Drucilla and I decide to leave the trail and cut across the meadow to intersect the Tall Tupelo Trail at the edge of the woods ahead. The meadow is muddy, and we have to skirt around several areas of ponding water. There are numerous animal tracks, primarily raccoon and deer, but I spot small fox-size canid tracks, too. We notice a tall, slender-stemmed, blue flower standing alone in an open area and identify it as blue toadflax (*Linaria canadensis*). Grape hyacinths (*Muscari botryoides*) are sprinkled here and there among numerous dandelions. A lone flea-bane (*Erigeron* sp.) stands near the woods ahead.

Now approaching the edge of the field, we notice several dragonflies sunning on a dead log. These are male and female common whitetails (*Plathemis lydia*). The male is easy to identify with his white abdomen and dark wing bands, but we almost miss the female. Her brown coloration and the oblique, white lateral dashes on the abdomen allow her to blend well with the brown tones of the log.

At the sign marking the Tall Tupelo Trail, we enter the woods where we found dwarf wakerobin (*Trillium pusillum*) in bloom two weeks ago. Dwarf wakerobin, also called least trillium, is a member of the lily family (Liliaceae). Although native to riparian habitats such as the Sanctuary, this plant is rare in Alabama. The *Alabama Plant Atlas* shows dwarf wakerobin occurring in only five counties: Limestone, Madison, Jackson, Marshall, and Morgan in the north central part of the state. The United States Department of Agriculture plants profile lists *Trillium pusillum* var. *pusillum*, the variety we find here, in only seven southeastern states and shows it as endangered in Tennessee, Kentucky, and North Carolina. This is why we are delighted to find this native, facultative wetland plant thriving here in the Sanctuary. Land use by humans, soil conditions, amount of sunlight, presence of pollinators, seed dispersal, and other types of vegetation growing nearby, as well as damage to the plant by animals in the area, are all important factors in the conservation of this rare plant.

Above: **Common whitetail dragonfly female** (*Plathemis lydia*)

Left: **Common whitetail dragonfly male** (*Plathemis lydia*)

Drucilla stops and points to the ground near a large oak. Several dwarf wakerobins are clustered around the base of the tree, but today the plants have no blooms. Instead, light green seeds have begun to develop where we saw the blooms a few weeks ago. Finding the plants today assures us that they are thriving and were not harmed by recent flooding. We are delighted to discover that they are producing seeds here in the tupelo woods.

We walk a few yards farther to the Tall Tupelo Observation Point where we find numerous water tupelos (*Nyssa aquatica*). These trees are deciduous and grow in swampy areas such as this. Tupelos can reach a height greater than 90' (27 m). Here, their buttressed trunks disappear into the murky water of the swampy, vernal pool. Looking around, I spot a tupelo with its trunk perfectly reflected in the still swamp water.

Above: **Bobcat tracks** (*Lynx rufus*), courtesy of Nicholas W. Sharp, Alabama Nongame Wildlife Program, Division of Wildlife & Freshwater Fisheries

Left: **Spring cress** (*Cardamine bulbosa*)

This area, dense with large and small water tupelos and trailing vines, conjures images of swamp monsters. My imagination is rewarded when I spy a huge tree shadowed by vines just beyond where we stand. The lower two feet in the center of the trunk might be construed, at dusk or on a dark day, as a large, open mouth. Two knotholes a few feet above "the mouth" seem to peer at me like beady eyes. It's a perfect Halloween tree.

Continuing on the Tall Tupelo Trail as it winds beside the swamp, we find other wildflowers in the woods on our right. Spring cress, phlox, rue anemone, blue violets, twisted trillium, violet woodsorrel, and spring beauties make this a perfect spring woodland. The sound of a barred owl drifts through the trees. I search with binoculars but I cannot find the owl. As we walk deeper into the woods, we hear a pileated woodpecker far off in the distance and catch a glimpse of downy and red-bellied woodpeckers in the tall trees. The raucous call of a blue jay nearby splits the air.

We continue through the woods to the Flint River. Here we pick up Deer Run Trail and find a number of animal tracks in a damp area. It appears that a wildlife drama recently played out here. Deer tracks and indistinct canid tracks—perhaps coyote (*Canis latrans*) or gray fox (*Urocyon cinereoargenteus*)—slide and crisscross in the soft ground. But of greatest interest to me is an indistinct track about 1.5" to 2" (3.8 cm to 5.1 cm) wide with almost round toe prints and no claw marks. This pugmark is typical of a cat. Indeed, this looks like the track of a bobcat (*Lynx rufus*). A little farther along the trail, skid marks show that the animal made a sliding stop. Perhaps it was chasing prey. Bobcat diet consists of rabbits, rats, squirrels, ground birds, turkeys, and even small deer. This would be a perfect location to install a motion-activated, night-vision camera. From the tracks and other signs, it appears that wildlife is active, abundant, and varied here beside the river.

About 50 yd (46 m) north of the Flint River Observation Point, we notice great blue herons (*Ardea herodias*) flying around the treetops on the opposite side of the river. We scan the area with binoculars and

Great blue herons at the rookery

discover several nests. One nest in a very tall tree has a heron standing on it. We will certainly return to observe this rookery and its heron activity in the coming months.

We backtrack on the Deer Run Trail through the woods to a raised area that was probably once an Indian midden. Here, we notice an interesting fungus growing against the trunk of a fallen and decaying oak limb. Arranged in graduated sizes in a row, these fungal bodies resemble cups. The hymenium, or inside lining of the cups, is dark brown—almost black—and the exterior is a grayish color. These are the fruiting bodies of *Urnula craterium*. *Urnula* means little urn and *craterium* refers to krater, a vessel used in ancient times for mixing wine and water. The fruiting bodies we have found are not quite mature. At maturity, the tops will become wider and look even more like cups. Sometimes called devil's urn, this goblet-shaped cup fungus is

Devil's urn fungus (*Urnula craterium*)

common but not conspicuous because its dark interior is easily missed in shadowy woods. Devil's urn is widely distributed throughout eastern North America and found in deciduous woods in the spring.

We've been exploring the Sanctuary for almost three hours and noon is approaching. We head back across the meadow and walk past patches of buttercups, grape hyacinths, and dandelions. Several crayfish chimneys made of balls of wet clay dot the area.

Across the meadow, we intersect Deer Run Trail and follow it toward the parking lot. On the way we notice orange, trumpet-shaped blooms high in the trees on our left as we pass Jobala Pond. This high-climbing vine is crossvine (*Bignonia capreolata*). Its flowers are beautiful, but dull compared to the bright orange of trumpet creeper, which blooms later in the spring. Crossvine is so named because of the cross-shape appearance of the pith in a cross-section cut of the stem.

A little farther, we notice another vine. This one has heart-shaped, pubescent (covered with fine, short hairs) leaves that are larger than Drucilla's hand with fingers spread wide. Curious-looking, light yellow blooms resembling old-fashioned pipes drape among the leaves. This

Crossvine (*Bignonia capreolata*)

woody vine is wooly dutchman's pipe vine (*Aristolochia tomentosa*). Endemic to the Appalachian region, this vine is found in forest edges from Pennsylvania to Georgia, throughout Alabama, and west to Texas, Oklahoma, and Kansas. Here in the Sanctuary, wooly dutchman's pipe vine blooms from early May through June.

We stand for a moment beside Jobala Pond to listen to the Eastern towhee (*Pipilo erythrophthalmus*) singing across the marsh. Towhees have seed-cracking bills and are a large member of the sparrow family. Males have rich rufous sides, a touch of white on the wings, a white belly, and black breast and back. Females are a rich brown instead of black but otherwise have the same markings. A colorful and handsome species, towhees are a year-round resident of the Sanctuary and the southeastern United States.

This has been a fine morning to visit the Sanctuary and a wonderful introduction to the diversity of species I expect to find as I explore here in the next months. We've seen or heard a number of birds, and the variety of spring wildflowers in bloom is amazing. The most exciting discovery, I think, is finding what looks like bobcat tracks beside the river. We make plans to come back soon to look for the bobcat and discover how the Sanctuary's scenery, flora, and fauna will change through the seasons.

Wooly dutchman's pipe vine (*Aristolochia tomentosa*)

Species List: April

Wildflowers and Plants

Alligator weed (*Alternanthera philoxeroides*)

Arrow arum (*Peltandra virginica*)

Beaked cornsalad (*Valerianella radiata*)

Blue toadflax (*Linaria canadensis*)

Blue violet (*Viola* sp.)

Buttercup (*Ranunculus* sp.)

Butterweed (*Packera glabella*)

Cattail (*Typha latifolia*)

Common duckweed (*Lemna minor*)

Crossvine (*Bignonia capreolata*)

Cutleaf geranium (*Geranium dissectum*)

Dandelion (*Taraxacum* sp.)

Dwarf wakerobin (*Trillium pusillum*)

Early saxifrage (*Saxifraga virginiensis*)

Fleabane (*Erigeron* sp.)

Giant duckweed (*Spirodela polyrhiza*)

Grape hyacinth (*Muscari botryoides*)

Mayapple (*Podophyllum peltatum*)

Parrot feather watermilfoil (*Myriophyllum aquaticum*)

Phlox (*Phlox* sp.)

Poison ivy (*Toxicodendron radicans*) bloom buds

Rue anemone (*Anemonella thalictroides*)

Sensitive fern (*Onoclea sensibilis*)
Smartweed (*Persicaria* sp.)
Spring beauty (*Claytonia virginica*)
Spring cress (*Cardamine bulbosa*)
Twisted trillium (*Trillium stamineum*)
Violet woodsorrel (*Oxalis violacea*)
Wild garlic (*Allium canadense*)
Wild peppergrass (*Lepidium virginicum*)
Wooly dutchman's pipe vine
  (*Aristolochia tomentosa*)

Trees and Shrubs

American sycamore (*Platanus
  occidentalis*)
Black locust (*Robinia pseudoacacia*)
Eastern redbud (*Cercis canadensis*) in
  bloom
Red buckeye (*Aesculus pavia*)
Red maple (*Acer rubrum*)
Water tupelo (*Nyssa aquatica*)

Birds

Barred owl (*Strix varia*)
Blue jay (*Cyanocitta cristata*)
Canada goose (*Branta canadensis*)
Carolina chickadee (*Poecile carolinensis*)
Carolina wren (*Thryothorus ludovicianus*)
Downy woodpecker (*Picoides pubescens*)
Eastern towhee (*Pipilo erythrophthalmus*)
Goldfinch (*Carduelis tristis*)
Great blue heron (*Ardea herodias*)
Northern cardinal (*Cardinalis cardinalis*)
Pileated woodpecker (*Dryocopus pileatus*)
Red-bellied woodpecker (*Melanerpes
  carolinus*)
Song sparrow (*Melospiza melodia*)
Tufted titmouse (*Baeolophus bicolor*)

(Note: The woods surrounding the
Tall Tupelo Observation Point and the
Forest Glen Pond proved to be excellent
birding sites. The list includes birds
identified visually and/or by call.)

Mammals

Bobcat (*Lynx rufus*) indistinct tracks
Canidae—probably Coyote (*Canis
  latrans*) tracks
North American raccoon (*Procyon lotor*)
  tracks
Rabbit (*Sylvilagus* sp.) tracks
White-tailed deer (*Odocoileus
  virginianus*) tracks

Insects

Common whitetail dragonfly (*Libellula
  lydia*)
Dragonfly nymphs in a vernal pool in
  the field
Falcate orangetip butterfly (*Anthocharis
  midea*)
Mayfly nymphs in a vernal pool in the
  field

Fungi

Devil's urn fungus (*Urnula craterium*)

Other Species

Crayfish (chimneys)
Midland water snake (*Nerodia sipedon
  pleuralis*)

MAY

Fish, Lichen, and a Gentle Garter Snake

Date: May 27
Begin: 9:00 A.M.
End: 12:30 P.M.
Weather: 9:00 A.M., 67°F (19°C), cloudy, humid
    12:30 P.M., 78°F (26°C)
Participants: Drucilla, Susan, Larry, Marian, and two guests from
    the Alabama Forestry Commission
Purpose: To explore the Sanctuary and to introduce it to guests
    from the Alabama Forestry Commission

As we begin our hike on Hidden Springs Trail this cloudy, humid morning, bright yellow goldfinches flit among new leaves in the tree canopy ahead. A great blue heron glides over the open field on our right, and, sitting among young maple leaves above us, a great crested flycatcher with a mouthful of nesting material watches us. Leaving the tree, the flycatcher drops to the ground about 20' (6 m) ahead and, still holding the nest material, he or she (plumage is similar for both) seems unafraid of us. Great crested flycatchers (*Myiarchus crinitus*) build nests of grass, twigs, feathers, and leaves, and as we see today, they also use cattail seed head fluff. These flycatchers construct nests in log or stump

Great crested flycatcher (*Myiarchus crinitus*) with a beakful of nest material

cavities or rotten fence posts. Sometimes they include shed snakeskin or a piece of cellophane in the nest. The reason for doing this is a matter of conjecture. A large species of flycatcher, the great crested has a body length of 7" to 8" (17.8 cm to 20.3 cm) and a wingspan of about 13" (33 cm). We leave this one to nest building and continue on the trail toward Jobala Pond.

Catalpa trees are in bloom now. Their large, showy, white flowers, dotted with yellow and purple markings, grace the left side of Hidden Springs Trail. This native southern tree (*Catalpa bignonioides*) belongs to the trumpet-creeper family (Bignoniaceae). Catalpas are found in warm regions across North America. William Bartram, the famous American botanist, described this tree in 1773 when he found it growing in southeastern Georgia. Hummingbirds, butterflies, and bees sip nectar from the blooms, and this fall when the trees lose their leaves, the fruit, which looks like long, slender bean pods, will be easy to see. Catalpa leaves are 5" to 10" (12 cm to 25 cm) long and 3" to 8" (8 cm to 20 cm) wide. They are heart-shaped and have sharply pointed tips.

Parrot feather watermilfoil (*Myriophyllum aquaticum*)

Although toxic to most species, catalpa leaves are the host and sole food source of catalpa sphinx moth (*Ceratomia catalpae*) caterpillars, which are not affected by the toxic substances in the leaves. The caterpillars, also called "catalpa worms," are prized as bait, a fact well known by fishermen.

We reach the head of the pond and notice a bright green frilly aquatic plant growing in the marsh in about 3' (0.9 m) of water. This is parrot feather watermilfoil (*Myriophyllum aquaticum*), not to be confused with the invasive Eurasian milfoil (*Myriophyllum spicatum*) that tangles in boat propellers and is the bane of boaters in large lakes across the country. Parrot feather watermilfoil has numerous leaves arranged in whorls around the stem. Most of the plant is submerged, and the leaves on the above-water part are different from those below water. Both submerged and emerged leaves are pinnately dissected (divided), but leaf length and number of dissections per leaf differ. Parrot feather is a perennial occurring in freshwater streams and lakes throughout North America.

In another area where the stream is free of vegetation, there are

several fish beds. We notice a medium-sized smallmouth bass (*Micropterus dolomieu*) attending one of these. Later at home, I read that smallmouth bass spawn in May and June. They begin building nests when water temperatures reach 55°F (12.8°C) to 60°F (15.6°C), but females lay eggs only when the water temperature is 61°F (16.1°C) to 65°F (18.3°C). Smallmouth bass may live as long as fifteen years and usually return to the same spawning area each year. Females lay between two thousand and fifteen thousand eggs. The eggs stick to small stones in the middle of the nest and hatch one to two weeks later. Males guard the nest and protect the young for another two weeks after they hatch.

As we approach Jobala Pond, two geese rise from the water and fly toward the open field on the opposite side of the pond. A few feet ahead of us near the bank, something is making ripples in the water. As we watch, a brown animal about the size of a large cat swims into view and then disappears into the marsh. It's a muskrat. This one was probably feeding on aquatic vegetation near the bank when we startled it as we came near. I'm happy to see this animal—I've long suspected muskrats as the engineers of holes in the bank at the head of the pond. These native North American, semi-aquatic rodents are the only species in the genus *Ondatra*. Muskrats belong to the family Cricetidae, which includes almost six hundred species of rodents. They thrive in a wide range of wetland habitats and spend much of their time in water where they forage for cattail roots, bur-reed stems, and other plant materials. They also include small frogs, crayfish, fish, and small turtles in their diet. Muskrats get their name from the musky odor used to mark territory and the fact that they somewhat resemble rats. However, muskrats are not true rats, which belong to the genus *Rattus*. Muskrats weigh 1.3 lb to 4.4 lb (0.6 kg to 2 kg). They can be 16" to 28" (41 cm to 71 cm) in length, of which almost half is tail. The tail is covered with scales rather than hair and is slightly flattened vertically (in contrast to the paddle-like, horizontally flat tails of beavers). This vertically flat tail design is unique to muskrats, and they use tails rather than legs as their primary aid in swimming. Muskrats had an important role in Earth's

Muskrat (*Ondatra zibethicus*)

creation according to several American Indian myths. After other animals had failed, it was the muskrat that dove to the bottom of the primordial sea to bring mud for creation of the earth. Muskrats probably live two to four years in the wild. I hope this interesting little animal will continue to make its home and raise families here in Jobala Pond.

Just ahead, Larry and several others have discovered a spotted gar (*Lepisosteus oculatus*) resting near the surface of the pond. The gar seems oblivious to us even as we slowly gather on the bank to watch it. Gars are facultative air breathers—they have gills as well as a primitive atmospheric air-breathing organ. This enables them to survive for several weeks in water that has a very low oxygen content. The air-breathing organ is a highly vascularized swim, or air, bladder. It is connected to the pharynx by a duct, which is regulated by air pressure (pneumatic). Gars breathe atmospheric air by gulping it at the surface and swallowing it. State of Alabama surveys list the spotted gar as one of the most abundant and widespread of the gar species in the state. Spotted gars can adapt to a wide range of habitats. Adults may attain a length of 2.9' to 3.9' (0.9 m to 1.2 m), but I estimate this one to be around 24" (0.6 m) long.

A little farther along Hidden Springs Trail, I notice turkey tracks in the mud beside Jobala Pond. We often find turkey tracks in the woods and meadows, but this is the first time I've found them in this area of the Sanctuary. We continue across the footbridge to the Forest Glen Observation Point. Here we notice a shrub about 12' to 15' tall (3.7 to 4.6 m). It bears spikes 3" to 6" long (7 cm to 15 cm) with bluish-purple flowers at the apex of stems. This is false indigo (*Amorpha fruticosa*), a member of the family Fabaceae. This native perennial shrub typically blooms in May in North Alabama. Later in the summer, small fruit pods will develop. Pods are barely 0.75" (0.64 cm) long and are not easy to see. False indigo is a facultative wetland species found from the Great Plains to the Gulf States and in most counties throughout the South. Often used as a landscaping plant, false indigo may have been cultivated in the United States since 1724. It thrives well in moist soils and provides cover for wildlife, especially in riparian environments such as this.

We backtrack to Jobala Pond, circle around it on the east side, and walk to the small stream that flows through a marshy meadow into the pond at the Jobala Haven Observation Point. Looking east toward the edge of the marshy meadow, I notice several dragonflies near low-growing vegetation. One is pruinose blue (overlying pigment producing a frosted appearance). It has dark eyes, slightly amber coloring on the front edge of the wings, and a noticeable white stigma on the leading edge of each of the four wings. In entomology, stigma refers to a prominent bar-like, opaque, or colored cell near the tip of each wing of some dragonflies and damselflies. I notice that stigmata of this dragonfly have a smaller black bar on the distal end of each white bar. The stigmata are bright and seem to glitter in the sun. This is a male spangled skimmer dragonfly (*Libellula cyanea*). The female perches nearby. Her thorax is dark brown with yellow patches on the sides. A broad yellow stripe extends along each side of the abdomen and converges into a single stripe over the thorax toward the head. The abdomen has a dark brown dorsal stripe. The prominent white stigmata on each wing are like those of the male, but the female's wings are darker amber, especially on the

Above: Spangled skimmer dragonfly male (*Libellula cyanea*)

Below: Spangled skimmer dragonfly female (*Libellula cyanea*)

leading edges. The female's eyes, set in her brown face, are light brown. Spangled skimmers are found in vegetated areas near ponds and in marshes such as this pond-side meadow.

We skirt the marsh on our left and continue around the meadow. Here, we find another interesting dragonfly. This one is a male blue dasher (*Pachydiplax longipennis*). His distinguishing features include

Male blue dasher dragonfly (*Pachydiplax longipennis*)

a pruinose blue abdomen, amber wings, striking green eyes, mostly white face, and a brown thorax with yellow stripes. Blue dashers are about 1.4" (3.6 cm) long and are abundant throughout most of the United States. Grasping the edge of a crinkled lichen, this one perches in a drooped forward pose characteristic of blue dashers. The flight season for blue dashers in our region is March through November. This is my first sighting of this colorful dragonfly in the Sanctuary, and I am delighted to discover it here.

Now, we turn left at the edge of the woods on the Tall Tupelo Trail and walk to the loop trail leading to the Tall Tupelo Observation Point. It was here that we discovered dwarf wakerobin blooming in late March and seeding in April, but today the plants have neither blooms

Green dragon (*Arisaema dracontium*)

nor seeds. The season of glory for this little plant appears to be over. We rejoin the Tall Tupelo Trail and walk through the woods toward the Flint River.

In the tupelo woods, we notice a cluster of low-growing plants that resemble young trillium. However, closer examination reveals branched leaflets at the top of the stems. These are young green dragons (*Arisaema dracontium*), an herbaceous perennial related to Jack-in-the-pulpit; both belong to the arum family (Araceae). Green dragons grow in damp woods and, when mature, produce a single flower stem that grows to a height of about 12" to 18" (30.5 cm to 46 cm). The flower stem is separate from the single leaf stem, which can grow over 3' (0.9 m) tall.

Further along the trail near the edge of the woods, we find a more mature green dragon. The leaf is curved and has fifteen leaflets that are held, umbrella-like, over the plant. This one has a slender spathe beginning to develop on the flower stem. A spathe is a large modified bract

or specialized leaf that encloses flower clusters of some plants. When mature, this spathe will be about 1" to 2.4" (2.5 cm to 6 cm) long. It will form around a spadix, which is a type of spike inflorescence consisting of small flowers. Later in the summer, the flowers will eventually develop into as many as one hundred and fifty berries in columns that resemble kernels on a corncob. As berries develop, they will turn from green to brilliant red by late summer. Each berry may contain one to three seeds. The roots of green dragons contain calcium oxalate and are toxic. These plants grow well in moist areas in the Sanctuary woods and woods bordering the Flint River.

We continue on the Tall Tupelo Trail to the Flint River Observation Point, then turn left and walk a short distance on Deer Run Trail. Looking across the river, we locate the great blue heron rookery that we discovered here in March. Today the leaves are dense, but we can make out one of the herons standing like a sentinel on a nest.

We reverse our course and continue on Deer Run Trail as it diverges from the river and meanders around the small meadow. The ground is drier now than in April, and there are no obvious tracks today. When we hiked here last month, Drucilla and I found what looked like bobcat tracks, among others. Ahead, young air potato vines (*Dioscorea polystachya*) climb vegetation on the left side of the trail. These vines are attractive with their heart-shaped leaves, but air potato is an invasive species and a serious threat to native trees and plants. Potato vines climb to the tops of trees and grow as much as 8" (20 cm) in a day. Vines die back in winter but grow again from underground tubers in the spring. A native of Africa, potato vine is a member of the yam family (Dioscoreaceae), and in many tropical countries people use it as a food source.

Another noteworthy plant growing here beside Deer Run Trail is the mock or Indian strawberry (*Duchesnea indica*) now displaying showy red berries that look very much like edible wild strawberries. This weedy plant grows low as a ground cover. A member of the family Rosaceae, it displays attractive yellow flowers in spring through early fall. The leaves are palmately compound and leaf edges are serrated. The berries and leaves are edible, and while the berries look good enough to eat, they are

Air potato vines (*Dioscorea polystachya*)

said to be tasteless. Apparently wildlife is of the same opinion; the plant is of little interest as food for animals or birds. In China, Indian strawberry is considered to be a medicinal plant. It is said to have value as a fever reducer, antiseptic, and anticoagulant and can be used for treatment of snake bites and various other injuries and maladies.

Farther along, we notice a colorful fungus growing on a log beside the trail. A fringe of creamy white and bands of brown, tan, dark brown, and greenish gray decorate it. This is a turkey tail fungus (*Trametes versicolor*). Turkey tail mushrooms are one of the most common species of mushrooms in North America. A member of the family Polyporaceae, they grow in overlapping clusters on dead hardwood logs and stumps.

Turkey tail fungus (*Trametes versicolor*)

Caps, only millimeters thick, are 0.8" to 4" (2 cm to 10 cm) across with tiny pores on the underside. Also found in Canada, Europe, Siberia, and Japan and first recorded during the Ming Dynasty (1368–1644) in China, this mushroom is not only attractive to the eye, but also has compounds that are reported to be useful in the treatment of cancer.

Looking up, I notice and photograph gray-green formations on the surface of a dead twig. These are lichens. One is frilly and looks like a beard lichen (*Usnea* sp.). The other is a foliose type (characterized as having a more or less "leafy" thallus or body). It belongs to the genus *Parmotrema* and has broad lobes, a gray-green color, ruffled margins, and dark cilia on the margins of the lobes. There are thirty-two species of *Parmotrema* reported in North America, of which about a third are found in Alabama.

Two lichens coexisting side by side: leaf-like (*Parmotrema* sp.) on the left
and beard lichen (*Usnea* sp.) on the right

Lichens are fascinating organisms that exist as an association between a lichen fungus (which has no chlorophyll) and a chlorophyll-
containing organism (a photobiont) that is capable of producing food
by photosynthesis. In the process of photosynthesis, the green pigment
chlorophyll, in the presence of sunlight, converts carbon dioxide and
water into glucose. Because fungi cannot produce their own food, lichen fungi must exist in a symbiotic relationship with the photobionts,
green algae or cyanobacteria (blue-green algae), or both of these. The
function of the fungus is to protect the photobiont sequestered within
its thallus (fungal body) and to provide a more constant supply of moisture by allowing movement of water within its cell walls. Also, the pig-
ments produced by the fungus protect light-sensitive green algal photobionts from excess light. Many photobionts could not survive outside of

the habitat provided by the lichen fungus. The fungus gains from the relationship because cell walls of the photobiont become more permeable when associated with the fungus. This allows carbohydrates produced by photosynthesis in the photobiont to leak out. Fungal cells then absorb these leaked carbohydrates as fungus food.

To initially form the fungus-photobiont combination of lichen, a fungus surrounds and presses its fungal hyphae against the cell walls of algae or cyanobacteria to secure them. Remarkably, a fungus can detect the proper algal partner. The fungus does this by sensing certain target proteins in the algal or cyanobacteria cell walls. The form of a lichen is determined by the fungus, which contains the genetic information for lichen development, but presence of the alga or cyanobacterium is required to turn on or activate the fungal genes that control morphogenesis into the form of the lichen. The mechanisms involved in this process are not fully understood.

Lichens produce more than five hundred specialized biochemical products. Extracts of lichens can be used to boost the immune system, and some lichen products can kill certain bacteria. Lichens protect the space around themselves by producing substances that reduce competition from other types of organisms in their environment. If I were a cat and had nine lives, I would devote one of my lives to the study of lichens. They are fascinating, but for now, I will pay more attention to the varieties of lichens here in the Sanctuary.

We continue to the Gravel Bar beside one of the Flint River's minor streams, but we do not cross this stream to the island that was formed when the river split into smaller streams here. Instead, we take advantage of shade under the trees to talk with our two guests from the Alabama Forestry Commission about the Treasure Forest Program. Our resulting discussion confirms their interest in helping us establish the Sanctuary as a Treasure Forest. The Alabama Treasure Forest Program was started by the Alabama Forestry Committee in 1974. This program assists landowners in protecting their forests and provides guidelines for stewardship. Treasure Forest status will ensure that trees in the

Goldsmith Schiffman Wildlife Sanctuary will be protected from harvest and abuse. Today's meeting is a step in the process of establishing the Sanctuary's Treasure Forest status.

Now ready to move on, we decide to leave the trail and take a shortcut across the field to the woods on the other side. A short distance into the woods, we find a wide depression with trees standing in several inches of water. Susan points out overcup oak (*Quercus lyrata*), American hornbeam (*Carpinus caroliniana*), and water tupelo (*Nyssa aquatica*). Typical of riparian bottomland woods, this depression is a seasonally flooded, temporary or vernal pool. The characteristics of these types of pools include their location in wooded areas, lack of continuously flowing inlet or outlet water (unlike sloughs), relatively small size, shallow depth, and absence of fish but presence of other aquatic fauna. Usually these pools contain water during the spring rainy season, but later in the year they can be completely dry. The wetland tree species growing here are well adapted to such fluctuations.

As we walk across the field, we notice the usual raccoon and deer tracks. Crayfish chimneys are distributed throughout, and in several places I notice scratch marks made by raccoons in search of something edible. Buttercups are still blooming, but the wild peppergrass (*Lepidium virginicum*), a member of the mustard family (Brassicaceae), and the beaked cornsalad (*Valerianella radiata*) we found here last month are no longer blooming. In fact, the peppergrass has gone to seed. Young leaves of this plant are edible and taste peppery. They are good in salads, or so I'm told. And there—in a very wet place—are two bobcat-sized tracks. These pugmarks are fresh, and I believe this animal visited the field not long before we came here today.

Not far from these tracks, I notice a small butterfly clinging to a short, vertical stem. Except for the bright orange on the forewing, I might have perceived it as a dead leaf. This strange creature has a very long snout and forward-positioned antennae. It is appropriately named snout butterfly (*Libytheana carinenta*). The snout actually consists of the butterfly's elongated, prominent labial palps (mouthparts). This, along with the mottled, gray-brown color on the underside of the wing, give the appearance of a dead leaf and stem. The wingspan of this small butterfly is about 1.4" to 2" (3.6 cm to 5.1 cm). Snouts are commonly found in moist areas in fields and wooded habitats. Hackberry trees, which grow here in the Sanctuary, are their sole host plant. These butterflies seek salts and minerals and belong to the "puddle club," defined by Bright and Ogard in *Butterflies of Alabama* as "a gathering of butterflies (usually males) at wet spots." Snout butterflies occasionally go on migrations. This seems to happen when populations become overcrowded. *Libytheana carinenta* is the only snout species in North America. They are not rare or endangered, but I am glad to find this one in the Sanctuary.

Now as we continue to the edge of the field joining the Deer Run Trail, we notice something moving in a clump of grass. It's a small snake. Susan reaches quickly into the grass and catches it just behind the head. As a naturalist, she knows which snakes should not be approached. She recognized this one as a non-poisonous eastern garter snake. Grasping it gently, she holds it still while I photograph it. When she releases the little snake, it quickly disappears into the grass.

Snout butterfly (*Libytheana carinenta*)

Eastern garter snakes (*Thamnophis sirtalis sirtalis*) live in habitats that include marshes such as this, as well as hillsides and gardens in both wet and dry locations. As adults, garter snakes eat insects, amphibians, fish, small rodents, and even small birds and bird eggs. Juveniles survive on spiders, tadpoles, earthworms, and other small creatures they may find. The most widely distributed snake in North America, garter snakes range in size from 18" to as long as 36" (0.5 m to 0.9 m). Coloration varies, but typically three yellow stripes run the length of the body and dark blotches are sprinkled between the stripes, thus giving the appearance of a garter, perhaps.

When Susan held the little snake for us to see its face, I noticed that it had round eyes with dark, round pupils. The round pupil is one feature that helps to distinguish venomous from non-venomous snakes. Most of the poisonous snakes in North America have elliptical pupils (coral snakes are an exception). Other characteristics of non-venomous snakes include the absence of a triangular-shaped head and the indentations (pits) in front of the eyes (characteristics of rattlesnakes and other pit-vipers). Also, the tail of this little garter snake is slender and tapered, not blunt like those of most venomous snakes. And, of course, there are no fangs, though we do not check to confirm this. I don't recommend handling any snake unless a person is trained and knowledgeable. It can be difficult to tell the difference between venomous and non-venomous snakes. Even the bite of a non-poisonous snake can cause serious damage from bacterial infection. Today we have had an excellent opportunity to learn more about one type of snake that inhabits the Sanctuary. Snakes are beneficial in helping to sustain biodiversity, and they are a part of the natural history and treasure of the Sanctuary. We need only to respect them.

Now, nearing Jobala Pond on the way back to the cars, I notice a bright orange butterfly nectaring on the blooms of Chinese privet (*Ligustrum sinense*) at the edge of the field on our right. The butterfly is an American lady (*Vanessa virginiensis*). This butterfly is almost identical to the painted lady (*Vanessa cardui*) I've seen in the Sanctuary at other

American lady butterfly (*Vanessa virginiensis*)

times. The primary difference is in the number of eyespots on the ventral side of the hindwing. The American lady has two large eyespots while the painted lady has four small ones. The American lady also has a white dot that shows on the dorsal and ventral sides of the forewing in the subapical field (the orange area just under the darker tip of the forewing). This spot is not found on the wings of the painted lady. Both species are common in Alabama, but American lady butterflies are a constant resident while painted lady butterflies are not tolerant of the cold. They must recolonize an area each year. The American lady is the most common species in the genus *Vanessa* in Alabama.

On our left as we continue on Hidden Springs Trail beside Jobala Pond, we note wooly dutchman's pipe vine (*Aristolochia tomentosa*) with its U-shaped blooms. We found this vine here in April. Today several black caterpillars with orange spots and two black horns on the head

Pipevine swallowtail caterpillars (*Battus philenor*)

are nibbling the edges of the leaves. These are pipevine swallowtail butterfly caterpillars (*Battus Philenor*). The caterpillars ingest leaves of their host plants, the pipevines and Virginia-snakeroot, which contain cardiac glycosides and aristocholic acids. The toxic substances are incorporated into the body of the caterpillars. Molecules of the toxic substances persist through metamorphosis and are passed to the adult butterflies. Consequently the caterpillars, as well as the mature butterflies, are rendered unpalatable to birds and other would-be predators.

In addition to pipevine, we find Cherokee rose (*Rosa laevigata*) blooming in a riot of pale pink farther along the trail, and leatherflower (*Clematis viorna*) twines over vegetation beside Jobala Pond. A question mark butterfly (*Polygonia interrogationis*) is sipping moisture from a damp place on the trail ahead. The two white spots on the underside of the up-folded wing distinguish it from the comma butterfly, which has only one white spot on the underwing. Question marks range

Question mark butterfly (*Polygonia interrogationis*)

throughout the eastern United States and nectar on butterfly bush and common milkweed. This is a medium-sized butterfly with a wingspan of 2.25" to 3" (5.7 to 7.6 cm). We skirt around this one and do not disturb it.

As we walk this stretch of trail, I am reminded of another day in May when, glancing at the vegetation on my left, I noticed a gray form that looked inconsistent with the limb and foliage. I walked closer for a better look. The gray hump on the limb turned out to be an eastern gray treefrog, probably *Hyla versicolor*. The frog opened an eye wider as my camera clicked, but it did not move from the limb on which its color blended so well. Gray treefrogs are capable of changing color from shades of gray to shades of green to blend with the environment. This type of coloration that conceals or disguises an animal's shape is called cryptic coloration. Gray treefrogs are masters of disguise. Cope's gray treefrog (*Hyla chrysoscelis*) also inhabits the same territory as *H. versicolor*, and the two are indistinguishable in appearance. The

Gray treefrog (*Hyla* sp.)

only differences are in the length of vocalizations of the males and the number of chromosomes (*H. versicolor* has twice the number of chromosomes as *Hyla chrysoscelis*). Determining the exact species of the little tree frog resting on the limb here would depend on analysis of its call or on chromosome studies in someone's molecular biology laboratory. Considering such subtle differences, I will simply call this one a *Hyla species*.

I've heard tree frogs singing high in trees on several occasions as I walk in the Sanctuary, but this is the first one I've actually seen. Gray tree frogs are found in the eastern United States and southeastern Canada and range in size from about 1.5" to 2" (3.8 to 5.1 cm). They hibernate under logs, leaf litter, and roots in winter. Because their blood

contains glycerol, they can tolerate freezing temperatures down to 17.6°F (-8°C). This permits them to exist in colder months at the northern end of their range. In order to live in trees, these frogs have specialized toe pads with mucous glands that enable them to adhere to vertical surfaces such as tree trunks. Small bones in the pads, and cartilage between these bones, help support the frog's weight. Tree frogs breed once a year in late April through May or when local evening temperatures rise above about 60°F (15°C). Their choruses can be heard on warm, cloudy nights from dusk to midnight usually in April and May, but may also be heard into the summer months.

Now approaching a slowly flowing section of the stream that drains from Hidden Springs Marsh into Jobala Pond, we notice a large number of black striped, blue damselflies. I believe these are bluets (*Enallagma* sp.). There are at least thirty-five species of bluets known in North America, and differentiating them can be a challenge. Looking with binoculars, I can see a nymph (naiad) clinging to a dead stem a few inches above the water. We have arrived serendipitously, at a time when damselflies are emerging from their weeks or months (depending on the species) of life underwater to become colorful, mature flying insects. I notice several cast-off skins (exuviae) left by previously emerged individuals. There are a number of other damselflies perching on vegetation or flying over the water. After emerging from their underwater life, damselflies fly around for a period of several days or longer (again depending on species) and then mate, lay eggs, and begin the cycle again. My camera catches a mating pair in the typical damselfly wheel formation.

Now hot and a bit tired, but happy with our morning of discovery, we reach the red gates just past noon. It has been a fine day with abundant wildflowers, smallmouth bass, a garter snake, a few fungi, an opportunity to witness stages in the life cycle of damselflies, and good company. And, of prime importance, I believe the Alabama Forestry Commission representatives are favorably impressed with the remarkable diversity and beauty of the Sanctuary.

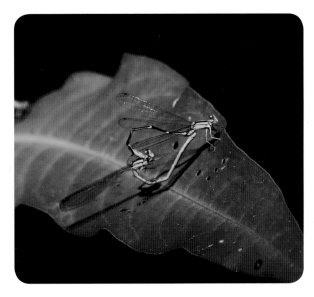

Bluet damselflies (*Enallagma* sp.) in wheel formation

Species List: May

Wildflowers and Plants
Air potato vines (*Dioscorea polystachya*)
Arrow arum (*Peltandra virginica*)
Beaked cornsalad (*Valerianella radiata*)
Buttercup (*Ranunculus* sp.)
Canada germander (*Teucrium canadense*)
Carolina wild petunia (*Ruellia caroliniensis*)
Cherokee rose (*Rosa laevigata*)
Chinese privet (*Ligustrum sinense*)
False indigo (*Amorpha fruticosa*)
Green dragon (*Arisaema dracontium*)
Horsenettle (*Solanum carolinense*)
Leatherflower (*Clematis viorna*)

Mock strawberry or Indian strawberry (*Duchesnea indica*)
Parrot feather watermilfoil (*Myriophyllum aquaticum*)
Sensitive fern (*Onoclea sensibilis*)
Wild peppergrass (*Lepidium virginicum*)
Wooly dutchman's pipe vine (*Aristolochia tomentosa*)

Trees
American hornbeam (*Carpinus caroliniana*)
Black locust (*Robinia pseudoacacia*)
Black walnut (*Juglans nigra*)

Catalpa (*Catalpa bignonioides*)
Overcup oak (*Quercus lyrata*)
Red maple (*Acer rubrum*)
Swamp or stiff dogwood (*Cornus foemina*)
Sycamore (*Platanus occidentalis*)
Water tupelo (*Nyssa aquatica*)

Birds

Canada goose (*Branta canadensis*)
Goldfinch (*Carduelis tristis*)
Great blue heron (*Ardea herodias*)
Great crested flycatcher (*Myiarchus crinitus*)
Turkey (*Meleagris gallopavo*) tracks

Mammals

Bobcat (*Lynx rufus*) tracks
Muskrat (*Ondatra zibethicus*)
North American raccoon (*Procyon lotor*) tracks
White tailed deer (*Odocoileus virginianus*) tracks

Insects

American lady butterfly (*Vanessa virginiensis*)
Blue dasher dragonfly (*Pachydiplax longipennis*) male
Bluet damselfly (*Enallagma* sp.)
Ebony jewelwing damselfly female (*Calopteryx maculata*)
Pipevine swallowtail butterfly (*Battus philenor*) caterpillars
Question mark butterfly (*Polygonia interrogationis*)
Snout butterfly (*Libytheana carinenta*)

Spangled skimmer dragonfly (*Libellula cyanea*) male and female

Fungi

Beard lichen (*Usnea* sp.)
Foliose lichen (*Parmotrema* sp.)
Turkey tail mushroom (*Trametes versicolor*)

Other Species

Eastern garter snakes (*Thamnophis sirtalis sirtalis*)
Gray treefrog (*Hyla versicolor*) or (*Hyla chrysoscelis*)
Pond slider turtle (*Trachemys scripta*)
Smallmouth bass (*Micropterus dolomieu*)
Spotted gar (*Lepisosteus oculatus*)

JUNE

Pond Sliders and a Muskrat

Date: June 28
Begin: 7:10 A.M.
End: 9:00 A.M.
Weather: 7:10 A.M., 70°F (21°C), partly cloudy, wind calm
    9:00 A.M., 81°F (27°C)
Participants: Margaret Anne and Marian
Purpose: To note wildflowers blooming in June and other
    interesting features

MARGARET ANNE AND I BEGIN our hike at 7:10 this morning. Temperatures have been in the mid-nineties for almost two weeks and, while spring rains were frequent in April and May, no significant rain has fallen during the past several weeks. Aquatic vegetation in Hidden Springs Stream has increased since May, and now alligator weed and pond scum (various types of floating algae) cover the surface except where water is flowing rapidly.

Queen Anne's lace (*Daucus carota*) blooms beside the trail opposite the stream. This plant is a member of the carrot family (Apiaceae), the same family and species as the carrots that grow in our gardens. Clumps of the woody shrub, buttonbush (*Cephalanthus occidentalis*), also grow

Buttonbush (*Cephalanthus occidentalis*)

beside Hidden Springs Trail near the stream. The round fuzzy balls with diameters of about 0.8" to 1.2" (2 cm to 3 cm) that hang from long stems are actually flowering clusters. Buttonbushes provide food for songbirds as well as waterfowl, including mallards and wood ducks, and the flowers are a nectar source for butterflies and other insects.

Now we quietly approach Jobala Pond. We hope to find Canada geese swimming here as they were in April and May, but today they are elsewhere. Continuing along Hidden Springs Trail, we cross the footbridge and walk around the end of the pond. Then we follow the woods on our right and head toward the Tall Tupelo Trail. The trail here beside the woods has been bush-hogged, and on this dry day walking is easy. Aside from enjoying the beauty of the Sanctuary, our hikes provide another benefit. We sharpen our observational and awareness skills and see common things in a different or new way. For instance, the discarded feather of a hawk or turkey leads us to speculate about its role in the Sanctuary's ecology. Discovery becomes an objective as Margaret Anne notices a hawk wing feather lying beside the trail. We wonder if it belonged to a red-shouldered or perhaps a red-tailed hawk. Are they nesting in the woods beyond the meadow? Although we do not see hawks flying over the woods or fields today, we are holding evidence of their presence. Farther along, we discover another feather. We examine it carefully. This one is about 9" (20 cm) long and has dark brown, horizontal stripes—a turkey feather. We often see turkey tracks in several places in the Sanctuary. I hope to catch a glimpse of these shy birds one day.

We continue to the Tall Tupelo Trail loop leading to the tupelo swamp. Margaret Anne stands beside a water tupelo (*Nyssa aquatica*) and comments on the huge size of the trunk. Trunk diameter at water level appears to be about 5' (1.5 m). The knee-high, dark-green band of moss around the trunk indicates that water in the tupelo swamp recently stood for some time at 2.5' to 3' (0.8 m to 0.9 m) deep.

Riparian habitats like the Sanctuary are characterized by periods of rain-induced river overflow and flooding, especially during winter and spring months. Tupelos have adapted morphologically to live in this environment by developing buttressed trunks to facilitate diffusion of gases (primarily oxygen and carbon dioxide) and to add support to trees growing in soft, swampy soil. Swelling of the trunks—and the height of the swelling—are responses to continual wetting and soaking.

Tree roots require oxygen for respiration and metabolic processes. When roots are underwater, oxygen is much less available because the diffusion rate across a water interface is many times slower than across a gas (air) interface. The enlarged trunks provide more surface area to allow gas exchange by increasing the number of lenticels (pores through which gases can be directly exchanged between internal tissues and atmosphere). This facilitates diffusion of oxygen and other gases into and out of the tree. Wetlands like this one are tremendously interesting and important, not only because of the adaptations of tupelos and other trees, but also because wetlands carry out critical functions of maintaining biodiversity, water storage, and production of food and habitat for wildlife.

Now we leave the tupelo swamp and continue through the woods on the Tall Tupelo Trail. Here we find a small blue wildflower. This is Carolina wild petunia (*Ruellia caroliniensis*). The stem has grown through a dead leaf in the once swampy but now dry habitat. Carolina wild petunia adapts to either wetland or non-wetland habitats and is at home here in the edge of the tupelo swamp. The plant is about 5" tall (13 cm) and has soft, hairy leaves and stems. We do not see other wildflowers blooming in the area today, and there is no sign of the dwarf wakerobins we found here in March and April. A few tiny mushrooms nestle beside a dead log.

We follow the trail to the Flint River Observation Point, turn left at the river, and walk a short distance to a clearing in the vegetation where we can see the tops of the tall trees on the other side of the river. Scanning with binoculars, I can make out a cluster of dead sticks, the remnants of a nest, now barely visible through the dense foliage. In March when I came here the first time, I saw herons on at least three nests. In April and May, some birds were on nests while others flew around above the rookery. Now in June, I do not see herons in the area. Apparently the young ones have matured and flown away to forage for themselves.

We backtrack and continue walking beside the river on Deer Run Trail. This is where we found canid, deer, and what looked like bobcat tracks in April. Today there are no discernible tracks. It's been too dry. A clump

Left: Carolina wild petunia (*Ruellia caroliniensis*)

Right: Chanterelle mushroom (*Cantharellus* sp.)

of Christmas fern (*Polystichum acrostichoides*) is growing in the woods on the right side of the trail. These ferns occur throughout eastern and central North America in rich woods and open woodlands. The fronds can reach a length of about 2' (61 cm). Christmas ferns are evergreen, and, as the name implies, they can be used for Christmas decorating.

Farther along on the right side of the trail, we find a loamy depression about 10' (3 m) wide with hardwood trees growing nearby. Several mushrooms the color of egg yolk are scattered among woody debris. They have funnel-shaped, depressed centers and the margins of the caps are wavy. I photograph one close up to show the broad stalk that tapers downward from the cap. These look like edible chanterelles (*Cantharellus* sp.), but some types of poisonous mushrooms have similar characteristics. We leave these as they stand, simply appreciating them for form and color.

About 15' (5 m) farther, we discover another interesting mushroom. There are actually two stages represented here. The one we spot first has a red cap emerging from a white material that looks like a battered Styrofoam cup. This is the egg or button stage of the Caesar's mushroom (*Amanita caesarea*). A few inches away, there is an almost round ball of the white material. This is an earlier stage before the red cap has begun to appear. Over the next few days, the red cap will continue to grow and become a flat-topped mushroom with a slender stalk 4" to 7" (10 cm to 18 cm) tall. The universal veil, which is the layer of tissue that covers the entire mushroom during early development, pulls away as the stem grows upward and the cap expands. The remnants of this tissue form a cup-like structure called the volva at the base of the stalk. When mature, this mushroom will also have a ring of tissue called an annulus near the top of the stalk. The annulus is formed when the partial veil, the tissue under the cap of the mushroom covering the gills or pores during initial stages of development, breaks away from the margin of the growing cap to form the ring around the stalk. In Italy *Amanita caesarea* is considered a delicacy, but in North America there are several poisonous mushrooms that resemble Caesar's. These are not found in Europe. People who harvest mushrooms in this country must exercise extreme caution. A look-alike may not be a Caesar's.

Continuing, I notice a young tuliptree or yellow poplar (*Liriodendron tulipifera*) growing beside the part of Deer Run Trail that follows the river to the edge of the woods. When mature, tuliptrees reach heights of 80' to 150' (24 m to 46 m) and produce large, tulip-shaped, light green flowers with an orange band in the center. Tuliptrees belong to the magnolia family (Magnoliaceae).

As the trail veers away from the river and into the open meadow, we make our way around a fallen tree. Margaret Anne stops suddenly and calls my attention to a turtle a few feet ahead. It is a pond slider (*Trachemys scripta*). The length of the carapace (top of shell) is about 10" (25 cm) from front to back and perhaps 6" or 7" (15 cm to 18 cm) wide. This female has been digging a nest; mud surrounds the hole and her back feet as well. When she sees us, she becomes still, and with her head mostly drawn into the shell, she watches us. Although she is

Button stage of Caesar's mushroom (*Amanita caesarea*)

more than 20 yd (18 m) from the river, she has carried water to soften the hard ground here in the edge of the field where she has chosen to dig her nest. Female pond sliders carry water in an accessory bladder located under the shell. They release the water to soften hard ground as they dig. Pond slider nests are usually 2" to 4" (5 cm to 10 cm) deep and about 4" (10 cm) across. Females deposit four to twenty-three eggs per nest depending on the size of the female. Eggs are covered with soil removed from the hole and will hatch in sixty to eighty days. A mother turtle has nothing more to do with her eggs or her offspring after she deposits the eggs and covers the hole.

The temperature during egg incubation is an important factor in determining the sex of the hatchling turtles. The baby turtles will be females if the temperature of the environment is 86°F (30°C) or above. But if the temperature is 72.5°F to 80.6°F (22.5°C to 27.0°C), hatchlings will become males. Egg hatching in the Sanctuary usually occurs between July and September. Females may lay one to five clutches a year.

A female pond slider (*Trachemys scripta*) digging a nest

The latest clutches are laid in July or August. If the baby turtles hatch late in the fall, they may overwinter inside the nest and emerge the next spring.

Foxes, coyotes, raccoons, skunks, and crows often destroy turtle nests. The leathery remains of broken eggs near a nest we found in May were the result of a raid by a predator. A little farther down the trail we find a raided nest with one round, speckled, leathery egg remaining. It appears to be about 0.75" (2 cm) in diameter. Perhaps the turtle Margaret Anne and I have found digging her nest today will be luckier. Pond sliders eat aquatic vegetation, insects, tadpoles, and small fish. They also scavenge for creatures that are no longer living. The lifespan of pond sliders in the wild can be as long as forty-two years.

We continue on Deer Run Trail as it winds along the edge of the field and discover an ant nest. It has been disturbed and the worker ants are scurrying around to move the brood of immature hatchlings to safety. Some of the adult ants are large and amber-colored; others are

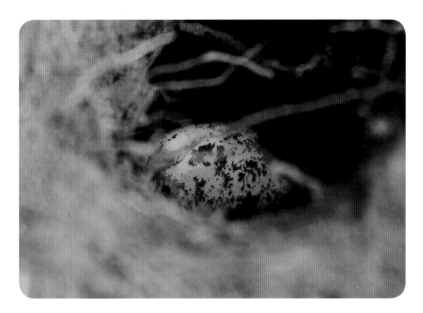

Lone turtle egg remaining in a nest raided by a predator

smaller and darker. The large size of the mound, the variation in the size of the ants, and their reddish brown color are characteristics of red imported fire ants (*Solenopsis invicta*). It is generally believed that a species of black imported fire ant (*Solenopsis richteri*) entered the United States through the port of Mobile around 1918. A red species appeared later, between 1933 and 1941. By 1953, imported fire ants had spread to ten states. Now they are found in all sixty-seven counties in Alabama. Their range, which is still expanding, currently covers all the southern states, up the East Coast as far as Maryland and west throughout Texas and into southern regions of New Mexico, Arizona, and California. As we know from experience, fire ant stings are painful to humans. They are a danger to chicks of ground nesting birds and other species; however, fire ants can be beneficial to cotton and sugar cane farmers by helping to control the number of caterpillar pests.

On other hikes in the Sanctuary, I have observed ant activity near Jobala Pond, but those ants were small and their 2" (5.1 cm) diameter hills were built of red soil. In the 1950s, the noted entomologist and Alabama native E. O. Wilson studied these native ants as he traveled the state collecting a range of species from different areas. More recently, a 2005 report by Joe A. MacGown (Alabama ant curator) and Jason A. Foster presents a compilation of Alabama ants, identifying 166 species in thirty-eight genera and nine subfamilies in the state.

I had not been aware before my search for information about ants that two species of fire ants are native to Alabama. One is *Solenopsis xyloni*, the southern fire ant. Its range includes the southern states and extends through the southwest to the California coast. The second native species is the tropical fire ant, *Solenopsis geminata*. These ants have spread almost worldwide through large-scale trading among different countries. In the United States, their range includes the southeastern states extending west to Texas. All fire ants sting, but stings of the native species are reported to be less painful than those of the imported species. Native fire ants have been reduced significantly over their range by the expansion of the more aggressive and invasive red and black imported species.

As we continue, a patch of tall, lavender-blooming plants beside the trail catches our attention. When I press a stem between my forefinger and thumb I can feel ridges, and my first impression is that this plant belongs to the mint family (Lamiaceae). I identify it as Canada germander (*Teucrium canadense*), a native perennial. Stems end in a terminal spike of numerous, small, oddly shaped flowers. I spend considerable time looking through wildflower books before I realize that the feature which distinguishes Canada germander from other mint species is the long lower lip on each tiny bloom. The upper lip of the germander bloom can be either absent or greatly reduced. The lower lip hangs below the main flower and serves as a landing platform for several types of bees, as well as other pollinating insects. Skipper butterflies, certain flies, hummingbirds, and hummingbird moths harvest nectar. The leaves are bitter, and deer and other mammals do not eat this plant.

Farther along the edge of the field, we notice another interesting plant. It has small, white blooms with bright yellow centers and spines on the stems and leaves. This is Carolina horsenettle (*Solanum carolinense*). Horsenettle is a member of the nightshade family (Solanaceae) and not a true nettle. Also growing here on the edge of the field are tired-looking daisy fleabanes and a wilted false dandelion. Just a month ago, these wildflowers were blooming profusely throughout the Sanctuary.

Walking along, we notice several colorful insects in the open field. Among these are eastern pondhawk dragonflies (*Erythemis simplicicollis*). This is one of the few dragonfly species that habitually perches on the ground. Females and immature males are a beautiful grass-green color. The adult male has a pruinose, pale blue body and blue-green eyes with dark spots set in a green face. The face of the female is bright green also. Eastern pondhawks belong to the skimmer family and are about 1.7" (4.3 cm) long. Voracious predators, they capture and devour other dragonflies, even ones larger than themselves. This female certainly adds color to the drab ground on which she rests.

Another colorful inhabitant of moist areas in the field is the pipevine swallowtail butterfly (*Battus philenor*). This is the adult form of the pipevine caterpillars we saw in June. These butterflies are harmful or distasteful to vertebrate predators, a gift from their infantile stage caterpillars that feed on plants belonging to the genus *Aristolochia*. Pipevine swallowtail butterflies are beautiful with their aposematic warning coloration of orange and blue on the underwings and an iridescent blue shine on the top of the hindwings. The wings glimmer in sunlight and may serve as a warning to would-be predators.

Leaving the field now, we follow Deer Run Trail toward Jobala Pond but stop at the Forest Glen Observation Point on the way. The small pond here is carpeted with duckweed, giving it a mossy, green appearance bank to bank. In the woods beside the pond there is a healthy growth of eastern poison ivy (*Toxicodendron radicans*). Poison ivy is a woody, perennial, climbing vine. The leaves are alternate and compound, and the three large, shiny, pointed-tip leaflets fit our image

Above: Female eastern pondhawk dragonfly (*Erythemis simplicicollis*)

Below: Male eastern pondhawk dragonfly (*Erythemis simplicicollis*)

Above: Underwings of a pipevine swallowtail butterfly (*Battus philenor*)

Below: Dorsal view of a pipevine swallowtail butterfly (*Battus philenor*) of this do-not-touch plant. Now in June, the green fruits have formed where small flowers bloomed in leaf axils last month. Eastern poison ivy is found throughout the eastern half of North America. To its credit, many birds and some animals feed on the seeds. I know from experience to leave it alone, but my horse often took a bite as we rode past an ivy-covered tree. The horse suffered no ill effects from her stolen bite.

Back on Deer Run Trail, we come to the footbridge at the south end of Jobala Pond. Here we notice arrow arum in the stream below us and pause to look at its arrow-shaped leaves. Suddenly something moves in the stream beside the plant. It's a snake about 3' (1 m) long. Chocolate-brown bands are bordered with black edges and alternate with caramel-colored bands. The snake's head is a metallic tan and the eyes are yellow. I know this is not a venomous snake because its head is not triangular, the pupils are not elliptical, and the tail is long and tapered, not blunt. This is a midland water snake (*Nerodia sipedon pleuralis*), a species common in ponds, lakes, and streams throughout Alabama except the southernmost portions of the Coastal Plain. It is the most frequently found water snake in the northern two-thirds of the state. We watch this attractive reptile glide gracefully out of sight under the bank's overhang.

Now we direct our attention back to the arrow arum (*Peltandra virginica*) in the stream below the footbridge. Categorized as an emergent, this aquatic plant lives at the edges of streams and ponds and in areas that are sometimes under water. Roots are buried in the soft soil, and leaves and stems grow above water. Arrow arum is common in the Sanctuary and proliferates in swampy habitats throughout. The flowers are small and whitish, greenish or light yellow, and occur on a spike surround by a largebract called a spathe. Arrow arum belongs to the family Araceae, and the spathe and spadix are very similar to the land plant known as green dragon (*Arisaema dracontium*) that we found near the Tall Tupelo woods in May.

A beautiful, metallic blue-green damselfly with black wings lands on a leaf about 10' (3 m) away. It's a male ebony jewelwing (*Calopteryx*

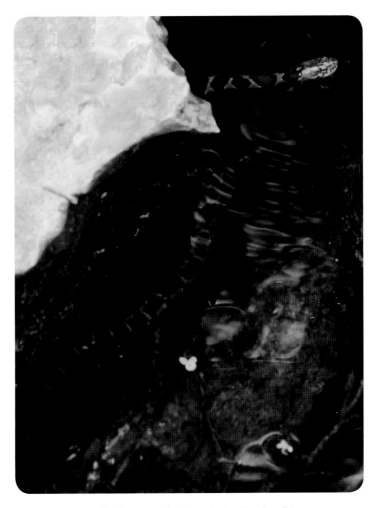

Midland water snake (*Nerodia sipedon pleuralis*)

maculata). Females have smoky wings with a bright white stigma near the tip. Their bodies are dull brown. Ebony jewelwings generally inhabit wooded areas near streams, but unlike other damselflies, they sometimes fly a distance from the stream or pond. These damselflies

Above: Ebony jewelwing damselfly male
(*Calopteryx maculata*)

Left: Ebony jewelwing damselfly female
(*Calopteryx maculata*)

are found in at least thirty-four states throughout North America. They mate in summer, and females lay eggs inside the stems of soft-stemmed water plants. After hatching, the nymphs, called naiads, spend their early life in water and then crawl up the stem to molt into adult form. According to Greek mythology, Naiads were female spirits who presided over springs, streams, and other freshwater features. Adult damselflies prey on mosquitos, willow aphids, gnats, crane flies, and a number of other insects. Great crested flycatchers and other birds, bats, ducks, turtles, frogs, and bass and other fish prey on damselflies.

In the shallow water about 15' (5 m) from where we're standing just past the footbridge, two spotted gars (*Lepisosteus oculatus*) swim into view. We saw a spotted gar in Jobala Pond in May. Gars spawn in April through June in ponds and streams where aquatic vegetation is present

Male and female spotted gar (*Lepisosteus oculatus*)

and where the water is about 3' (1 m) or less deep. Females are usually larger than males. Here the smaller male swims persistently beside the large female. Females can lay up to 20,000 eggs, but the number varies. Their eggs are green and coated with an adhesive so that they stick to leaves of aquatic vegetation. In ten to fourteen days, eggs hatch, and we hope the young will develop here in Jobala Pond and ensure a gar population for the future. Male gars live about eight years and the average lifespan of the female is about ten years.

Farther along Hidden Springs Trail, we find clusters of beautiful unripe red and ripe black dewberries (*Rubus trivialis*) beside the trail. This is the southern species of the genus, and it is probably one of the most important plants in the southeast for mammals, songbirds, and game birds. Deer and eastern cottontail rabbits browse on the leaves. Dewberries and blackberries belong to the rose family (Rosaceae). Dewberries are found from Pennsylvania, south to Florida and west to Texas and Colorado. Species of blackberries are found worldwide.

As we walk beside the stream, something ahead splashes loudly. We look in that direction and see a muskrat, perhaps the same one we found here in May. It is swimming in the middle of the stream. Occasionally it makes a dramatic splash as it dives under the surface. This fellow does not seem perturbed by our presence and allows me a great deal of time and many camera clicks before it disappears into the alligator weed upstream. Muskrats can swim under water for up to seventeen minutes and can close their ears to keep water out. On land, they get around in their territory by making trails through the vegetation. Where water freezes over in swamps and marshes, muskrats continue to follow their trails under the ice. This is an interesting fact, although muskrats living in the Sanctuary would not find this necessary as winters in North Alabama are relatively mild. We are delighted to have this animal in its natural habitat in the Sanctuary.

As we walk the last few hundred yards to our cars, we enjoy the bright blue color of a spiderwort (*Tradescantia* sp.) blooming at the edge of the woods. A patch of lizard's tail (*Saururus cernuus*) bends in the breeze beside the swamp, and a widow skimmer dragonfly (*Libellula luctuosa*) rests on a stem nearby.

So ends another fine expedition of discovery in the Sanctuary. As always, there is something new to discover and new mysteries to solve each time we go exploring in this habitat.

Above: **Lizard's tail** (*Saururus cernuus*)

Below: **Widow skimmer dragonfly** (*Libellula luctuosa*)

SPECIES LIST: JUNE

Wildflowers and Plants

Alligator weed (*Alternanthera philoxeroides*)

Arrow arum (*Peltandra virginica*)

Buttonbush (*Cephalanthus occidentalis*)

Canada germander (*Teucrium canadense*)

Carolina horsenettle (*Solanum carolinense*)

Carolina wild petunia (*Ruellia caroliniensis*)

Christmas fern (*Polystichum acrostichoides*)

Dewberry (*Rubus trivialis*)

Duckweed (sp.)

Eastern poison ivy (*Toxicodendron radicans*)

Lizard's tail (*Saururus cernuus*)

Queen Anne's lace (*Daucus carota*)

Spiderwort (*Tradescantia* sp.)

Trees

Tuliptree (*Liriodendron tulipifera*)

Water tupelo (*Nyssa aquatica*)

Mammals

Muskrat (*Ondatra zibethicus*)

North American raccoon (*Procyon lotor*) tracks

White tailed deer (*Odocoileus virginianus*) tracks

Insects

Eastern pondhawk dragonfly (*Erythemis simplicicollis*)

Ebony jewelwing damselfly (*Calopteryx maculata*)

Imported fire ants (*Solenopsis invicta* and *Solenopsis richteri*)

Pipevine swallowtail butterfly and caterpillar (*Battus philenor*)

Six-spotted fishing spider (*Dolomedes triton*)

Widow skimmer dragonfly (*Libellula luctuosa*)

Fungi

Caesar's mushroom (*Amanita caesarea*)

Chanterelle mushroom (*Cantharellus* sp.)

Snakes, Turtles, and Fish

Midland water snake (*Nerodia sipedon pleuralis*)

Pond slider turtle (*Trachemys scripta*)

Spotted gar (*Lepisosteus oculatus*)

JULY

Aquatic Life, Dragonflies, and Butterflies

Date: July 29
Begin: 3:30 P.M.
End: 5:30 P.M.
Weather: 3:30 P.M., 88°F (31°C), very windy and cloudy
     5:30 P.M., 88°F (31°C)
Participants: Richard and Marian
Purpose: To photo document flora and fauna in the Sanctuary in July

TODAY AS WE BEGIN OUR hike on Hidden Springs Trail, we notice a passion flower vine with colorful white and lavender frilly blooms and an egg-shaped, green fruit about 2" (5 cm) long and 1" (2.5 cm) in diameter. The genus and species name of the passion flower, also known as maypop and purple passion flower, is *Passiflora incarnata*. Its flower structure is complex. Ten white to pale lavender tepals (sepals modified to resemble petals) form the base of the flower. Above the tepals is an array of frilly purple and white filaments that form the corona. Extending up from the center of the corona, five pollen-producing stamens hang on filaments below the three central stigmas. The stigmas are sticky and collect pollen transported by hummingbirds, butterflies, and bees from other passion flower blooms. This perennial, vascular

Passion flower (*Passiflora incarnata*)

vine is native to the southeastern United States. Its range extends from Florida to Pennsylvania and west to Kansas, Oklahoma, and Texas. Passion flowers grow well along roadsides, edges of fields, and in sunny and moist habitats. Maypop fruit consists of a number of seeds, each surrounded by soft, juice-filled pulp that, when ripe, tastes delicious. Other members of the passion flower family (Passifloraceae) are used to provide flavor to some of the fruit-flavored drinks.

As we proceed along Hidden Springs Trail we notice tall pokeweeds (*Phytolacca americana*) growing at the edge of the woods on our right. Pokeweed can reach a height of 8' to 10' (2 m to 3 m). Small,

Unripe maypop (*Passiflora incarnata*)

greenish-white flowers continue to bloom along the stem while berries develop at the base. By September, these berries will have ripened to a deep purple. Dark red juice from ripe berries was used many years ago as an ink, and in the Algonquian Indian language poke refers to a plant used for staining. The juice was also used at one time to darken pale wines. This is no longer done because berries, seeds, and roots contain several toxic substances. Some people still harvest the young leaves in the early spring and cook them like spinach. However, pokeweed is so highly toxic that it must be boiled several times and the water discarded each time to remove the toxins. This plant is not a food for amateur outdoorsmen. It can be very dangerous if improperly cooked or if berries are ingested. The American Cancer Society cautions that all pokeweed parts are toxic. Pokeberries are poisonous to mammals, but birds are not affected by the toxins. Among bird species fond of pokeberries are robins, catbirds, finches, woodpeckers, orioles, northern mockingbirds, brown thrashers, eastern bluebirds, blue jays, common grackles, tufted

Aquatic Life, Dragonflies, and Butterflies

titmice, Carolina chickadees, Carolina wrens, scarlet tanagers, and cedar waxwings (all of which either visit or live in the Sanctuary). The plant and its berries are visually attractive and good food for birds—and I will leave pokeweed for them.

Now in late July, other seeds, nuts, and berries are developing on the plants we saw blooming in April, May, and June. Red buckeye bushes bear 1"-diameter (2.5 cm) buckeyes. Clusters of seedpods hang from black locust trees that border the trail near the swamp. Black walnuts the size of golf balls cling in singles, pairs, and triplets on low-hanging branches of young black walnut trees. The dewberries, abundant as they ripened on vines beside Hidden Springs Trail in June, have disappeared without a trace—eaten by birds, insects, and perhaps a few *Homo sapiens*.

On our right as we walk along, we notice numerous clumps of ragweed. This plant belongs to the family Asteraceae. The genus name *Ambrosia* is said to derive from Ancient Greek, meaning food for the gods—obviously a misnomer for ragweed. Ragweed, of which there are twenty-one species in North America, is best known for producing summer and fall pollens that cause allergies. The two common species in the Sanctuary are giant ragweed *Ambrosia trifida* and common ragweed *Ambrosia artemisiifolia*. The latter is the most widespread and grows to a height of about 3' (1 m). Giant ragweed may reach a height of 13' (4 m). Flowers are wind-pollinated during the summer and into the fall in this area. Caterpillars of many butterflies and moths feed on ragweed leaves, and birds eat the seeds in winter. A species of fruit fly, two weevil species, and a moth species feed on seeds, and field mice, earthworms, and carabid beetles eat seeds of giant ragweed in the soil.

Growing beside the ragweed, white vervain (*Verbena urticifolia*) stands with its spikes of tiny white blooms stiffly reaching upward. Flowers of this native, perennial, vascular herb are fertilized by small butterflies, wasps, honeybees, bumblebees, and some types of flies. Caterpillars feed on the foliage; juncos and several species of sparrows eat the seeds.

On the opposite side of Hidden Springs Trail at the edge of the marsh, a patch of arrow arum (*Peltandra virginica*) is growing in the shallow water. Its leaves are about twice as large as they were a month ago. Smartweeds (*Persicaria* sp.) line the banks and display their knobby spikes of pale pink flowers. A verdant patch of parrot feather watermilfoil (*Myriophyllum aquaticum*) covers a large area of the stream that slowly meanders through the marsh. Milfoil is a choice food for the little muskrat that lives here at the head of Jobala Pond. Muskrats consume the whole plant, and ducks, geese, and other waterfowl eat the leaves. Species of milfoil are so plentiful nationwide that it has been suggested as a biofuel and a source of ethanol for the future.

As we walk beside the stream at the head of Jobala Pond, we note several smallmouth bass (*Micropterus dolomieu*) swimming in the swifter flowing section of the stream. This is where we discovered bass tending fish beds last month. On the far bank, the catalpa trees that bloomed so beautifully in May now host 6"-long (15 cm) immature green pods.

Farther along Hidden Springs Trail, we find large patches of shrubby St. Johnswort (*Hypericum prolificum*) growing on the banks of the stream. The bright yellow, cushiony blooms of this perennial shrub add a dash of color to the green vegetation that dominates the area. Also colorful are the bright orange, trumpet-shaped blooms of trumpet creeper (*Campsis radicans*) that add a decorative touch to the trees along this section of the trail. This climbing, perennial vine is native and found in the eastern and midwestern states in North America as well as Oregon, California, Utah, and Colorado.

Another type of vine weaves its way through the foliage of low-growing bushes near the stream. This one has a delicate stem with reddish purple areas, heart-shaped leaves, and clusters of small, pale, cream-colored flowers. It's a honeyvine milkweed (*Cynanchum laeve*), a climbing vine belonging to the milkweed family (Asclepiadaceae). Like the swamp milkweed (*Asclepias incarnata*) that also grows here in the Sanctuary, honeyvine milkweed is food for monarch butterflies and other insects. It is locally common across the eastern United States and may grow to

Above: **Shrubby St. Johnswort** (*Hypericum prolificum*)

Below: **Trumpet creeper** (*Campsis radicans*)

Honeyvine milkweed (*Cynanchum laeve*)

a height of 15' (4.6 m) climbing on other vines, corn stalks, and fences.

Nearby, horsenettle (*Solanum carolinense*) presents its spiny stems. This plant, a member of the family Solanaceae, was blooming in the Sanctuary in June. In searching for more information about horsenettle, I learned that it has an interesting collection of relatives that includes members of the nightshade family that are well known to us. These include tomatoes, potatoes, red and green bell peppers, hot peppers such as chili and paprika, and eggplant. This family also embraces tobacco, poisonous belladonna (*Atropa* sp.), and the toxic plants henbane (*Hyoscyamus* sp.), mandrake (*Mandragora* sp.), and jimsonweed (*Datura* sp.).

Just beyond the horsenettle, we notice a yellow, stringy, spaghetti-like net of vine trailing over low-growing vegetation. This is love vine or common dodder (*Cuscuta gronovii*). This native, vascular vine is called love vine because it clings and appears to hug its host plant. Love vine is a parasite. It does not have chlorophyll and cannot make its own food. The vine attaches its twining stems to a host by use of tiny suckers

Above: **Common dodder or love vine** (*Cuscuta gronovii*)

Below: **Mosquitofish** (*Gambusia affinis*)

called haustoria. These suckers draw water, minerals, and carbohy-drates from the host; dodder is a true sap-sucker. It produces tiny, scale-like leaves in July and numerous clusters of very small, cream-colored flowers from July through October. Seeds are produced and fall to the ground where they sprout. Sprouts then attach to a host plant and there-after, they lose all contact with the ground.

Now at the footbridge over the outflow from Jobala Pond, we pause to watch a school of small, stout fish swimming in the shallow water. They have large eyes and their heads and bodies are covered with relatively large scales that seem to form patterns. These are gambusia or mosquitofish (*Gambusia affinis*). The name gambusia is derived from a Cuban Spanish word "gambusino," meaning useless. The name "mosquitofish" is earned because they feed on the aquatic larvae of mosquitoes. These little fish are found in freshwater ponds and streams in the eastern and southern United States. They were brought into this country in the early 1900s as a means to control mosquitoes. They are more efficient at this than some native fishes, but mosquitofish also eat eggs of desirable species of fish. Mouths of mosquitofish are curved upward to enable feeding at the surface of the water. Females are about 2.8" (7 cm) long and males grow to a length of about 1.6" (4 cm). They are a hardy species and can live in water with low oxygen levels and high salinity and temperature. Because of their ability to withstand such environmental diversity, mosquitofish may be the most widespread freshwater fish in the world. They do not lay eggs but instead bear live offspring. Mosquitofish live for two to three years and are prolific.

We cross the footbridge and pause at the south end of Jobala Pond. On this hazy afternoon, colors are muted by water vapor—everything is a greenish monochrome. The scum on the pond's surface is green algae, probably a *Spirogyra* species. *Spirogyra* filaments are slimy to the touch. They form long strands that may become numerous and assemble into mats like those we see on the pond today.

Rounding the curve at the south end of the pond we walk toward the Jobala Haven Observation Point. There in the water under the overhanging vegetation is a spotted gar (*Lepisosteus oculatus*) lying very still near the surface (*Lepisosteus* in Greek means bony scale). As we noted in Chapter 3, spotted gars spawn from April through June, and now in July perhaps this one is waiting in the shade for a fish to swim by. Primarily fish eaters, gars are equipped with many teeth and are voracious, opportunistic feeders and efficient ambush predators. Richard

Head of a spotted gar (*Lepisosteus oculatus*)

tells me about his observations of gar feeding behavior. Some years ago when he was in graduate school, he watched a young gar in a university aquarium. The gar lay still until an unwary fish swam near; then in a flash the gar snapped sideways and captured the fish. Spotted gars apparently are surviving very well in Jobala Pond. The maximum life span of the species is about eighteen years and they normally grow to weights of 4 lb to 6 lb (1.8 to 2.7 kg).

Continuing toward the Jobala Haven Observation Point, I notice that most of the ground cover in this area is lespedeza (*Lespedeza* sp.), a small, annual member of the pea family Fabaceae. Lespedeza can capture free atmospheric nitrogen through a symbiotic relationship with certain types of bacteria. The process is called nitrogen fixation. Nitrogen is an inert gas that comprises 79 percent of the atmosphere. But it is not directly accessible to most organisms, including humans and plants. Bacteria of the genus *Rhizobia* are able to fix atmospheric nitrogen after becoming established inside root nodules of legumes. Nitrogen fixation occurs when atmospheric nitrogen is converted into ammonia within the root nodules. Ammonia is subsequently converted into components of plant proteins, nucleic acids, and other molecules. When the plant dies, nitrogen compounds are released into the soil for use by other plants. In this case, lespedeza serves as a host by developing the root nodules where bacteria live. The bacteria require the plant host; they cannot independently fix nitrogen outside the plant's root nodules. Lespedeza has considerable value in addition to its nitrogen fixing capability. It prevents erosion and provides food for wildlife.

Now, instead of crossing the small stream that feeds Jobala Pond at the Jobala Haven Observation Point, we walk north across the field. Rose mallow or swamp rose (*Hibiscus moscheutos*) blooms beside the stream on our left. Swamp rose is a shelter for frogs, snakes, insects, mammals, and birds including northern bobwhites (which I hope to discover in the Sanctuary) as well as ducks. Japanese beetles eat the leaves. Flowers are pollinated by visiting hummingbirds and bumblebees as they come to sample nectar.

Looking across the near end of the field, we note several clumps of the soft rush (*Juncus effusus*). The *Juncus* genus consists of two hundred twenty-five to three hundred species. The clumps we see today are growing in a low-lying corner of the field in a marshy area. Certain Lepidoptera (the order of insects that includes butterflies and moths) feed exclusively on juncus. Larvae of moths in the genus *Coleophora* (case moths) feed on the seeds, flowers, and leaves. As these larvae mature they make silken cases that incorporate material from the plant. I will look for discarded larval cases among the stems and flowers of juncus on future visits to the Sanctuary.

Buttonbushes (*Cephalanthus occidentalis*) line the stream on our left, and the fruiting balls have turned from the white of a month ago to dark pink now. Pink buds of swamp milkweed (*Asclepias incarnata*) are ready to open at the edge of the woods ahead. Also called swamp silkweed and white Indian hemp, this herbaceous perennial plant is native to North America and grows in damp to wet areas. It produces large amounts of nectar and attracts butterflies; among them are the monarchs, as well as other pollinators. The relationship between monarchs and milkweed is well known. Milkweeds are the host plant for monarch caterpillars. The caterpillars incorporate toxic substances from the sap of milkweed leaves into their bodies (just as pipevine swallowtail caterpillars

Juncus (*Juncus effusus*)

incorporate toxic materials from their host pipevine plants). The caterpillars, and subsequent butterflies, are thus made distasteful to predators. Of course this is beneficial, by means of mimicry, to any other
species of butterfly that resembles monarchs or pipevine swallowtails.

Here beside the stream in this wetland area, several dragonflies pose

Swamp milkweed (*Asclepias incarnata*)

long enough for me to photograph them. Today, two species predominate: the great blue skimmer (*Libellula vibrans*) and the slaty skimmer (*Libellula incesta*). Among the principal joys I find in exploring the Sanctuary are seeing a familiar plant, vine, wildflower, or creature in a different way and the discovery of species that I had not noticed before. This is the case with the Odonata, the order to which dragonflies and damselflies belong. I have been a watcher of these insects since childhood when I drifted around a pond in a flat-bottomed boat powered by a homemade paddle and soft summer breezes. In those days, I knew dragonflies as snake doctors (revivers of deceased snakes) and darning needles (for sewing children's ears closed). Now, as I explore the marshes, swamps, ponds, and streams in the Sanctuary, I have rediscovered the joy of dragonfly and damselfly watching.

In the eastern United States and Canada, 336 species of odonates are presently identified. Their compound eyes afford excellent vision. The very large dragonflies may have as many as 30,000 simple eyes, or

Great blue skimmer dragonfly male (*Libellula vibrans*)

lenses, that comprise a single compound eye. Each lense is a component of a prismatic unit known as an ommatidium. If we look closely at the surface of a dragonfly's eye, ommatidia appear like single polygons or facets. Each ommatidium is a visual receptor, and together they provide a mosaic enabling the dragonfly to detect the slightest movement even at a distance. Dragonfly eyes are large and extend around the head to allow a visual range of almost three-hundred-and-sixty degrees, a valuable characteristic making dragonflies efficient carnivorous predators.

Because all four wings move independently, dragonflies can fly straight up or down, hover and fly backward as well as forward. Forward flight speeds can be very slow or accelerate to 30 mi (48 km) per hour.

In researching habits and attributes of dragonflies and damselflies, I learned that they sleep at night. Damselflies generally roost in thick

Smooth ground cherry (*Physalis longifolia*)

weeds while dragonflies choose shrubs or roost higher in trees. I now have a renewed fascination with these amazing dragons of the air. Through the seasons except in winter, the Sanctuary provides an array of colorful odonates and the opportunity to discover amazing facts about them.

We backtrack on the trail and stop by the Jobala Haven Observation Point. Here we notice a light yellow flower with a turks-cap shape. The flower is about 1" (2.5 cm) across and petals have ruffled edges that are not clearly serrated. Several green, papery pods dangle like small lanterns from stem intersections. Richard turns a bloom upside-down so I can photograph the center of the flower. Five dark brownish, oval patterns superimposed on the yellow background of petals form an image that looks like a miniature gingerbread man. I identify this plant as smooth ground cherry (*Physalis longifolia*). Ground cherries belong to the family Solanaceae along with tomatoes, horsenettle, and the other members of the nightshade family. Ground cherry blooms develop into fruit, each separately housed in a heart-shaped, papery package that hangs downward from the stem, as we see. The spherical fruit will turn yellow or red when it ripens in the fall. Several types of bees and insects feed on this plant. Bobwhites, turkeys, skunks, and white-footed mice eat the ripe fruit.

We continue toward the Deer Run Trail leading to the Flint River. As we approach the far end of the field, we discover a group of small butterflies. They appear to be intent on licking moisture from a damp place. Three different types are present and each type seems to keep to itself. The largest group consists of twelve individuals. Their up-folded wings are about 0.75" (1.9 cm) from top to bottom. Standing tall on their whitish legs and with their wings folded up, they look like small, yellow windsails. All face the same direction. When they spread their wings, we see that the wing tops are bright orange with a wide, black, scalloped border and one black crescent marking on the forewings. This is a sulfur butterfly called sleepy orange (*Abaeis nicippe*). In the larval stage, these butterflies feed on plants of the pea family. Sleepy sulphurs are common in the south. Males often gather in large numbers around puddles. According to Bright and Ogard in their book *Butterflies of Alabama*, "sleepy" refers to the small black crescent marking on the top of the forewing that might remind one of a sleepy eye. These authors note that there is nothing "sleepy" in this butterfly's flight pattern as was sometimes conjectured to be the origin of their name.

Within a few feet of the sleepy orange butterflies, there are several gray, fuzzy-looking ones. But these are smaller than sulphurs and are gray to brownish in color with prominent white spots on the under- and uppersides of the wings. They have very prominent black eyes. These are common checkered skipper butterflies (*Pyrgus communis*).

The third group consists of three individuals, smaller than the other two types. They are gray with small black dots and a bright orange

Above: **Sleepy orange butterflies** (*Abaeis nicippe*)

Below: **Common checkered skipper** (*Pyrgus communis*)

Eastern tailed-blue butterflies (*Cupido comyntas*)

patch on the undersides of their up-folded wings. A short "tail" projects from the edge of their hindwings. These butterflies also have very large black eyes and their antennae are banded with black and gray. We identify them as Eastern tailed-blue butterflies (*Cupido comyntas*). They belong to a group called "hairsteaks" and are common across the United States. Most species of hairstreaks have short thread-like tails on their hind wings. We notice their visible bright-blue upper wing surfaces when they fly.

We continue toward the Gravel Bar at the west branch of the Flint River. The stream has only a trickle of water today, so we walk across it and continue along the Gravel Bar Trail. This is actually a primitive road that leads through Grayson's Island toward the main branch of the Flint River. Along the way, I photograph a fully unfurled resurrection fern (*Pleopeltis polypodioides*) resting on top of a tree limb. When we reach the bank of the main branch of the Flint, I notice a motion-activated, night-vision camera attached at a height of about 20' (6 m) on the trunk of a nearby tree. It was placed here by the city's parks department to monitor this remote area of the Sanctuary. I'm sure the camera captured us, too. This is the first time I've been on Grayson's Island. The trail is shady and pleasant to walk as it winds through the woods.

Ricefield flatsedge (*Cyperus iria*)

On our way back past the Gravel Bar we rejoin the Deer Run Trail at the edge of the field. Where the field meets the woods that border the west stream, there is an area that remains wet throughout most of the year. Sedges and other marsh plants commonly grow here. I pause to photograph a good example of a sedge (*Cyperus iria*) and a spike rush *Eleocharis species*. Spike rushes are also members of the sedge family and have solitary spikelets topped by a nutlet and tubercle at the tip of the stems. The following well-known and often recited verse helps me remember the differences among sedges, reeds, and rushes:

Sedges have edges,
Rushes are round.
And reeds abound
Where water is found.

This rhyme is not entirely accurate. Some sedges of the genus *Eleo-charis* and some species in the genus *Schoenoplectus* are round. The term "reed" is a collective botanical term that describes a number of tall, grass-like plants that grow in wet environments. Among plants called reeds are members of the grass and sedge families, cattails, and other water-loving plants. Rushes usually have cylindrical stalks or hollow, stem-like leaves. Juncus, mentioned earlier, is a common rush.

Now wet with perspiration and comfortably tired, we head back toward the cars. As we walk along the Hidden Springs Trail, we notice a yellow-blooming plant. It is about 7' (2 m) tall and has foliage and flowers characteristic of the pea family (Fabaceae). This is the robust perennial herb, wild senna. Here in the south, the common native species is Maryland senna or southern wild senna (*Senna marilandica*). The

Spike rush (*Eleocharis* sp.)

bright yellow flowers have a small club-shaped gland that secretes nectar to attract certain kinds of insects including bumblebees, ladybugs, and ants. Caterpillars of some of the sulfur butterflies rely on senna for food. Deer and other herbivores usually avoid eating the foliage. Senna has a purgative effect. Seeds are eaten by some game birds.

In the marsh at the head of Jobala Pond, there are a number of aquatic plants. One of these is cattail (*Typha latifolia*), also called broad-leaf cattail or common cattail. This perennial wetland obligate (meaning it always grows near water) occurs throughout the United States except Hawaii. Native Americans used the rhizomes as well as young flower spikes and stems of this plant for food. Roots were used medicinally. Now in mid-summer, cattails in the Sanctuary are colorful and visible in the marsh.

Nearing the parking lot, we find bitterweed or bitter sneezeweed (*Helenium amarum*) growing beside the road. In pastures where cows eat young bitterweed in the spring, their milk acquires a distinctively unpleasant taste.

This has been a hot day for hiking, but a very good day for finding butterflies and other insects, photographing wildflowers in bloom, learning about aquatic and wetland plants, and looking for seeds, nuts, and fruits maturing in the Sanctuary.

LIST OF SPECIES: JULY

Wildflowers and Other Plants
Arrow arum (*Peltandra virginica*)
Bitterweed (*Helenium amarum*)
Buttonbush (*Cephalanthus occidentalis*)
Common cattail (*Typha latifolia*)
Common dodder (*Cuscuta gronovii*)
Common ragweed (*Ambrosia artemisiifolia*)
Giant ragweed (*Ambrosia trifida*)
Honeyvine milkweed (*Cynanchum leave*)

Horsenettle (*Solanum carolinense*)
Lespedeza (*Lespedeza* sp.)
Lizard's tail (*Saururus cernuus*)
Man of the earth vine (*Ipomoea pandurata*)
Maypop (*Passiflora incarnata*)
Parrot feather watermilfoil (*Myriophyllum aquaticum*)
Passion flower (*Passiflora incarnata*) bloom and fruit

Pokeweed (*Phytolacca americana*)
Resurrection fern (*Pleopeltis polypodioides*)
Rose mallow (*Hibiscus moscheutos*)
Sedge (*Cyperus iria*)
Shrubby St. Johnswort (*Hypericum prolificum*)
Smartweeds (*Persicaria* sp.)
Smooth ground cherry (*Physalis longifolia*)
Soft rush (*Juncus effusus*)
Spike rush (*Eleocharis* sp.)
Swamp milkweed (*Asclepias incarnata*)
Trumpet creeper (*Campsis radicans*)
White vervain (*Verbena urticifolia*)
Wild senna (*Senna marilandica*)

Trees
Black locust (*Robinia pseudoacacia*)
Black walnut (*Juglans nigra*)
Catalpa (*Catalpa bignonioides*)
Red buckeye (*Aesculus pavia*)
Water tupelo (*Nyssa aquatica*) in dry season

Birds
Great blue heron (*Ardea herodias*)
Green heron (*Butorides virescens*)

Mammals
White-tailed deer (*Odocoileus virginianus*)

Insects and Bugs
Common checkered skipper butterfly (*Pyrgus communis*)
Eastern tailed-blue butterfly (*Cupido comyntas*)

Ebony jewelwing damselfly (*Calopteryx maculata*) female
Great blue skimmer dragonfly (*Libellula vibrans*)
Leaffooted bug (family Coreidae)
Periodiocal cicada (*Magicicada* sp.) shells
Slaty skimmer dragonfly (*Libellula incesta*)
Sleepy orange butterfly (*Abaeis nicippe*)

Other Species
Inky cap mushroom (*Coprinus* sp.)
Mosquitofish (*Gambusia affinis*)
Smallmouth bass (*Micropterus dolomieu*)
Spotted gar (*Lepisosteus oculatus*)
Toad (*Bufo* sp.)

AUGUST

A Sunrise Venture

Date: August 15
Begin: 5:45 A.M.
End: 9:15 A.M.
Weather: 5:45 A.M., 75°F (24°C), a misty morning
    9:15 A.M., 81°F (27°C)
Participants: Margaret Anne, Clayton, Sam, Sara, Jimmy, and
    Marian
Purpose: To visit the Sanctuary in the early morning and view the
    sunrise

A FEW WEEKS AGO, WE agreed to meet in the Sanctuary at dawn (the time of twilight just before sunrise) on August 15. Our goal would be to experience the Sanctuary in its various moods and presentations; to absorb its colors and fragrances; to feel the stirrings and changes in its wind and weather; and to be a part of its earth, forest, streams, vegetation, and wildlife as they evolve at the beginning of a day. A week ago, Margaret Anne asked me to let her know when to expect sunrise so we could arrive at dawn and walk to a place in the Sanctuary where we could watch and photograph sunrise best. I consulted a website (www

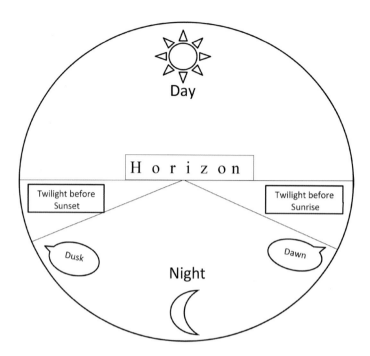

Types of twilight (drawn by the author)

.gaisma.com/en/location/huntsville-alabama.html) and found that sunrise should occur around 6:05 A.M. on the day chosen for our hike.

So this morning, having extrapolated the time between expected dawn and sunrise, we arrive at the Sanctuary at 5:45 A.M. and quickly set our course toward the chosen site in the big field near the intersection of Deer Run and Gravel Bar Trails. It's a cloudy, misty morning. Green Mountain stands veiled in the distance and the mist-covered leaves of soybean plants in the field near the Sanctuary entrance appear to be cloaked in velvet. As we follow Hidden Springs Trail beside Jobala Pond, we notice pea-sized, green berries on the greenbrier vines (*Smilax tamnoides*), and farther along at the intersection of Hidden Springs and Deer Run Trails, goldenrod is beginning to bloom in the edge of the field.

Ahead, our trail seems to disappear into the mist, but it reappears as we approach the intersection of Deer Run and the Gravel Bar Trail. Here we pause to look around. It's getting lighter, and the time for sunrise is near. It won't be an orange orb sun rising today; it's too cloudy, but perhaps this sunrise will reward us with spectacular colors. To the east, trees block our view of the lower sky, but looking west we see orange sky with light playing on billowing clouds. This contrasts sharply with the almost black of the trees in the woods across the field. Muted, gray mist rises ghost-like from the field in the foreground. We photo document the beauty and color of the landscape as the sun gradually illuminates it. Clayton mentions that he wanted a misty morning to photograph. His wish is certainly granted this morning. The artistic potential is superb.

Now we turn and follow the Gravel Bar Trail through the deciduous woods toward the west branch of the Flint River. Numerous leaf-bare trees make a still, dark tunnel where light is slow to penetrate. A broken, golf ball–sized puffball sits in the sand beside the trail. Puffballs belong to a group of mushrooms called gasteromycetes (stomach mushrooms). Spores are produced and mature within the "ball" instead of being borne on gills or in pores like other types of mushrooms. As the spores mature, they form a mass in the center of a spheroidal fruiting body. When the surface of the ball cracks from impact of a raindrop, a curious animal, or the toe of someone's boot, clouds of brown dust-like spores are released. Spores are distributed by the wind. The broken puffball here may be a member of the genus *Lycoperdon*, but to confirm this we would have had to see the color of the spore mass inside before the spores matured and the puffball cracked open. Young puffballs can also resemble early stages of some of the poisonous mushrooms.

We come to the stream on the west side of Grayson's Island, a small island about 0.2 mi (0.3 km) wide, formed by small, divergent streams in the Flint River. Now in late summer, water in the stream is shallow. We walk across its 10'-wide (3 m) bed without getting the tops of our boots wet, then we continue on the Gravel Bar Trail as it winds across

Ringless honey mushrooms (*Armillaria tabescens*)

the island. The island is heavily wooded and moist, a good habitat for mushrooms. In fact, we find several clusters growing around the base of an oak tree. These appear to be ringless honey mushrooms (*Armillaria tabescens*). Found across eastern North America, ringless honey mushrooms are common in the southern United States. The caps are 2" to 4" (5 cm to 10 cm) across and can be straw-colored, tawny brown, or yellowish. A few dark scales are concentrated toward the center of the caps. The stems are a whitish color and do not have a ring (collapsed veil). The gills are decurrent (gills extend down the stem at a slant). Ringless honey mushrooms are edible, and these look good enough to eat, but we are not mushroom experts so we will leave them as they are.

As we come nearer to the main stream of the Flint River, Sara notices a thick rope of vines twisted around each other like a loaf of braided bread. How do vines twine? I wonder. They obviously climb upward toward sunlight, but how? This complexity of twining vines appears to consist of three separate woody stems, all about 0.75" (0.19 cm) in diameter, wrapped tightly around each other. This unusual and determined coil has piqued my interest.

Twining vines

Back at home later, my search discloses that, although all vines must depend on some kind of support structure, there are fundamental vine types based on the way each one interacts with its support. The manner and direction in which a vine twines is determined by its genetic code. If no tree or other support is available, a twining vine will wrap itself around its nearest neighbor, even another vine. An example is trumpet creeper (*Campsis radicans*), which uses its woody stems to twine. Other vines clasp their support. There are three ways in which clasping vines do this. One is by use of tendrils like those of grape and smilax (greenbrier). Virginia creeper sticks to tree trunks with disk-like suction cups,

Split gill mushrooms (*Schizophyllum commune*)

and poison ivy clings to its host support by use of aerial roots.

Now at the Flint River's edge, we watch the gray-green water swirl 5' (1.5 m) below us at the bottom of the steep bank on which we are standing. Eddies form hundreds of intricate patterns in the flowing water. I wonder what those patterns look like from underneath the surface—from a turtle's-eye-view.

On the way back across the island, we notice part of a dead tree that has broken from the stump beside the trail. The horizontal trunk is almost covered with a cluster of stemless fungi that apparently developed on the vertical, dead trunk before it fell. This looks like the split gill mushroom *Schizophyllum commune*. This fungus is very common and is reported to be the world's most widespread species of mushroom. It is found on every continent except Antarctica, where there is no wood. The individual mushrooms range in size from about 0.4" to 1.6" (1 cm to 4 cm). They are leathery, shell-shaped, wavy, and lobed. The top surface, when dry as we see today on this dead tree trunk, is mostly an ashy gray. This mushroom can shrivel in dry weather and revive and

Above: **Browneyed Susan** (*Rudbeckia triloba*)

Below: **Wild potato vine** (*Ipomoea pandurata*)

expand after rains. When it dries, the gills split longitudinally. *S. commune* grows on dead wood from autumn to spring, but it can persist all year if winter is not too severe.

We intersect the Deer Run Trail and turn right to follow it around the edge of the big field. Here we see several browneyed Susans (*Rudbeckia triloba*) in bloom, and man-of-the-Earth vines, also known as wild potato vine (*Ipomoea pandurata*), are abundant with their clusters of large, purple-centered, white blossoms.

Partridge pea (*Chamaecrista fasciculata*)

We also notice several bright yellow blooming plants, 6" to 8" (15 cm to 20 cm) tall. They have numerous leaflets that look like mimosa leaves; indeed, they both belong to the legume family Fabaceae. The flowers are showy and the stamens have six purple and four yellow anthers in the center of the bloom. This is the partridge pea (*Chamaecrista fasciculata*). Partridge peas provide food for larvae of sulphur and hairstreak butterflies like the ones we saw in this field in June.

Suddenly Clayton and Margaret Anne call my attention to something across the field. With camera ready, I scan the far woods, but I can only see the three-foot tall soybean plants and the forest beyond. But then, like a magic rabbit popping out of a hat, a deer rises from the verdant field, head and shoulders above the surrounding plants. It's a young white-tailed deer (*Odocoileus virginianus*), and it looks as if he's aiming for the sky. I point the camera and click the shutter to capture the image. But the "leaping deer show" is not over yet. Another leap, and this time my camera records the downward half of his arc. He has almost reached the woods, but I can still see the tip of his white flag tail just before he disappears entirely.

We continue on our way and note that conditions today must be ideal for mushrooms. As we walk in the woods beside the Flint River, we find several more large clusters. One group exhibits smooth, weak-looking, whitish to brownish velvety stems, and the caps are light yellow with brown centers. These look like another of the ten or eleven *Armillaria* species found in North America. Placed flat in a dish, they would resemble baked teacakes.

Farther along and now entering the woods where the trail diverges from the course of the river, we discover a cluster of light brown mushrooms with dark scales. These are growing in a wooded area. The caps are funnel-shaped and the gills are decurrent. The stalk surfaces are scaly. These mushrooms show the characteristics of aged *Armillaria* species.

Identifying mushrooms in the field is challenging. During the course of their development, they change shape as well as size and form. At different stages, they often resemble an entirely different species, and poisonous and non-poisonous specimens may be confused easily. This is why harvesting mushrooms is always best left to the experts.

In the course of writing this book, I have become aware of several facts and concepts about fungi that had escaped my notice before. For instance, exactly what is a mushroom? Mushrooms are not plants—they more closely resemble animals. Their cell walls are made of chitin, the same substance that constitutes the exoskeletons of insects. Under the surface of soil, leaves, forest detritus, and our lawns, there exists a network of fungal fibers, strands, and tiny hairs, called mycelia. These make up the actual body of the fungus. The mycelial mass of hundreds of fungal species can persist underground for many years. Periodically, when conditions are optimal, the fungal universe under our feet sends up fruiting bodies above ground. The form of the mushroom fruiting body that we see depends on which of the myriad types of underground fungi produce it. The function of mushrooms is to create and disperse spores for the next generation. Spores are produced by gills or pores usually under the mushroom's cap. Millions of spores are produced and dispersed by wind, by animals feeding on the mushroom, or by other means. The variations in the design of mushrooms for the purpose of housing spores for the next generations are almost unimaginable. We are discovering some of these forms on our hike today.

Fungi serve several purposes. One is to aid in ridding the forest of decaying dead wood. Mushrooms are also fare for squirrels and other rodents, turtles, and slugs. Certain types of flies live their entire lives in or on mushrooms. Fungi are not always beneficial, however. They can be poisonous and fatal to humans and cause diseases in trees and crops. In British Columbia, conifers were severely damaged in the late 1980s and early 1990s by a root disease caused by *Armillaria ostoyae*. As we see today, our deciduous woods in the Sanctuary are home to several members of the *Armillaria* genus. Hopefully these will serve the beneficial purpose of ridding the woods of dead limbs and stumps rather than causing disease.

We follow the Deer Run Trail through a sparsely wooded area, and here we discover another type of mushroom growing under hardwood trees. These are white and about 4" (10 cm) tall with a cap diameter of approximately 3" (8 cm). I notice one lying on its side a few feet away. It has a cup or volva at the base and the remnant of what looks like a partial veil, but this is insufficient information to allow precise identification. When I talk later with a person who has knowledge of fungi and experience identifying edible mushrooms, she tells me that these may be an *Amanita* species.

Finding this potentially deadly mushroom gives me an excellent reason to think about the characteristics of poisonous *Amanitas*. Not all *Amanitas* are poisonous, but the destroying angel complex (*Amanita virosa* and *Amanita bisporigera*) and the death cap (*Amanita phalloides*) are well known poisonous ones. These are common and found in woodlands, lawns, or other places where buried organic tree material occurs, such as here in the open woods in the Sanctuary. Destroying angels are characterized by stark white stalks, gills, and caps. They have a partial veil (ring) that circles the stalk near the top, and the gills are not

Mushroom with characteristics of an *Amanita* species

attached to the stem (as I observed when I examined the overturned mushroom). The most important features for identifying species of destroying angels of the *virosa/bisporigera* complex are the presence of the universal veil and the cuplike structure at the base of the stalk. Other white mushrooms may have either a veil or a ring, but no other mushroom has both veil and ring. However, these structures are not always visible if the mushroom is old or damaged. Death cap mushrooms (*A. phalloides*) have a greenish cap, a broad ring around the stalk, and no volva, and the gills are free (not attached to the stalk).

Identification of these deadly mushrooms is tricky, and taking a bite or eating as little as half a cap can result in death. *Amanita* are found worldwide. They are mycorrhizal, meaning that they colonize the roots of a host tree and live in a mutualistic association with the tree. This type of fungal-plant relationship is common among fungal types and occurs in about 90 percent of the world's plant families, including all trees. The tree contributes carbohydrates (glucose and sucrose) to the fungus, and in return the tree benefits from the fungal mycelia's higher absorptive capacity for water and minerals. In this way, the fungus helps make water and phosphates available to tree roots.

Amanita are among the most beautiful mushrooms. Some have red caps, such as the Caesar's mushroom discussed in chapter 3, and some are even edible. However, it is best to leave all *amanita* alone—it is difficult to tell which are edible and which are toxic.

As we follow the trail a little farther, we find ourselves in the middle of a stand of very tall water tupelos (*Nyssa aquatica*). The tupelo swamp is dry today. The trunks of these trees, large at the base, taper upward to substantial heights; tupelo wood can be used for lumber. In September, these trees will bear fleshy, oblong, purple, 1"-long (2.5 cm) fruit. Many types of wildlife, including wood ducks, squirrels, raccoons, and deer, eat this fruit. The blooms provide nectar with which bees make tupelo honey.

Walking back along the Deer Run Trail, we notice a few clumps of pale blue wild ageratum, also called mistflower (*Conoclinium coelestinum*). We continue to the Tall Tupelo Trail and walk through the woods to the edge of the field and then continue around the woods. I notice young acorns on the water oaks (*Quercus nigra*) growing here. I'll watch as these mature through autumn. We walk beside the field toward the stream that flows into Jobala Pond at the north side. I notice a woody vine with red stems and whitish green berries that look as if they have been sprinkled with black pepper. This is peppervine (*Ampelopsis arborea*). Peppervines are deciduous and climb by use of tendrils. As the berries ripen, they turn from green to shiny red and finally to black. Peppervines are so named because the seeds resemble peppercorns and have a peppery taste. Raccoons include the berries of peppervine in their diet.

As we near the Jobala Pond Observation point, an elderberry bush (*Sambucus canadensis*) with ripe berries stands out among neighboring vegetation. It's growing beside the stream that runs into the pond. As I focus my camera to photograph the berries, I see that the bush harbors a disreputable-looking mockingbird. This is probably a young bird in the process of molting. However, its ruffled feathers, the wild look in its eye, and position among the ripe berries suggest that it may have succumbed to overindulgence and berry intoxication.

Northern mockingbird (*Mimus polyglottos*) on elderberry bush

Up ahead at the edge of the pond, Margaret Anne and Sara are calling me. They have found a box turtle (*Terrapene carolina*). I hurry over to photograph it. Box turtles are quite different from the pond sliders that we often see in the Sanctuary. Pond sliders are usually found in the water or sunning on a log, while box turtles are land reptiles. In addition to obvious differences in shape and form, box turtles have a hinged section on the underside of the shell and can almost completely close themselves within the shell. This one does just that when Margaret Anne picks it up and holds it upside down so I can photograph the underside (plastron). The plastron of pond sliders is solid, and the animal cannot close itself in the shell.

Box turtles may live for more than a hundred years (unlike pond sliders that live about forty-two years maximum in the wild). The usual territorial diameter for a box turtle is about 750' (229 m). Sometimes they go wandering out of this range; no one knows exactly why. Box turtles nest from May through July. Like the pond sliders, they dig nests

Ventral view of an eastern box turtle (*Terrapene carolina carolina*)

with their hind legs. Females usually lay four or five elliptical, thin, white, flexible-shelled eggs. Box turtles are omnivorous; they eat plant and animal materials, including snails, insects, berries, fungi, slugs, worms, roots, flowers, fish, frogs, salamanders, snakes, and bird eggs. They even eat mushrooms, and this makes it dangerous for humans to eat box turtles because the toxins from poison mushrooms may absorb into the turtle's flesh. They are diurnal and dig shallow holes in which to spend the night. In very cold weather, box turtles hibernate sometimes in burrows 2' (0.6 m) deep that they dig in loose earth or mud. They also use unoccupied mammal burrows, holes in stream bottoms, and old stumps.

We have been enjoying the Sanctuary for almost four hours this morning and now the sun is becoming quite warm. We walk back along Hidden Springs Trail toward the cars. On the way, I photograph several interesting plants. One is the 8' to 10' (2 m to 3 m) tall, giant ironweed (*Vernonia gigantea*), spaced here and there beside Hidden Springs Trail.

Giant ironweed (*Vernonia gigantea*)

This showy purple-blooming wildflower belongs to the aster family. Giant ironweed grows throughout the Sanctuary but is usually found in the drier areas and around the fringes of woods.

We notice an unusual vine twining through the bushes on the edge of Jobala Pond. The vine resembles wisteria in the way the lavender flowers with their darker purple wings are borne in densely clustered, fragrant racemes. This is the perennial herb known as groundnut (*Apios americana*). Wisteria and groundnut both belong to the family Fabaceae. Found throughout eastern North America, west to the Dakotas, and south to Texas, groundnut also grows in Ontario and Quebec. This twining vine has an underground stem with many small fleshy tubers ranging from pea-size to the size of a hen's egg. These tubers are edible. Indeed, groundnuts were cultivated as food by American Indian tribes. According to Jack Sanders in his book *The Secrets of Wildflowers*, a British explorer in 1602 documented the use of groundnuts for food by the Indians of Martha's Vineyard. Until I discovered the vines here beside Jobala Pond, I had not been aware of this plant, although it has been known in this country for at least four hundred years. Even Henry David Thoreau reportedly found groundnuts quite tasty. Groundnut vines bloom from June through August. We will look for their seedpods here later in the fall.

On a twig beside the trail, a dragonfly poses long enough for me to photograph it. Dragonflies seem to land effortlessly on vegetation. This one grasps the twig with the spines on its legs—a characteristic of dragonflies.

While I stand photographing the dragonfly, a hackberry emperor butterfly (*Asterocampa celtis*) lands on my arm. Luckily, I brought the camera with the close-up lens today and can photograph, at very close range, this fearless butterfly licking salt from my arm. Hackberry emperors are noted for such behavior, and this one stayed with me for several minutes as I walked along.

Hackberry emperors dine on sap, fruit, damp dirt, and forest detritus rather than on the nectar of flowers like other butterflies. The hackberry trees that live in bottomland habitats such as this are the host plant for the caterpillars of these butterflies. When winter comes, the caterpillars that have not undergone metamorphosis bind leaves together with silk threads and attach the "nest" to a tree limb. They go inside and, with time, they turn brown to match the color of dead leaves. In this way, they spend the winter in diapause in which development is

Above: Groundnut vine in bloom (*Apios americana*)

Below: Hackberry emperor butterfly (*Asterocampa celtis*)

suspended until spring. The caterpillar's leaf nests are known as hibernaculums. When other leaves fall from the trees in winter, hibernaculums remain attached to the tree. In spring the hackberry emperor caterpillars emerge, feed on new leaves, turn green again, and finally become butterflies. Fascinating.

Cardinal flowers (*Lobelia cardinalis*)

At the head of Jobala Pond we notice a bright, red cardinal flower in bloom in a wooded area beyond the marsh.

Finally we arrive at the cars. This was a fine morning to explore the Sanctuary at sunrise. We were privileged to see a deer bounding through the field; a number of interesting mushrooms; the maturing seeds, berries, vines, and colorful late-summer flowers; and a traveling box turtle. A visiting hackberry emperor butterfly gave us the opportunity to learn that it spends winter months in a hibernaculum. This has been a delightful morning in the Sanctuary.

SPECIES LIST: AUGUST

Wildflowers and Other Plants

Alligator weed (*Alternanthera philoxeroides*)

American black elderberry (*Sambucus canadensis*)

Cardinal flower (*Lobelia cardinalis*)

Blue morning glory (*Ipomoea* sp.)

Broadleaf arrowhead (*Sagittaria latifolia*)

Browneyed Susan (*Rudbeckia triloba*)

Buttonbush (*Cephalanthus occidentalis*)

Common dodder (*Cuscuta gro*)

Foxtail grass (*Setaria* sp.)

Giant ironweed (*Vernonia gigantea*)

Goldenrod (*Solidago* sp.)

Greenbrier (*Smilax tamnoides*)

Groundnut (*Apios americana*)

Horsenettle (*Solanum carolinense*)

Kudzu (*Pueraria montana*)

Maryland wild senna (*Senna marilandica*)

Parrot feather watermilfoil (*Myriophyllum aquaticum*)

Partridge pea (*Chamaecrista fasciculata*)

Peppervine (*Ampelopsis arborea*)

Pokeweed (*Phytolacca americana*)

Sensitive fern (*Onoclea sensibilis*)

Spiderwort (*Tradescantia* sp.)

Swamp milkweed (*Asclepias incarnata*)

Trumpet creeper (*Campsis radicans*)

Wild ageratum or mistflower (*Conoclinium coelestinum*)

Wild potato vine or man of the earth vine (*Ipomoea pandurata*)

Trees

Water oak (*Quercus nigra*)

Water tupelo (*Nyssa aquatica*)

Birds

Northern cardinal (*Cardinalis cardinalis*)

Northern mockingbird (*Mimus polyglottos*)

Mammals

White-tailed deer (*Odocoileus virginianus*)

Insects

Eastern pondhawk dragonfly (*Erythemis simplicicollis*)

Hackberry emperor butterfly (*Asterocampa celtis*)

Tent caterpillars (*Malacosoma* sp.)

Reptiles

Box turtle (*Terrapene carolina*)

Fungi

Amanita mushrooms (*Amanita* sp.)

Puffball (*Lycoperdon* sp.)

Ringless honey (*Armillaria tabescens*) and *Armillaria* species

Split gill mushrooms (*Schizophyllum commune*)

Lichens

Crustose lichen

Lichen (*Usnea* sp.)

Other

Smallmouth bass (*Micropterus dolomieu*)

SEPTEMBER

Unexpected Discoveries and Seeing Small

Date: September 10

Begin: 1:30 P.M.

End: 4:00 P.M.

Weather: 1:30 P.M., 75°F (24°C), humid, hazy to sunny

    4:00 P.M., 84°F (29°C)

Participants: Richard and Marian

Purpose: To photo document flora and fauna in the Sanctuary in

    September

TODAY THE LEAVES OF RED maples (*Acer rubrum*) in the Hidden Springs Swamp are beginning to show early fall colors. Red maples are adapted to wetlands and may attain a height of 50' to 80' (15 m to 24 m). They grow rapidly in swampy environments. As we expected, the water level in the swamp is higher than usual due to recent rains. We also notice that the arrow arum (*Peltandra virginica*) we saw growing here in the early summer is still thriving. Green Mountain rises in the distance, shrouded in summer haze from moisture transpired by lush vegetation growing in woods and surrounding fields.

A number of blooming fall wildflowers border Hidden Springs Trail today. One of these is field bindweed (*Convolvulus arvensis*), a member of the morning glory family Convolvulaceae. Field bindweed is a herbaceous perennial vine that twines around other vegetation in a counter-clockwise manner, as dictated by its genes. The blooms can be white or pale pink with white streaks radiating from the center. Leaves are arrow-shaped and roots of this vine may penetrate deep into the soil. It is common in moist thickets, such as this one beside Hidden Springs Trail. When I look closely at the blossom I notice several small insects, and a bee glares back at me from deep inside the bloom. I snap the photo without disturbing the bee. Several nature observers have reported that bees on foraging missions sometimes do not return to their home nest at night. Instead, they camp out and sleep inside of a fragrant flower. After the sun warms them the next morning, they go on their way. Now in the afternoon, I have probably caught this bee inside the bloom gathering pollen.

Just beyond, we note a patch of yellow-blooming wildflowers. This is wingstem (*Verbesina alternifolia*), a member of the aster family. Wingstem has very narrow, toothed leaves and gets its name from the way the leaves wrap around the stem. Another identifying characteristic is the mop-like center of the blooms. Common wingstem is a fall-blooming native perennial found through eastern North America. It grows to a height of 3' to 8' (1 m to 2.4 m).

In the grass beside the trail a frothy substance on the stems of several plants catches our attention. This is the habitat of a spittlebug. The appellation "spittlebug" is the common name applied to several families of bugs in which the nymphs feed on plant sap and create a substance that looks like spittle. Froghoppers and leafhoppers are among the bugs represented in this group. As they feed, the nymphs face head down to drink sap from the plant stem. Spittle is produced from the posterior of the nymph as plant sap is pumped through its body and expelled at a rapid rate. One opinion held by bug experts is that in the process, plant juice is mixed with air in a special abdominal chamber. Another theory suggests that as the sap flows over the bug's body, the

Above: Field bindweed
(*Convolvulus arvensis*) with a foraging bee

Right: Wingstem (*Verbesina alternifolia*)

bug thrashes about creating air bubbles and then uses its legs to move the bubbles to cover itself.

Spittle serves as a hiding place, insulating the nymphs from uncomfortable temperatures and protecting them from dehydration. Adult species of the spittlebug group lay eggs on plant debris in late summer. Eggs hatch in early spring, and the bugs develop through five stages (called instars) to reach adulthood. Nymphs are very small but resemble adults. Froghoppers, so named because of their resemblance to the head region of a frog, are related to leafhoppers but are larger. Froghoppers jump from plant to plant and some adult species can jump to a height of 28" (71 cm). There are about eight hundred and fifty species of spittlebugs worldwide. These bugs are associated with a wide variety of plants.

We are not making great progress toward the interior of the Sanctuary today because of the interesting plants we're finding at the beginning of Hidden Springs Trail. About 30' (9 m) beyond a group of black walnut trees on the left side of the trail, there are several wildflowers that I had not noticed before. One of these is woodland lettuce (*Lactuca floridana*). The thin-stemmed, spindly plants growing here are bent over, but standing upright they would be about 5' (1.5 m) tall. Numerous blooms on short stems extend from longer stems that are perpendicular to the main stem. The 0.5" (12 mm) diameter, starburst-like flowers are a beautiful, delicate blue. Leaves are triangular, arranged alternately, and do not have lobes except for the basal leaves, which are pinnately lobed and toothed. Here beside the trail, this plant has been overtaken by a twining vine. Although the lettuce has a very slender stem, it is sturdy enough to support the vine and still produce numerous flowers. A member of the aster family, this species thrives in damp thickets, along riverbanks and the edges of fields and may reach a height of 10' to 15' (3 m to 4.6 m).

In the grass beside the trail, a non-native, common Asiatic dayflower (*Commelina communis*) displays its two vivid blue petals that stand in sharp contrast to the one white petal barely showing below the yellow stamiodes (rudimentary stamens that do not produce pollen). Each flower remains for only one day, hence the name dayflower. I have found this member of the spiderwort family (Commelinaceae) blooming in several locations in the Sanctuary.

In the same area, we notice a plant with a bloom that looks like a funny face with yellowish eyes and a long nose. The blooms are tiny, only 0.2" to 0.47" (6 mm to 12 mm) across. The plant has numerous leaves along the stem and three leaflets per leaf. This is common beggarweed or largebract ticktrefoil (*Desmodium cuspidatum*). A member of the pea family (Fabaceae), this native perennial grows well in thickets and wet areas and along roadsides. It is found throughout eastern North America. The triangle-shaped fruits are fuzzy and occur in two to six distinct segments. In October when the fruits ripen, they will turn brown and break apart easily. Fruits with the seeds inside are distributed by clinging to animal fur as well as to clothing of humans who

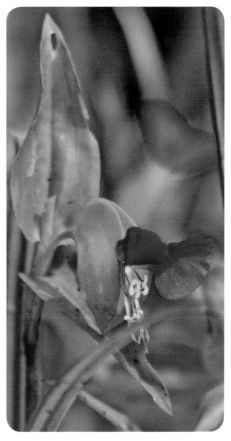

Clockwise from upper left:

Woodland lettuce (*Lactuca floridana*)

Asiatic dayflower (*Commelina communis*)

Beggarweed (*Desmodium cuspidatum*)

unknowingly may brush against the plant. I have had a lot of experience removing the little hitchhikers, one by one, from socks and jeans cuffs after a hike in the Sanctuary.

Beggarweeds are beneficial to wildlife. In addition to blooms providing showy color along roadsides and trails, the plant's seeds are eaten by northern bobwhites, wild turkeys, and white-footed mice. Leaves provide food for white-tailed deer, rabbits, and groundhogs, while bees and some butterflies enjoy the nectar. Clouded sulphur, eastern tailed-blue, and silver-spotted skipper butterflies find shelter in the plant as well.

At the very edge of the Sanctuary property on the right side of Hidden Springs Trail, there is a large-leafed, trailing vine decorated with fragrant purple blooms. This is kudzu (*Pueraria montana* var. *lobata*). The seedpods, which develop even while the vine continues to bloom, are covered with short, bristly hairs. Kudzu is an invasive plant. It was introduced from Japan in 1876 as an ornamental. From 1936 into the 1950s, kudzu was promoted in the South as a way to control erosion. This semi-woody vine grows rapidly by twining and trailing. It has no natural enemies in this country, and if uncontrolled it can overgrow large areas, outcompete native plants, and damage trees. In rural areas, kudzu can cover cars in a junkyard in just a few years.

In some ways, kudzu is beneficial. Until frost kills the leaves in the fall, white-tailed deer feed on them. Kudzu thickets provide excellent cover for young fawns, and the larvae of the silver-spotted skipper butterfly spend time developing in kudzu. Extracts from the plant produce compounds that some say may be used as a herbal remedy to treat a wide range of ills, including allergies and migraine headaches. Kudzu is a nitrogen fixer and thus provides some benefit in restoring nitrogen to the soil. It has been suggested as a source of ethanol for fuel.

Now we pass the red gates into the Sanctuary. Beside the marsh, we notice bright scarlet flowers at the top of a tall, slender stem. This is the native perennial, cardinal flower (*Lobelia cardinalis*), once described by Roger Tory Peterson as America's favorite wildflower. The brilliant red flowers definitely add color to the landscape in this part of the Sanctuary. The leaves of cardinal flowers are toothed, and the 1"- to 1.5"-long (2.5 cm to 3.8 cm) flower tubes are split down the middle between the upper lobes. Long stamens extend through the split. Cardinal flowers bloom from July to September and grow along stream banks and in swamps. Hummingbirds and several species of butterflies find the nectar palatable. However, cardinal flowers, as well as several other lobelia species, can be toxic to wildlife although white-tailed deer sometimes browse on this plant.

Looking across Hidden Springs Trail from where we stand at the head of Jobala Pond, I notice a cluster of black berries borne on an upright shrub that is about 8' to 10' (2.4 m to 3 m) tall. This is a clump of common elderberry (*Sambucus canadensis*). The leaves of this shrub are opposite and pinnately compound with five to eleven oval-shaped leaflets along the central stem. Berries have a diameter of about 0.08" to 0.24" (4 mm to 6 mm) and would be soft and juicy if we pressed them. This deciduous, soft-stemmed shrub is native in our area. It produces flat clusters of white blooms from April through July, and seeds from July through October. Elderberries serve as food for more than fifty species of birds including robins, northern bobwhites, wild turkeys, and mourning doves. Sometimes deer forage on the foliage.

In addition to animals and birds, humans make use of elderberries. For hundreds or perhaps thousands of years, these purple-black berries have been used to make wine. They are rich in vitamin C and antioxidants, and I'm told the wine is pretty good. The leaves, stems, bark, and roots are toxic, however, so be wary about taste-testing this plant.

Growing near the elderberry bushes on the same side of the trail, we find late boneset or late flowering thoroughwort (*Eupatorium serotinum*). This fall wildflower blooms in September and October and is common in our area. It has flat-topped clusters of white flowers and elongated leaves. The edges of the leaves are dentate (meaning with pointed or tooth-shaped projections). Thoroughwort grows from 4' to 8' (1.2 m to 2.4 m) tall and thrives in dry and wet woods, clearings, and low-growing thickets. You may recognize this plant blooming in the fall in uncultivated fields and along roadsides, as well as in the Sanctuary. Flowers appear hairy or fuzzy on the surface. In December the seeds form as nutlets with white bristles; they remain through February. We will look for the seeded version of thoroughwort this winter.

As we approach the widest part of the stream that flows into Jobala

Late-flowering thoroughwort (*Eupatorium serotinum*)

Pond, we notice a colony of plants with lily pad leaves. Some leaves are floating on the surface while others are slightly elevated above the water. Leaves appear to be about 6" to 7" (15 cm to 18 cm) across and are cleft from one side toward the middle. Leaf veins radiate from the junction of the leaf and stem (petiole). There are several white-tipped, pointed bloom buds among the pads. Blooms of water lilies are usually open between early morning and early afternoon, but now it is probably too late in the afternoon for us to find an open bloom. After consulting with aquatic biologist Richard Modlin, who is hiking with me today, we determine that this is a species of water lily in the genus *Nymphaea*, family Nymphaeaceae. It is most likely the fragrant, native American white water lily *Nymphaea odorata*. This species is found in Madison County and is common in other counties across the state and, indeed, across North America. Here, these water lilies are growing in a swampy area where water depth is about 2' or 3' (0.6 m to 0.9 m). An interesting fact about water lilies is that the stomata, or pores through which the

Mild water pepper (*Persicaria hydropiperoides*)

leaf breathes, are located on the upper surface of the leaf rather than on the lower surface as in leaves of most plants. Water lilies are a source of food for a number of insect species. Small bees and species of flies and beetles gather pollen from the blooms. Foliage and roots are favorite muskrat foods, and sometimes even white-tailed deer may enter the water to feed on water lily foliage.

Farther along, the main stream diverges and flows on either side of a small marshy island. Here we notice a large patch of smartweeds. The predominant type appears to be mild water pepper (*Persicaria hydropiperoides*). Mild water pepper has slender bloom spikes with pale pink flowers arranged around the spike. The leaves are slender and lack the dark spot of lady's thumb (*Persicaria maculosa*) that also grows in this area. Mild water pepper flowers are loosely arranged on the bloom spikes. This is another characteristic that differentiates it from the more densely packed flowers of other *Persicaria* species we find growing beside Jobala Pond. The stems of smartweeds are jointed and leaves are alternately arranged on the stems. Leaves have smooth (entire) edges. These abundant marsh plants have provided a soft pink tint to vegetation at the head of the pond all summer.

Later, when I look more closely at an enlarged photograph of the smartweed, I notice an interesting bug. It has two whitish-yellow lines across its flat, dark brown body and flattened leaf-like expansions on its hind legs from which it gets its name. This is an eastern leaffooted bug (*Leptoglossus phyllopus*). There are eleven species in this genus in the United States. Adults are about 0.75" (2 cm) long. Leaffooted bugs are widespread and common in the southeast where they feed on peaches, blackberries, and grain crops. They also feed on bean seeds, developing cotton, citrus, tomatoes, and the stems and tender leaves of potatoes. In immature stages they resemble ants and congregate on fruit where their egg masses were laid. Leaffooted bugs belong to the very large insect order Hemiptera (about eighty-two thousand known species worldwide). This order includes a diversity of species, all having piercing mouthparts that suck juices from plants or animals. Cicadas, hoppers, scale insects, spittlebugs, and aphids belong to this order along with the leaffooted bugs.

Also beside the marshy area at the head of Jobala Pond, we find the giant ironweeds we noted blooming on our earlier trips in June, July, and August. But now some of the blooms are going to seed. Seeds are borne at the base of beige-colored, hair-like tufts. Later at home when I look carefully at a close-up photograph, I find a tiny, gray-striped caterpillar arching across the side of one of the remaining blooms. This immature caterpillar is about 0.25" (0.6 cm) long. It belongs to the measuring worm family (Geometridae). The name has Latin and Greek derivation and means earth-measurer because of the looping mode of locomotion.

Caterpillars in this family have several common names including spanworms, loopers, cankerworms, measuring worms, and inchworms. They do not have legs (prolegs) in the middle of the body like other lepidopteron caterpillars. This is why inchworms move with a looping motion. This little creature has two pairs of leg-like appendages (called false legs) in back, and there are no such legs in the middle of its body. At maturity, inchworms are about 1" (2.5 cm) long. It is interesting to note that inchworms go through metamorphosis to become drab brown adult moths 1" to 1.5" (2.5 cm to 3.8 cm) long in fall or early spring. Female moths have small wings and are flightless. Mating is dependent upon the males finding a waiting female.

Now, as we make our way a little farther along Hidden Springs Trail beside Jobala Pond, we find the peppervines (*Ampelopsis arborea*) that we identified in this location last month. But then the berries were pale green or pinkish. Now, they are a darker pink and within the next two months, they will turn purplish black as they mature.

On the other side of the trail there are bright orange flowers dangling from slender stems. They resemble small vases tipped on the side. The plant is called spotted touch-me-not or orange jewelweed (*Impatiens capensis*). Jewelweeds are annual, native, herbaceous plants. They grow 2' to 5' (0.6 m to 1.5 m) tall, bloom during summer months, and produce seedpods that ripen in the fall. If you touch a ripe seedpod, it will explode and shoot seeds in multiple directions. This is the source of their common name, "touch-me-not." Jewelweed sap is reputedly good for treating poison ivy and other rashes, though this is not definitively confirmed in controlled studies. The name "jewelweed" may also derive from the rounding up of water droplets on leaf surfaces after a rain. The droplets look like jewels sparkling in the sun. Many creatures drink jewelweed nectar. These include hummingbirds, long-tongued bees like bumblebees and honeybees, and a number of species of butterflies and flies. Caterpillars of several moth species as well as white-tailed deer dine on the foliage, and northern bobwhites and white-footed mice eat the seeds. Not only colorful and a delight to see blooming at the edge of the trail, this plant is widely beneficial to wildlife.

Now we stop beside a shallow, temporary pool just off Deer Run Trail on our right. Here we discover sprigs of duckweed among the pads of what appear to be miniature water lilies. Closer inspection reveals that these aquatic plants are not water lilies at all. This is mudplantain or kidneyleaf mudplantain (*Heteranthera reniformis*). This aquatic belongs

Spotted touch-me-not or jewelweed (*Impatiens capensis*)

to the Pontederiaceae or water-hyacinth family. It is often found float-ing in colonies in shallow water or creeping over mud. The leaves, or blades, are 0.4" to 2" (1 cm to 5 cm) wide and either float on, or stand above, the surface of the water. Flowers are white to bluish in color. They are borne on a spike that arises from a spathe that extends above the water. Flowers are about 0.5" (1.3 cm) across, and usually there are two to eight flowers per spathe. Although they all open on the same day, all of the flowers may not extend outside the spathe. This species of mudplantain is found in the southern United States and flowers are present from August through October. We can see several bloom buds and one spathe with open flowers.

Later when I looked carefully at my enlarged photographs of mud-

Kidneyleaf mudplantain (*Heteranthera reniformis*)

plantain, I discovered several creatures I had not noticed while I was taking the photos. One such creature is a small damselfly perched on a leaf of alligator weed. Damselflies (order Odonata) catch and hold mosquitoes and other small flying insects with their front legs. In the larval stages, damselflies live from a few weeks to two or three years submerged in ponds, lakes, or streams. During this time they go through as many as twelve instars (the stage between successive molts). After the last aquatic instar, they climb up a plant stem and out of the water to molt a final time and become adult flying insects. Adult damselflies are short-lived and usually survive for only a few weeks except in hot, dry climates where they may live for six to seven months. After mating, the females deposit eggs on emergent plants or floating vegetation, and the life

cycle begins anew. Damselflies usually produce one generation per year.

Another insect I found in the mudplantain photograph is a small fly (order Diptera) sitting on a pad. It is about 0.25" (6.4 mm) long. This is a colorful little insect. Its shiny green thorax and iridescent wings reflect the light in a rainbow of colors. It casts an interesting shadow on the mudplantain pad.

I wonder how many other small creatures I've missed in my hurry to continue on my way. I take a look at a magnification of another photograph and sure enough, there's a tan and brown insect with large wings. It has long, gangly legs anchoring it to aquatic plants just above the water. This is a crane fly. Now I'm really excited about finding small, hidden, or camouflaged creatures. I recommend carrying binoculars in the field to look for insects or other creatures in unexpected places.

There are more than fifteen hundred species of crane flies (order Diptera) in North America. This one has a distinctive pattern of dark brown bands on its wings. Based on wing markings and size, this resembles a giant eastern crane fly (*Pedicia albivitta*), but without further examination I cannot confirm the identity of this one. Giant eastern crane flies are one of the largest species of crane flies found in Canada and the northeastern United States, as well as in North Carolina and Tennessee. These insects live only a few days as adults and do not feed. Their sole purpose is to mate and lay eggs. They emerge as adults usually at two distinct flight periods, one in May and June and the other in September and October. Because they have such long legs, they are not skillful flyers and seem to collide with things. Some people are afraid of them because of this and because they may look like huge mosquitoes. But crane flies are harmless; they do not bite or sting. In fact, they serve as food for everything from birds to fish, even fungi and bacteria. As larvae, called leatherjackets, they feed on small aquatic insects and decomposing material such as grass roots and other plant debris. In doing this, they are considered beneficial insects and aid in nature's decomposition and recycling. The larvae of giant eastern crane flies are wormlike and live in the mud in streams, in wet soil, and seepages.

Broadleaf arowhead (*Sagittaria latifolia*)

Adults are nocturnal; the one we found is probably resting in the shadows and will become active after dark.

Near the edge of the pool, a patch of broadleaf arrowhead (*Sagittaria latifolia*) is in bloom. Bloom stalks have whorls of two or three flowers. The staminate (male) flowers are located at the top part of the bloom stalk and pistillate (female) flowers are below. Each of the staminate flowers is about 1" (2.5 cm) across and has three white petals and three green sepals between the petals. The golden-yellow stamens are numerous and stand above the petals of the staminate flowers. The green bur-like masses are carpels of pistillate flowers that contain the seeds. Seeds are produced as achenes, which are dry, single-seeded fruit. Achenes, packed as three-angled, flat, winged forms with beaks extending from the center, give the fruit its bur-like appearance. Arrowheads bloom for about a month from mid-summer to early fall. We were quite fortunate to find this patch in bloom in the small, temporary pool near Hidden Springs Trail today. If we could dig into the plant

Unexpected Discoveries and Seeing Small

cluster, we would find tufts of coarse roots. These develop into starchy tubers and long rhizomes, the thick underground stems that produce new roots and shoots that develop into new plants. As mentioned, sagittaria reproduces by seeds as well.

Growing on the bank beside the small pool, there is a plant that at first glance I mistakenly think is common ragweed. When I look more closely, I see that it has small bracts (reduced leaves) at the base of the tiny flowers that protrude from the spike. Ragweed does not have bracts. This plant is marsh elder or sumpweed (*Iva annua*). Sumpweed is an herbaceous plant native to North America and found here in Madison County. In eastern North America, indigenous people cultivated sumpweed for its seed. A benefit in the Sanctuary is that it attracts birds.

Mixed with the sumpweed patch on the bank is a pretty yellow-blooming plant. This is wingleaf primrose-willow (*Ludwigia decurrens*). A member of the evening primrose family Onagraceae, this native plant can reach a height of 6' (1.8 m). The ones growing here beside the pool are about 2' (0.6 m) tall. The characteristic that distinguishes wingleaf primrose-willow from the numerous other species of *Ludwigia* found in Alabama is its four-winged stem. The species name, *decurrens*, is derived from the manner in which leaves form a narrow wing below their attachment, termed decurrent. Leaves are narrow, smooth around the edges, and arranged alternately along the stem. They resemble slender leaves of willows. Flowers have four bright yellow petals separated by four pointed-tip sepals and eight to twelve stamens (most other species have only four stamens). The seed capsules, also called seedboxes, are four-sided, tapered at the bottom and can be up to 0.75" (1.9 cm) long. No other species of *Ludwigia* found in northern Alabama have such long seed capsules. Classified as an obligate wetland plant, wingleaf primrose-willow grows in swamps, in ditches, and around the edges of ponds.

When I looked closely at a photograph of the primrose-willow, I was surprised to discover a caterpillar on the underside of a stem. The caterpillar's bright green body with pink and white stripes is an excellent

Wingleaf primrose-willow (*Ludwigia decurrens*)

example of protective coloration. It blends well with the vegetation on which it rests. This appears to be a sphinx moth caterpillar.

Now we leave this area and walk along Hidden Springs Trail to the footbridge. There beside the stream I notice an emergent plant with its roots in the water and about 18" (46 cm) of stem and foliage above the surface. The jointed stem is almost as big around as my little finger. Several of the joint segments are pink. This is alligator weed (*Alternanthera philoxeroides*). The faintly fragrant flowers consist of small, 0.5" (1.3 cm), whitish, half-ball-shaped clusters of six to ten florets borne singly on branches 1" to 3" (2.5 cm to 7.6 cm) long. The submerged portion of the plant serves as a habitat for invertebrates. Decaying plants are a food source for several aquatic species. Other than providing food and shelter for aquatic creatures, this weed is not known to have any direct food value for wildlife. This is unfortunate because alligator weed is extremely abundant in the streams and marshes around Jobala Pond this year. The plant is a native of South America and an invasive in the United States.

As I walk across the footbridge and around the end of Jobala Pond, I notice the vines on my right. They have heart-shaped leaves and 0.6"-wide (1.5 cm) white blooms with purple anthers (the pollen-bearing part of a flower at the tip of stamens). This is a small white morning glory called whitestar (*Ipomoea lacunosa*). It belongs to the family Convolvulaceae. An herbaceous vine, it climbs by twining. This morning glory is native and blooms from July through October. It grows in thickets in moist soils and along roadsides.

The purple flowers of a lone giant ironweed (*Vernonia gigantea*) stand on the left side of a patch of sweet goldenrod (*Solidago odora*) blooming at the edge of the woods across from Jobala Pond. This goldenrod is identified by its narrow, lance-shaped, smooth-edged leaves, 2" to 4" (5 cm to 10 cm) across. It can grow to a height of 50" (1.3 m) and prefers dry woodlands and field edges. Crushed leaves of some goldenrods have an anise-like fragrance. Seeds provide food for birds, especially American goldfinches, and deer may browse on remains of the plant in winter.

Past Jobala Pond, we follow Deer Run Trail. As we turn right toward the Forest Glen Observation Point, we notice a vine with brilliant red, almost translucent ripe berries that hang among clusters of green unripe berries above us on the left. This is Carolina moonseed (*Cocculus carolinus*) also known as Carolina snailseed, coralbeads, and redberry moonseed. Now in September, the seeds are developing, though some green berries are still present. Berries will continue to ripen and turn a more brilliant red through October and November.

Another interesting discovery at the Forest Glen Observation Point is the carpet of duckweed that we find floating on the pond. It covers most of the surface in a pale green mass of tiny, rounded, swollen-looking leaf-like structures. Duckweeds are perennial floating herbs in the family Lemnaceae. Each plant occurs separately or in rafting groups. Common duckweed (*Lemna minima*) is 0.07" to 0.13" (1.7 mm to 3.2 mm) across and has only one root, while a species of larger duckweed grows to 0.25" (6.4 mm) and has at least three roots. Duckweeds reproduce mainly by budding but can also produce seeds from tiny flowers that

Above: A small white morning glory called whitestar (*Ipomoea lacunosa*)

Right: Tickseed sunflower (*Bidens polylepis*)

arise from the top surface of the plant. The roots may dangle 5.9" (15 cm) beneath the floating plant. Duckweed colonies serve as habitat for small invertebrates, and many kinds of ducks consume the plant. Waterfowl transport it to other locations on their legs and feathers.

Now walking along Deer Run Trail as it follows the road through the field, I notice a patch of bright yellow sunflowers rising above common ragweed and smartweed at the edge of the field. This showy fall-blooming wildflower is a member of the aster family. The leaves are deeply divided, opposite, and compound with three to seven slender, toothed leaflets. Based on the leaves and the number and length of outer bracts (longer than inner bracts), I identify this as tickseed sunflower (*Bidens polylepis*). These wildflowers grow in moist areas and bloom from August through October. They produce seeds (called beggar ticks), which have two barbs that aid in seed dispersal by hitching a ride on animals as they brush by, or on our clothing.

Farther along, we note a large green patch ahead and to the right of the trail. The patch is tightly populated by plants about 3' (1 m) tall. Their green flower spikes are covered with lighter green, very small, goblet-shaped cups that have frilly edges. Some of the cups contain spiny buds. Tiny, yellowish flowers reside in the uppermost cups. The heavily veined leaves are severely serrated and have spiny hairs along the top surfaces. This plant is three-seeded mercury, also known as hophornbeam copperleaf (*Acalypha ostryifolia*). It looks like a stinging nettle, but its hairs do not sting. It is a member of the spurge family Euphorbiaceae and is found across the southern United States, north to the Great Lakes to the eastern seaboard and west to New Mexico and Arizona. An annual herb, three-seeded mercury grows in fields, road-sides, and waste sites. This plant is native to North America.

Continuing on Deer Run Trail, we come to the far edge of the field. Here I notice a plant about 8" (20 cm) tall with a stem topped with a gracefully curving double row of tiny blue flowers. Some flowers have bright orange centers. The stems are hairy and leaves are coarse and crinkly. This plant, called turnsole or Indian heliotrope (*Heliotropium indicum*), belongs to the Boraginaceae or forget-me-not family. The tiny flowers are fragrant and attract bees and butterflies. Deer do not find it palatable. Indian heliotrope grows throughout the southeastern United States and thrives well in waste ground, as here in the middle of the field road, and in low, moist woods.

Now we come to the edge of the small stream on the Gravel Bar Trail. The two sides (valves) of an Eurasian clam (*Corbicula fluminea*) open like a butterfly's wings and nestle among the small, dark river stones on the bank. The clams that live here in the Flint River and its tributaries are freshwater bivalve mollusks (the shell has two sides). Adults usually don't grow larger than 1.5" (about 3.8 cm). This one is a bit smaller than a nickel, as are most we find along the riverbanks here. Clams draw food along with water and dissolved oxygen into the body through an incurrent siphon. Wastes and excess water are expelled by a second or excurrent tube.

Indian heliotrope (*Heliotropium indicum*)

Like another mollusk (snails), these clams use a muscular foot for locomotion. Asian clams were first introduced on the West Coast of the United States in the 1920s. By the 1970s, they had spread all the way to the East Coast and are now found throughout the United States where temperatures range between 35°F (2°C) and 86°F (30°C). Humans are responsible for their spread. Clams escape when people use them as fishing bait, and researchers may have inadvertently released them into streams and waterways during scientific research projects. Asian clams pose a serious problem for industries when they plug intake water pipes. They prefer flowing water and sand or gravel surfaces. Clams feed on plankton in the water, require high levels of dissolved oxygen, and do not thrive in polluted waters.

Here in the same area on the sandy beach by the stream, we notice a few small whitestar morning glories in bloom. Also, there is another type of vine creeping across the ground. This one has remarkably

coiled tendrils that resemble a tightly wound spring. The five-lobed, heart-shaped leaves are about 2.5" (6.4 cm) across. Blooms are whitish to cream-colored, about 0.25" diameter (6.4 mm), and have greenish-yellow centers and five petals. Bloom stems are very hairy. This is a one-seed bur cucumber (*Sicyos angulatus*). A member of the gourd family, this interesting small vine grows on riverbanks and in moist thickets.

About 15' (4.6 m) beyond the bur cucumber on the sand bar, a lone bush of wild ageratum or mistflower (*Conoclinium coelestinum*) stands by the stream. Blue, many-headed flowers form in clusters at the end of branched stems. Mistflowers grow to a height of 1' to 3' (0.3 m to 1 m). Leaves have rounded teeth and the surfaces are wrinkled. I've seen mistflowers growing in several other locations in the Sanctuary around edges of the fields and in moist areas in the woods. They bloom in late summer and early fall. Its soft, frilly blooms make this one of my favorite wildflowers.

We head back along Deer Run Trail to the intersection of Hidden Springs Trail and follow that toward the Jobala Haven Observation Point. Here we pause beside the pond to photograph a pond slider turtle sunning on a floating log. It watches us for a moment before slipping into the water. The surface of the water is still and clumps of algae float in thick patches, forming a mat that covers large areas of the pond this time of year. It's as if the pond is peacefully resting under a soft, green blanket anticipating the changes that will come with the approaching winter.

Richard turns and walks a short distance into the big field behind us. He stops and stands in a huge patch of ricefield flatsedge (*Cyperus iria*). The sedges are about as tall as his knee, and the ripe seeds at the apex of stems appear golden against the green background of the field and darker green woods beyond. This end of the field is marshy, a prime environment for sedges as we have observed in other months. They have indeed taken over the edge of the field bordered on one side by the stream that flows from the woods about 200' (61 m) away. This stream continues on its course and drains into Jobala Pond near the Jobala Haven Observation Point.

Six-spotted fishing spider (*Dolomedes triton*)

We head back around the pond toward Hidden Springs Trail. As we cross the footbridge over the stream at the outflow of Jobala Pond, I notice a spider resting on a leaf of lizard's tail below us. The spider's body is about 0.5" (1.3 cm) long, and its front legs are slightly longer than its body. It appears to be waiting for something, and indeed it is. It's a fishing spider waiting for some hapless insect to come near. The color pattern and characteristic light spots on the top of the abdomen help me to identify this as a six-spotted fishing spider (*Dolomedes triton*); however, the six spots for which this spider is named are on the underside of the cephalothorax and can be seen only from below.

Fishing spiders are diurnal (active and feed during the day). They are usually found near streams and ponds where they dine primarily on water striders (an insect that skates on the surface of the water), but these spiders are ambush hunters that will eat whatever they can capture. They may consume five times their weight in a day. In addition to water striders and small fish, they feed on tadpoles and insect larvae. Though they are stealthy hunters, their prey capture rate is not high.

Males are usually 0.4" to 0.5" (9 mm to 13 mm) long, and the larger females are about 0.6" to 0.8" (17 mm to 20 mm).

Fishing spiders do not spin webs but depend instead on their keen eyesight and stealth to ambush and capture prey. They sit very still on a leaf as this one is doing. If the spider sees a ripple, it will dive below quick as a flash to capture its prey. Fishing spiders can dive as deep as 7" (18 cm). The underside of their body is covered with water-repellent hairs, an aid when diving. They breathe air trapped in these hairs and can remain underwater for as long as forty-five minutes. Fishing spiders can be found around Jobala Pond from May through September. Females spin a silk sack and carry their eggs around in their jaws. Just before eggs hatch, the female deposits the egg sac among nearby leaves. She guards it well. She will watch over the baby spiders for about a week after they hatch and then leave them to busy herself with other spider activities.

Continuing back along Hidden Springs Trail beside Jobala Pond, we notice common dodder or love vine (*Cuscuta gronovii*). We found this vine growing over the vegetation here last month. Now it is in full bloom. I had not seen love vine blooms before. It's quite showy with numerous clusters of tiny, white, waxy flowers. Minute seedpods about 0.125" (0.3 cm) long will appear next month.

Just beyond the love vine on the same side of the trail, strange, spidery-looking, multiple-legged forms seem to march across the vegetation. These are the achenes of leatherflower (*Clematis viorna*) borne on long stems rising from the vine. A member of the buttercup family (Ranunculaceae), leatherflowers (also called vasevine) bloom in the spring and summer in moist woods and along stream and pond banks. Sanctuary artist Katrina Weber photographed a bud almost ready to open on a vine growing here beside Jobala Pond in August. When a bud opens, what looks like the flower is actually not; instead, the flower parts are housed inside four large, leathery, tough sepals fused at the base and modified to look like petals. The sepals are dark reddish-lavender on the outside and yellowish and fuzzy on the inside. When the flowers open, the sepals curl backward at the tips, thus forming

Leatherflower (*Clematis viorna*) achenes

an elegant-looking, vase-like structure. Leaves consist of three, five, or seven dark green leaflets. Leatherflower vines do not twine; they trail over other vegetation. After fertilization, the flowers develop into the spidery-looking fruits we find here today. Achenes are arranged in clusters and have long tails. This dramatic and decorative seed arrangement is wind dispersed and well designed for propagation of this plant.

A little farther along the trail, we find several milkweed seedpods among the vegetation on the bank of Jobala Pond. On close examination, we discover a group of bright orange and black bugs on one of the pods. Black wing pads are clearly visible on the larger bugs. The small bugs are also orange but lack the visible wing pads. Both sizes have long black antennae. At first I thought these might be two different types of bugs, but the small ones did not appear fearful of the larger ones. In fact, they seemed to be in very close company with each other. Checking several websites and insect books, I found that these are nymphal stages of the large milkweed bug. Their classification is as follows: Phylum, Arthropoda; Class, Insecta; Order, Hemiptera (true bugs);

Large milkweed bug nymphs (*Oncopeltus fasciatus*)

Family Lygaeidae (seed bugs); Genus and Species *Oncopeltus fasciatus*. Hemiptera means "half wing," and I thought it interesting that, in addition to having long, piercing, tube-like, segmented mouthparts, the forewings of most members in the order Hemiptera are hardened near the base and membranous toward the end. The adults of a related species, the small milkweed bug (*Lygaeus kalmii*), are 0.4" to 0.5" (10 mm to 12 mm) long and the nymphs have two black markings behind the head; the large milkweed bug nymphs we find here on the pod do not have these markings. Adult large milkweed bugs are 0.4" to 0.7" (10 mm to 18 mm) long. These bugs habitually congregate in clusters on milkweed seedpods. They pierce the seed and secrete enzyme-containing saliva into the seed through one of two parallel tubes in the beak. The enzymes digest an area within the seed to render it soluble and edible. The bug uses the other tube to suck the mix of dissolved material into its body. Toxic cardiac glycosides from the milkweed plants are ingested by these bugs and, while the bugs are not harmed, the chemicals make them taste very bad to birds or other would-be predators. Once a bird has tasted a milkweed bug, it is unlikely to sample any orange and black bug again. The coloration of milkweed bugs is termed aposematic, meaning colors advertising toxicity.

Today we have enjoyed a most productive expedition into the Sanctuary in terms of species discovered. Our "closer look" yielded a number of surprises: a green caterpillar hiding on the stem of wingleaf primrose-willow, a fishing spider on a leaf above the stream, a colorful crane fly camouflaged in the shadows of sagittaria, a small damselfly on an alligatorweed leaf, the bright colors of milkweed bugs, the oddity of a leaf-footed bug, and a bee hiding inside a morning glory blossom. This has been one of our most exciting and inspiring forays into the Sanctuary.

The Language of Alders

I wonder if there is a language alders speak.
Do they whisper to insects on their leaves,
and stems and buds?
Do alders tell of cycles, and seasons,
and life beyond the meadow?
And do they translate the wisdom of the wind
to bobcat, bird, and deer?

And what do alders say to the spider
whose web balances life with death between the twigs?
For here by wingtips, a hapless dragonfly swings
suspended by a spider's web,
As if it were a shirt hung on a line to dry—
a player in Nature's timeless
dance of fortunes.

Species List: September

Wildflowers and Other Plants

Alligator weed (*Alternanthera philoxeroides*)

American black elderberry (*Sambucus canadensis*)

American white water lily (*Nymphaea odorata*)

Arrow arum (*Peltandra virginica*)

Asiatic dayflower (*Commelina communis*)

Beggarweed or largebract ticktrefoil (*Desmodium cuspidatum*)

Bur-reed (*Sparganium* sp.)

Cardinal flower (*Lobelia cardinalis*)

Carolina moonseed (*Cocculus carolinus*)

Common or broadleaf arrowhead (*Sagittaria latifolia*)

Common dodder (*Cuscuta gronovii*)

Common duckweed (*Lemna minima*)

Devil's darning needles (*Clematis virginiana*)

Field bindweed (*Convolvulus arvensis*)

Giant duckweed (*Spirodela polyrhiza*)

Giant ironweed (*Vernonia gigantea*)

Indian heliotrope (*Heliotropium indicum*)

Kidneyleaf mudplantain (*Heteranthera reniformis*)

Mild water pepper (*Persicaria hydropiperoides*) and other *Persicaria* species

Kudzu (*Pueraria montana* var. *lobata*)

Late-flowering thoroughwort (*Eupatorium serotinum*)

Leatherflower (*Clematis viorna*)

Lizard's tail (*Saururus cernuus*)

Marsh elder or sumpweed (*Iva annua*)

Milkweed (*Asclepias incarnata*)

One-seed bur cucumber (*Sicyos angulatus*)

Peppervine (*Ampelopsis arborea*)

Ricefield flatsedge (*Cyperus iria*)

Spotted touch-me-not or jewelweed (*Impatiens capensis*)

Sweet goldenrod (*Solidago odora*)

Three-seeded mercury (*Acalypha ostryifolia*)

Tickseed sunflower (*Bidens polylepis*)

Whitestar morning glory (*Ipomoea lacunosa*)

Wild ageratum or mistflower (*Conoclinium coelestinum*)

Wingleaf primrose-willow (*Ludwigia decurrens*)

Wingstem (*Verbesina alternifolia*)

Woodland lettuce (*Lactuca* sp.)

Trees

Black locust (*Robinia pseudoacacia*)

Black walnut (*Juglans nigra*)

Red maple (*Acer rubrum*)

Insects and Bugs

Crane fly species (Order Diptera, Suborder Nematocera)

Damselfly species (Order Odonata, Suborder Zygoptera)

Eastern leaffooted bug (*Leptoglossus phyllopus*)

Giant eastern crane fly (*Pedicia* sp.)

Large milkweed bug nymphs
(*Oncopeltus fasciatus*)
Measuring worm (*Geometridae*)
Six-spotted fishing spider (*Dolomedes triton*)
Spittlebugs (Order Hemiptera, Family Aphrophoridae)

Others
Eurasian clam (*Corbicula fluminea*)
Mosquitofish (*Gambusia affinis.*)
Mushroom (*Amanita* spp.)
Pond slider turtle (*Trachemys scripta*)

OCTOBER

Fall Colors and a Bobcat

Date: October 31
Begin: 3:00 P.M.
End: 6:00 P.M.
Weather: 71°F (22°C), sunny until sunset
Participants: Margaret Anne, Clayton, Larry, and Marian
Purpose: October sunset hike

It's a pleasant, sunny afternoon—perfect for hiking. Although we have not had frost, the nights are chilly, and Hidden Springs Swamp is sporting fall colors. Smartweeds and other plants add a rust hue to vegetation in the foreground. Mountains in the distance reflect the colorful tints of fall leaves in the hardwood forests. Now at the end of October, only remnants of arrow arum (*Peltandra virginica*) are visible above the dark swamp water. This aquatic plant flourished here from February through September. The tuber-like roots (rhizomes) will lie buried in soft mud all winter. In spring, new plants will emerge from rhizomes and arrow-shaped leaves will populate the swamp once again.

We follow Hidden Springs Trail past the red gate and pause to view the marsh at the head of Jobala Pond. Patches of bright green water parrot feather watermilfoil (*Myriophyllum aquaticum*) contrast with dark water and brown leaves trapped among its frilly plumes. Pond scum composed of green algae in the genus *Spirogyra* floats on the surface. Today the sun lights the trees so that a mirror image reflects on an area of water just beyond a patch of *Myriophyllum*. Not even a breath of wind stirs the surface. The image I see is upside-down on the water—milfoil at the top, treetops and azure sky at the bottom—it's a reflection of colors more vivid in water than what actually exists above. I have the sense that I should stand on my head to view this image of trees and sky.

Here the two streams that flow on each side of the marsh converge to isolate a small island. Most of the brown spikes of the common native cattails (*Typha latifolia*) that grew here all summer now show seeds attached to fluffy parachutes that will carry them to new locations on winter winds. A few of the more tenacious cattails still sport visible green leaf blades amid the brown and gray of other fall vegetation. Stems of goldenrod, late flowering thoroughwort (*Eupatorium serotinum*), and giant ironweed stand with their shriveled leaves and spent blooms marking the late fall phase of their life cycle. These wizened, graying, fuzzy, seed-bearing remnants of summer glory that house the promise for next year's vibrant blooming wildflowers also line the banks that border the upper end of Jobala Pond.

Extracts made from common boneset (*Eupatorium perfoliatum*), a member of the same genus as the late flowering thoroughwort we see here on the island, were used as a medicinal by Early Americans. Common boneset is also found in Madison County. The bitter concoctions made from the plant were used to treat everything from snakebites to fevers, including dengue fever, a mosquito-borne illness so painful that those infected feel as if their bones are breaking. A tea made from dried boneset leaves was used to relieve the pain. Extracts also seemed to aid the immune system in fighting illness. The name "boneset" may have derived from the way leaves of common boneset join as they grow opposite each other on the stalk. Some folk may have believed that the symbolic leaves would aid in knitting broken bones. In botanical

Above: **Goldenrod** (*Solidago* sp.) **going to seed**

Below: **Mature seeds of late flowering thoroughwort** (*Eupatorium serotinum*) terms, "wort" means plant, especially the types of plants once used to treat diseases.

A few feet farther down Hidden Springs Trail we find that beavers have built a solid dam across the stream. This is a choice location for us to visit some night to listen for a beaver to announce our intrusion by slapping its tail on the water. Also, it would be a good location to place a night-vision, motion-activated camera to capture a beaver's nocturnal activity.

As we walk along this segment of Hidden Springs Trail, I look for the seedpods of the wooly dutchman's pipe vine (*Aristolochia tomentosa*) that bloomed here on the right side of the trail in the summer. This plant employs an interesting mechanism for pollen dispersal. The S-shaped flowers are fragrant and attract flies that become trapped on hairs inside the tube of the bloom. Once a fly is trapped, the hairs wither and allow the insect to escape. In this way, pollen clinging to the fly is transferred to fertilize other blooms.

Now, looking up into the vines just above my eye level, I can see several boxy dutchman's pipe vine seedpods. These are about 3" (7.6 cm) long and 1.5" (3.8 cm) in diameter. One pod is broken open to reveal stacks of closely packed seeds. I focus my camera on the stack and note that one seed is precariously balanced on the bottom edge of the pod. This gives me an excellent view of an individual winged seed. The wing is about 0.5" (1.27 cm) at the broadest end and very flat. This plant does a first-rate job of packaging. Many individual seeds are tightly stacked into each of several pod chambers. Seeds are designed for wind dispersal; however, some may be distributed by birds.

Other seedpods hang from leafless vines beside Jobala Pond. The mature pods of trumpet creeper (*Campsis radicans*) are suspended by their arched necks from woody stems. Growing here beside the pond, this vine's trumpet-shaped, bright orange blooms added color and provided nectar for hummingbirds all summer. Also here beside the pond, 3"-long (8 cm) bean-shaped pods of groundnut (*Apios americana*) have formed on the vines I discovered in bloom here in August. Looking

Left: Wooly dutchman's pipe vine (*Aristolochia tomentosa*) seedpod and seed

Right: Trumpet creeper (*Campsis radicans*) seedpod

higher, I notice crinkled, black, drying berries of peppervine (*Ampelopsis arborea*) contrasting against the blue sky. These are the same berries that graced their vines with pink in early summer and then changed to purplish black last month.

We continue along the trail to the small temporary pool where we found mudplantain and sagittaria in September. The pool is now covered with brown leaves that float among small remnant sprigs of milfoil, but none of the mudplantain or sagittaria remains. Continuing across the footbridge at the end of Jobala Pond, we stop at the Forest

Glen Observation Point. Here, too, brown leaves are sprinkled over the surface of the pond. On visits to the Sanctuary during summer and fall months, I observed a large, healthy sensitive fern (*Onoclea sensibilis*) growing on the side of the small ditch that connects to the pond. Last month this fern stood dark green and sturdy, but now it is in decline and seems worn and in need of a rest. Aptly named "sensitive" fern, the fronds die quickly after frost. As the temperatures continue to drop, remaining fronds will turn black and disappear. Next spring, roots will send up new fronds and the fern will flourish again—the natural progression of nature's cycles.

Back on Deer Run Trail, we walk across the soybean field. This field is now bare except for the green fuzz of very small vegetation carpeting the ground. Near the Gravel Bar Trail entrance, a morning glory vine clings tenaciously to the larger stem of a greenbrier. The thorny greenbrier remains green, but the heart-shaped morning glory leaves wear fall colors of yellow and rust.

Sooty mold is still present on the leaves remaining on the vegetation here. This charcoal-colored fungus was evident on many of the Sanctuary's plants all summer. I had hoped the fall rains would wash the mold from leaves and vegetation in the Sanctuary, but this did not happen. Perhaps with winter's cold, the mold will disappear and the new leaves that develop next spring will be free of it.

I wonder where sooty mold comes from and why it doesn't show up every year. My research reveals that sooty mold is more common when temperatures are high and during drought conditions, which was the case this past summer and fall. But the real culprits that make it possible for sooty mold to cloak plant leaves in black are certain types of insects. These are the insects that feed on sap and subsequently secrete honeydew: a clear, sweet, sticky substance. When mold spores, carried by wind, come into contact with the sticky, nutrient-rich honeydew on a leaf surface, the spores stick, germinate, and send out filaments called mycelia that cover the leaf. The cells of these filaments contain the black pigment melanin, and this imparts the sooty color to vegetation.

The insects that facilitate growth of sooty mold all have something in common. They belong to the order Hemiptera, which includes insects with piercing, sucking mouthparts. Whiteflies, leafhoppers, mealybugs, scale insects, aphids, and spittlebugs fit the description. These are plentiful in the Sanctuary. Aphid populations increase when plants are stressed by drought. There were periods during the summer when no rain fell for days. An abundance of aphids and insufficient rainfall to wash away honeydew probably contributed to the extent of sooty mold in the Sanctuary. Several types of black fungi produce this mold. Common genera include *Cladosporium, Aureobasidium, Antennariella, Limacinula, Scorias,* and *Capnodium.*

Now as we approach the Gravel Bar Trail, we notice a patch of blooming wildflowers; each one is about 3' (1 m) tall. These are showy, yellow, tickseed sunflower (*Bidens polylepis*). The leaves are divided into lance-shaped, toothed leaflets, and the twelve or more outer bracts are wavy. A member of the aster family, these sun-loving wildflowers bloom from August through October. When most wildflowers in the Sanctuary have formed seeds and their leaves have turned brown and shriveled, tickseed sunflowers add color to the fall scene by blooming brightly in the late afternoon sun.

We turn right onto the Gravel Bar Trail and walk toward the stream. This tributary of the Flint River was so shallow and narrow that we walked across it in September. Now, as a result of recent rains, the stream is more than 10' (3 m) across, 2' (0.6 m) deep, and flowing swiftly. We elect to stay on this side today.

On the opposite bank a red maple blazes with brilliant fall color. It's getting late, and now the slanting rays of sun touch the leaves in time for Clayton and me to photograph this brilliant display of fall foliage. We are certain that this tree will be immortalized by Clayton's brush, and we look forward to seeing it in future art exhibits.

We walk back to the Deer Run Trail and turn right to skirt around the woods. A lone wingstem (*Verbesina alternifolia*) stands at the edge of the field. Some of its leaves are already curling and seeds are almost

Red maple tree (*Acer rubrum*) in the fall

Carolina moonseed (*Cocculus carolinus*)

ready to disperse. Wingstems bloomed in this location and around the borders of the field earlier in the fall.

A Carolina moonseed (*Cocculus carolinus*) vine with its clusters of red berries adorns the vegetation here also. This vine belongs to the family Menispermaceae. A twining type vine, Carolina moonseed may climb as high as 15' (4.6 m) into trees and other vegetation along road and field margins and near streams. The berries look good enough to eat—but don't. They have alkaloid compounds that are bitter and can cause gastric distress. The leaves are heart-shaped and somewhat resemble the shape of an elephant's head. These Carolina moonseed vines bloomed in the Sanctuary in late spring, but I missed seeing the small, greenish flowers. I'll look for them in this location next spring. Carolina moonseed is a deciduous native vine that grows throughout the southeastern United States. The seeds have a hard wall and resemble the curl of a snail shell, thus justifying the alternate common name, Carolina snailseed.

Farther along the trail we find a dead log near the edge of deciduous woods. A goblet-shaped fungus is growing on the bark. The caps have the brown, orange, tan, and greenish color similar to the turkey tail mushrooms we found in the Sanctuary in May. However, the funnel shape, rather than the flatter fan of a turkey tail fungus, tips me that this is a different mushroom. When I look more closely at the underside of the caps, I do not see pores and the surface is smooth. This is a crust fungus, not a polypore. Crust fungus is an unscientific term used to describe fungi with smooth or wrinkled pores on the spore-bearing surfaces. The fungus growing here is false turkey tail (*Stereum ostrea*). As evidenced by the greenish color indicating presence of green algae, this fungus appears to have reached old age. False turkey tail fungi are widely distributed in North America and can be found throughout the year.

We have taken our time photographing fall colors and interesting features as we walk along, and now the sun is sinking fast behind the row of trees across the field to the west. If we are to reach the tupelo swamp and return to the cars before dark, we must hurry. I quickly photograph bright red and dark purple sweetgum (*Liquidambar styraciflua*) leaves on trees beside the field. I don't want to miss documenting their contribution to fall colors in the Sanctuary.

We follow the Deer Run Trail along its tangent with the Flint River. Just past the Flint River Observation Point sign, a bright red spot on the ground catches my eye. It's a single berry, about 0.25" (6.4 mm) in diameter with a small but noticeable scar on the top surface. I notice another distinguishing feature on a second plant growing nearby. This one has two, almost round, opposite leaves. These are partridgeberries (*Mitchella repens*). In his book *Wildflowers of Tennessee*, Jack B. Carman writes that the genus name honors Dr. John Mitchell, a botanist living in Virginia in the eighteenth century. Carman also writes that the name implies that partridges should like the berries, but these berries

Above: **False turkey tail mushrooms** (*Stereum ostrea*)

Below: **Partridgeberry** (*Mitchella repens*)

are not an important food for wildlife. Partridgeberry is a creeping, branching evergreen perennial. It blooms in May and June, and the small, fragrant, white flowers are borne in pairs with ovaries united. A single berry develops from the two blooms. A scar on the berry forms where the two ovaries were originally connected during flowering.

A short distance beyond the Flint River Observation Point we stop to look for heron nests in the tall trees across the river. We have been checking this site each month since last March to determine if the nests remain intact. Today I can see two large balls of sticks in one of the trees. I'm reassured to find these nests because herons usually return to the same rookery year after year. I hope the nests will remain during winter and will be here when herons arrive next spring.

We walk along the river, then turn back to follow the trail through the woods to the tupelo swamp. This is the same swamp that extends from the Tall Tupelo Observation Point to wind through the woods here. The path through the south end of the tupelo swamp is an old logging road and easy to follow. Larry and I stop to photograph a cluster of stalkless mushrooms growing on the trunk of a maple. These mushrooms are white with yellowish pores under the caps. They are growing on the lower part of the trunk of a living tree and there is moss on the caps of some of the mushrooms. This is characteristic of the mossy maple polypore fungus (*Oxyporus populinus*). This fungus grows year-round on trunks and in wounded areas on hardwood trees, especially living maples.

We leave the woods and continue through a soggy area where a muddy trail, obviously traveled by a number of deer, dissects the field. Both small and large tracks, all going in the same direction, follow the narrow path. Margaret Anne and Clayton are ahead on the opposite side of the field. Margaret Anne is motioning to us. She seems excited. When Larry and I catch up, she tells us that she and Clayton have just glimpsed a bobcat as it bounded across the field into the woods.

"It wasn't a deer or a coyote, so it couldn't be anything but a bobcat," Margaret Anne exclaims, and Clayton concurs.

I am delighted that they actually saw this animal. I first discovered what looked like bobcat tracks last April when we hiked Deer Run Trail beside the river. Since then, I've noticed their faint, but possible, tracks

Mossy maple polypore fungus (*Oxyporus populinus*)

several times in various places in the Sanctuary. I'm disappointed that I missed seeing the bobcat today, but Margaret Anne reminds me that late afternoon is the best time to view wildlife. I will certainly join her to come back at dusk another day with the hope of finding the bobcat hunting again in this big field.

It is almost dark now. We follow the edge of the woods back and intersect the segment of the Tall Tupelo Trail that leads to the Jobala Haven Observation Point. From there we follow Hidden Springs Trail around the pond and back to the cars. By the time we reach them it is quite dark.

This has been a wonderful hike beginning with bright sun, comfortable temperature, good lighting, and fantastic fall colors. The bobcat sighting by Margaret Anne and Clayton adds a perfect conclusion to an exhilarating afternoon and early evening in the Sanctuary.

Species List: October

Wildflowers and Plants

Arrow arum (*Peltandra virginica*)

Carolina moonseed (*Cocculus carolinus*)

Climbing hempweed (*Mikania scandens*)

Common cattails (*Typha latifolia*) seeding

Coontail (*Ceratophyllum demersum*)

Foxtail grass (*Setaria* sp.)

Giant ironweed (*Vernonia gigantea*) seeding

Giant ragweed (*Ambrosia trifida*)

Goldenrod (*Solidago* sp.)

Ivyleaf morning glory (*Ipomoea hederacea* Jacq.)

Green algae (*Spirogyra* sp.)

Groundnut (*Apios americana*) seedpods

Late flowering thoroughwort (*Eupatorium serotinum*) seeding

Leatherflower (*Clematis viorna*) achenes

Myriophyllum (*Myriophyllum* sp.)

Partridgeberry (*Mitchella repens*)

Passion flower (*Passiflora incarnata*) leaves

Parrot feather watermilfoil (*Myriophyllum aquaticum*)

Peppervine (*Ampelopsis arborea*) ripening berries

Pokeweed (*Phytolacca americana*) berries

Sensitive fern (*Onoclea sensibilis*) with spore-bearing stems

Smartweed (*Persicaria* sp.)

Sumpweed (*Iva annua*)

Tickseed sunflower (*Bidens polylepis*)

Trumpet creeper vine (*Campsis radicans*) fall color, seedpod

Wingstem (*Verbesina alternifolia*) seeds

Wooly dutchman's pipe vine (*Aristolochia tomentosa*) seedpods

Trees

Red maple (*Acer rubrum*)

Sweetgum (*Liquidambar styraciflua*)

Sycamore (*Platanus occidentalis*)

Tuliptree (*Liriodendron tulipifera*)

Mammals

Bobcat (*Lynx rufus*)

Insects

Red imported fire ant *(Solenopsis invicta)*

Wooly alder aphid (*Prociphilus tessellatus*)

Fungi

Amanita mushroom (*Amanita* sp.)

False turkey tail mushroom (*Stereum ostrea*)

Mossy maple polypore mushroom (*Oxyporus populinus*)

Sooty mold spp.

NOVEMBER

chapter 8
NOVEMBER

Rain, Tadpoles, and Camouflaged Insects

Date: November 22
Begin: 2:30 P.M.
End: 5:30 P.M.
Weather: 54°F (12°C), rain and mist
Participants: Margaret Anne, Sam, and Marian
Purpose: Sanctuary Artists' November hike

It's INTERMITTENTLY MISTING AND sprinkling rain, but once Sam joins Margaret Anne and me to make our duo a trio, we brave the elements and enter the Sanctuary. Clouds cloak surrounding mountains and water drips from everything. Colors of wet vegetation are vivid—a good day for photography. Sam wants to capture the Sanctuary's moods in black and white, his photographic specialty, today.

We begin at the Hidden Springs Swamp overlook. The swamp is mysterious and dreary, except for the little color afforded by leaves of aquatic plants growing in patches. Yet, it is beautiful with its muted colors, gray tree trunks, and ubiquitous greenish algae covering the water's surface. The arrow arum is gone now, and trees stand leafless. There is a quiet beauty, a peacefulness about the swamp today.

Farther down Hidden Springs Trail, I find a maypop (fruit of the passion flower) with leaves still clinging to its vine. The maypop, about 1.5" (3.8 cm) in diameter, is green—a late developer. A Japanese honeysuckle vine (*Lonicera japonica*) blooms in the thicket nearby. I wonder why these plants are here so late in the season. Passion flowers bloomed in the Sanctuary last summer and their maypop fruit ripened in September. By October, most maypops were gone. Perhaps these particular plants were protected by the nearness of the water in the swamp and by their position low on the side of a protective bank.

On my right, a splash of color at the edge of the trail catches my eye. There, on last season's weathered cornstalk debris, is a tattered common buckeye butterfly (*Junonia coenia*). Coloration of this species is sometimes brighter in late fall than in spring and summer. This variation is probably a result of seasonally lower temperatures and shorter days. The butterfly here is easy to spot with its cream-colored patch on each forewing amid shades of brown, orange, yellow, and black. The large, dark eyespots on the wings, the buckeye's distinguishing feature, seem to stare back at me. These "eyes" may deter would-be predators. In the fall buckeyes become more abundant in the Sanctuary when they are joined by others migrating southward. They are intolerant of freezing temperatures, and now in November this one will have to travel farther south if it is to survive. Buckeyes belong to the family Nymphalidae, the brush-footed butterflies, characterized by furry forelegs that are too short for locomotion but serve well as sensors. At different times, we have found other members of this family in the Sanctuary. These include snout, monarch, hackberry emperor, American lady, question mark, and pearl crescent, making the Sanctuary a source of butterfly diversity.

At Hidden Springs Marsh just past the red gate at the head of Jobala Pond, I pause to photograph cattail remnants, spent flower stems and seed heads, and a patch of bright green milfoil. Now that the leaves have fallen from the trees on the other side of the trail, we can see the squirrel nest that I photographed last spring. But then it was occupied by a squirrel. Though the squirrel is not here today, I'm sure one will spend cold winter nights snuggled in that nest.

Common buckeye butterfly (*Junonia coenia*)

The beaver dam is still standing and it seems to be a little higher. More water has backed up behind it in the marsh. I am still hoping to find a beaver here to photograph one day. Farther along where the stream widens before flowing into Jobala Pond, we notice a clump of floating lily pad-like leaves with sprigs of *Myriophyllum* and red-brown fall leaves mixed among them. This is not the mudplantain we saw here in September, although the pad-like leaves, approximately 1" (2.5 cm) wide, are about the same size as those of mudplantain. The leaves of this aquatic plant have shallow, cleft margins with three to five well-rounded lobes. The margins of the lobes are scalloped (crenate). I notice that leaf blades have a reddish spot in the center. We have discovered swamp water pennywort (*Hydrocotyle ranunculoides*), a member of the carrot family (Apiaceae). This aquatic perennial grows in marshes where the water is shallow or in mud if there is no water. It spreads

Swamp water pennywort (*Hydrocotyle ranunculoides*)

horizontally and can form dense mats. This patch is attractive growing here in the headwaters of Jobala Pond.

We continue on our way, cross the footbridge at the far end of the pond and join Deer Run Trail. At the juncture of this trail and the path leading to the Forest Glen Observation Point, I pause to photograph Carolina moonseed (*Cocculus carolinus*) berries. They are bright red, almost translucent and shining, wet from the rain.

On my right lying in the small ditch beside the trail a cinnamon-colored, fan-shaped fungus covers one side of a dead limb. Individual caps are about 1" to 2.5" (2.5 cm to 6.4 cm) across and several are a larger size. The caps have a cream-colored fringe and several darker zones radiate around its semi-circular shape. Today the colors are made more vivid because of the rain and mist that settles on everything.

A colorful fungus (*Stereum* sp.)

This looks like crowded parchment fungus (*Stereum complicatum*). The caps of the parchment fungi, like those of the crust fungus (*Stereum ostrea*) mentioned in Chapter 7, are smooth on the undersurface and do not show pores, teeth, or gills. The spores, if visible, would be very small. Crowded parchment fungus is the most common of the parchment fungi. It is saprobic and decomposes dead wood, especially oak, from which it gains nourishment. This crust fungus is found across North America, except in the Rocky Mountains. It is also found in Europe. Crowded parchment fungus can overwinter, and we will watch for it as winter progresses.

Continuing on Deer Run Trail through the big field, we pause at an area where water ponds almost year round. The depth of this vernal pool is about 5" (12.7 cm) now, and grasses and weeds are still green under the surface. I notice something move beside a clump of submerged grass. Looking closely, I am surprised to see that it's a tadpole. There are a few others swimming randomly about. Focusing through

the water, I snap several pictures of the closest one. From tip of nose to tip of tail, this tadpole appears to be about 0.5" (1.3 cm) long. The color is grayish-brown with dark mottling. I believe this may be an upland chorus frog (*Pseudacris feriarum*) tadpole.

Upland chorus frogs are found in wetlands, including flooded fields and ditches. They are common and abundant in the state of Alabama except in some coastal regions. Upland chorus frogs breed in winter usually from December to April. To identify a frog species by the appearance of a tadpole, one must look closely at the tadpole's particular features such as the position of the eyes. Lateral eyes are positioned toward the sides of the head, and those placed near the top are termed dorsal. This tadpole seems to have eyes that are more lateral than dorsal. This feature, along with the vertical white stripe that runs down the middle of its nose between the nostrils, strongly supports the likelihood that this is an upland chorus frog tadpole. I would like to capture it to determine what kind of frog it will become, but I don't have a container. Besides, I do not want to interfere with the life of creatures I find in the Sanctuary by removing them from their natural habitat.

Walking on, we come to the Gravel Bar Trail and a west branch of the Flint River. This stream is still at least 10' (3 m) across and flowing rapidly, as it was last month when we walked this way. Two months earlier, it was so narrow that we walked across to Grayson's Island and continued east to the main branch of the Flint River. Today we pause at the Gravel Bar to look around.

Suddenly from upstream, the call of a pileated woodpecker splits the air. The large bird circles over us vocalizing loudly, and then it flies back upstream the way from which it came. The woodpecker repeats this behavior as we leave. We are not welcomed graciously into its territory.

Pileated woodpeckers (*Dryocopus pileatus*) are crow-sized, the largest woodpecker in North America. In April, the male attracts a female by chiseling a hole in a tree. This entices the female to begin nesting. These woodpeckers do not reuse the same nest holes, which make excellent homes for forest songbirds in subsequent years. Pileated woodpeckers eat insects, especially carpenter ants. They also like poison ivy berries, nuts, and fruits. We often see the large almost rectangular holes in the lower part of dead tree trunks in the Sanctuary. These were made by pileated woodpeckers hunting for wood-boring beetle larvae and insects.

Looking around, I notice several trees standing at the edge of a gulley where floodwaters have undercut the side of the bank. The clay has been swept away, leaving roots exposed and giving us an excellent view of their structure. I'm amazed that this shallow tangle of roots could support the weight and height of a tree. Later, I checked several information sources and found that most roots do not extend deeply into the soil to give support to large trees. Smaller roots like the ones we see here usually extend outward from the trunk to a distance two to three times wider than the tree's canopy above and to a depth of only 6" to 18" (15 cm to 46 cm). Shallow roots provide support by radiating in all directions around the tree. It's this even or balanced distribution that provides the necessary architecture for supporting large trees.

A primary function of roots is to absorb water and inorganic nutrients. Most trees spread roots near the surface of the ground where water, oxygen, and nutrients are most available. Some trees have tap roots as long as the tree is high, but these usually occur in deserts or where surface water is limited. Here in the Sanctuary where water and nutrients are readily available, tap roots may be short.

As we are leaving the gravel bar, I notice several small, round, light-colored spots on a tree trunk near the trail. These spots are about 0.3" to 0.4" (8 mm to 10 mm) in diameter and look like lichen, but they are not flattened against the bark around the edges in the manner of lichens. Also unlike lichens, they are nestled in patches of moss. I gently touch one with the tip of my finger. It's soft, and it sidles away. It's alive. I carefully remove it from the tree trunk and place it in my hand where it begins to move across my palm. What a surprise, a moving, lichen-covered mystery. I note that it has pincher-like appendages. This must be some kind of insect that camouflages itself with lichen. When

Larval stage of green lacewing insects covered with
lichen (family Chrysopidae)

I turn the creature over on its back, I can see that it has spiny legs and
its underside is almost white and ribbed. Sam photographs this strange
little being with his macro lens-equipped camera. Now that we have
documented it digitally, I put it back on the tree trunk where I found it.

Later at home, I searched my information sources, including several
insect identification books. I even bought a book about insects that feed
on trees and shrubs. But I was on the wrong track. For weeks this creature's identity remained a mystery until, browsing the Internet one day,
I read a blog describing an insect that slowly collects bits of lichen to

cover itself. Further research informed me that green lacewing (family Chrysopidae) larvae place lichen fragments on their body, and these fragments later become a component of the larvae's cocoon when it pupates. Fascinating.

I wanted to know more about green lacewings and discovered that they occur throughout North America and are useful in controlling a number of plant juice–sucking insects. The larvae of green lacewings are voracious, and with their pincers they grasp a victim and then suck fluids from its body. Lacewing larvae prey consists of beetle larvae, moths, small caterpillars, and plant sap–sucking insects such as aphids, whiteflies, and mealybugs. The larvae feed on the eggs of leafhoppers. I hope lacewings will thrive here in the Sanctuary—their larvae may help control future overabundance of the bugs and insects that contribute the honeydew that allowed sooty mold to establish and smudge vegetation last summer.

After the excitement of discovering an insect wearing a coat of lichen, we are ready to move on. But now the sun breaks through the clouds and finds its way past the tree canopy to shine like a spotlight on a patch of tan-colored fall grasses. This sunfleck emphasizes the grass; I would not have noticed it otherwise. I promptly photograph the scene, but the sun's light fades as quickly as it appeared. The sunfleck was brief, perhaps lasting thirty seconds, and I had time for only one shot. But it was long enough for me to capture the image of shining grasses and the mystical quality of the November woods with mist settling through the trees in the background.

We leave the Gravel Bar Trail, turn right onto the Deer Run Trail, and continue to the Flint River Observation Point. From there, we enter the woods and follow the Tall Tupelo Trail. Some yards ahead, a wet-looking orange mass about the size of a saucer coats a tree trunk. We walk closer to investigate.

The mass seems to expand upward from an injury on the trunk of a deciduous tree. My first thought is that this beautiful, shiny, brilliant orange jelly-like mass is an orange slime mold. But I have learned that

Mystic November woods

Witches' butter fungus (*Tremella mesenterica*)

fungi can be deceptive and identifying them is not a simple matter. I photograph this orange mass from several angles. Later, I send a picture to the mycology laboratory at the University of Tennessee in Knoxville, where Dr. Ronald Petersen kindly agrees to take a look. It turns out that this is not a slime mold after all. Dr. Petersen suggests that it may be "witches' butter," possibly a species of jelly fungus in the genus *Tremella* or *Dacrymyces*.

I check several sources and come to the conclusion that we have found a species in the genus *Tremella*, since *Dacrymyces* species grow on the wood of conifers. However, in a mixed growth forest, the two genera cannot be differentiated in the field, and only microscopic examination of the shape of the spore-bearing cells (basidia) can differentiate between them. The fungus here is growing on a deciduous tree and on a fallen limb of the same tree, in a wet habitat (the tupelo swamp) on a rainy day, all of which favor witches' butter in the genus *Tremella*. The likely species is *Tremella mesenterica*, which is widely distributed in North America and found in Central and South America, Europe, Africa, Asia, and Australia. It is interesting that this fungus is parasitic on the mycelium

Marbled orbweaver spider (*Araneus marmoreus*)

of species of crust fungi in the genus *Stereum*, which are also found in the Sanctuary on decaying logs of hardwoods. Witches' butter is beneficial to wooded habitats by helping to decompose dead wood.

From here, we walk briskly back through the woods to the field's edge. At the Jobala Pond Observation Point, we pause while I photograph a colorful spider on a shriveled leaf. This is a marbled orbweaver spider (*Araneus marmoreus*).

Continuing around the Pond on Hidden Springs Trail, we notice a gray catbird (*Dumetella carolinensis*) ahead on the ground. It interrupts its search for insects in the fallen brown leaves to watch us as we go by, but it does not fly away. A little farther along the trail, a brown thrasher (*Toxostomo rufum*) is searching in a vine overhead for seeds and insects.

Today's highlights include sighting vociferous pileated woodpeckers at the Gravel Bar and discovering the small, lichen-covered, larval lacewing insects on the tree trunks by the Gravel Bar. And Sam spotted a deer crossing the trail ahead of us on our way back to the cars. It was a fine outing, pleasant and productive in spite of, or possibly because of, the mist and wetness.

Above: **Gray catbird** (*Dumetella carolinensis*)

Below: **Brown thrasher** (*Toxostoma rufum*)

Species List: November

Wildflowers and Plants

Carolina moonseed (*Cocculus carolinus*)
  ripe berries

Common winterberry (*Ilex verticillata*)

Devil's darning needles (*Clematis
  virginiana* L.) feathery tailed
  achenes

Goldenrod (*Solidago* sp.) blooming

Horsenettle (*Solanum carolinense*)
  yellow fruit

Japanese honeysuckle (*Lonicera
  japonica*)

Meadow garlic (*Allium canadense*)

Mistletoe (*Phoradendron* sp.)

Parrot feather watermilfoil
  (*Myriophyllum aquaticum*)

Passion flower (*Passiflora incarnata*)
  vine and fruit

Smartweeds (*Persicaria* sp.)

Swamp water pennywort (*Hydrocotyle
  ranunculoides*)

Wintergreen or pipsissewa (*Chimaphila
  maculata*)

Wooly dutchman's pipe vine
  (*Aristolochia tomentosa*) seedpods

Trees

American sweetgum (*Liquidambar
  styraciflua*) red leaves

Honeylocust (*Gleditsia triacanthos*)
  spines, seedpod

Red maple (*Acer rubrum*)

Water tupelo (*Nyssa aquatica*)

Mammals

Common raccoon (*Procyon lotor*) tracks

Eastern gray squirrel (*Sciurus
  carolinensis*)

White-tailed deer (*Odocoileus
  virginianus*) tracks

Birds

American bald eagle (*Haliaeetus
  leucocephalus*)

Brown thrasher (*Toxostoma rufum*)

Dark-eyed junco (*Junco hyemalis*)

Eastern phoebe (*Sayornis phoebe*)

Gray catbird (*Dumetella carolinensis*)

Nodding bur marigold (*Bidens cernua*)
  blooming in the marsh

Northern cardinal (*Cardinalis
  cardinalis*)

Northern flicker (*Colaptes auratus*)

Northern mockingbird (*Mimus
  polyglottos*)

Pileated woodpecker (*Dryocopus
  pileatus*)

Red-headed woodpecker (*Melanerpes
  erythrocephalus*)

White-throated sparrow (*Zonotrichia
  albicollis*)

Insects, Bugs, and Spiders

Common buckeye butterfly (*Junonia
  coenia*)

Green lacewing insect larvae (family
  Chrysopidae) covered with lichen

Marbled orbweaver spider (*Araneus marmoreus*)
Sulfur butterfly (*Phoebis* sp.)

Fungi
Crowded parchment fungus (*Stereum complicatum*)
Gilled shelf fungus
Inky cap mushrooms (*Coprinus* sp.)
Polypore fungus
Witches' butter (*Tremella mesenterica*)

Amphibians
Upland chorus frog tadpole (*Pseudacris feriarum*) (probable)

Reptiles
Pond slider turtle (*Trachemys scripta*)

DECEMBER

chapter 9
DECEMBER

Winter Is Here: Flooding and Displaced Pond Weeds

Date: December 12
Begin: 10:30 A.M.
End: 11:30 A.M.
Weather: 42°F (6°C), cloudy and breezy
Participant: Marian
Purpose: To explore the Sanctuary after major flooding

HEAVY RAINFALL ON DECEMBER 8 resulted in significant flooding of low-lying areas surrounding the Flint River—including the Sanctuary. On December 9 and 10, the whole area around the north entrance remained underwater. At the east entrance, muddy water covered Hidden Springs Trail as far as I could see. By December 11, water had begun to recede, but trails remained soggy and impassable.

Today, December 12, I park at the main entrance to the Sanctuary at Taylor Road and walk to the Hidden Springs Swamp overlook. It's a monochrome, drab, wintery day and the fourth day after the heavy rainfall. Water now covers the swamp, but Hidden Springs Trail into the sanctuary is no longer flooded. I walk beside Hidden Springs Stream

Flooding at the east entrance of the Sanctuary

toward Jobala Pond and note that water flows swiftly through two breaks in the beaver dam. A patch of green, tattered milfoil remains in the pooled water upstream of the dam. No traces of the water lilies or mudplantain that grew here two months ago remain.

The recent flooding in the Sanctuary leads me to wonder about the characteristics of such riparian environments. Riparian ecosystems border rivers, lakes, and streams and include sloughs, springs, and wet weather streams and seeps. Although water standing in the Sanctuary for several days caused my concern for the survival of vegetation and animals, flooding is normal and necessary to replenish soil nutrients, refresh groundwater, and maintain the succession of plant species in this bottomland floodplain. Animals and plants that live here are adapted to life in flood zones. The characteristic short-term (two- to four-day) seasonal flooding scours vegetation from the pond and sloughs and clears the way for new growth in spring.

This scouring is quite obvious as I walk beside Jobala Pond and note debris on trees and bushes bordering Hidden Springs Trail. Most noteworthy is the distribution of the aquatic plants, coontail (*Ceratophyllum demersum*) and milfoil (*Myriophyllum aquaticum*), piled in the terrestrial vegetation all along the banks of the pond and across the trail on the right side. Muddy and damaged, the trailing sections of these plants cling to the sturdy 2' to 3' (0.6 to 0.9 cm) tall weeds. The force of the flooding water was obviously strong enough to rid Jobala Pond of most of its aquatic vegetation and deposit it, brown and tattered, onto bushes all the way to the footbridge at the far end of the pond. I am amazed at the mass of water plants transported.

Based on the appearance of vegetation surrounding the area, I estimate that floodwater reached a depth of 5' (1.5 m) or more as it flowed from the Pond and over Hidden Springs Trail southwest toward the soybean fields and beyond. I check the temporary pond on the right side of Hidden Springs Trail. It, too, is scoured of debris and the plants remaining are bent in the direction of flow. Continuing to the footbridge, which is about 4' (1.2 m) above the stream, I note a clump of debris containing sticks, broken corn stalks, and battered pond weeds trapped on the upright structures of the footbridge. This provides further evidence that floodwater was over 5' (1.5 m) deep here.

As I cross the footbridge, I hear a rustling sound in the leaves ahead. The woods are now open, a result of winter die-off of undergrowth vegetation. Only vines, stubby stems, and dry, brown leaves on the ground characterize these woods today. Looking toward the source of the sound, I notice several swamp sparrows foraging in the mud and among the dead leaves. I pause to watch them. They are about 20' (6 m) away and seem to pay no attention to me. This gives me a fine photographic opportunity. Swamp sparrows (*Melospiza georgiana*) prefer dense thickets around freshwater swamps and wetlands. The characteristics that distinguish them from other sparrows found in similar areas are their rust-colored wings, whitish throat (with a smaller white patch than white-throated sparrows), streaked head, gray face, and dark line

Swamp sparrow (*Melospiza georgiana*)

behind the eyes. Swamp sparrows winter in the southeastern United States and throughout the southwest to parts of the California coast. Their breeding range includes Canada and most of the northeastern United States. I am happy to see these birds spending the winter in the Sanctuary.

I turn right on Deer Run Trail and stop by the Forest Glen Observation Point. Here I check the banks of the small ditch that runs perpendicular to the pond and find no remnants of the sensitive ferns (*Onoclea sensibilis*) that grew here all summer and fall. I'm sure these ferns succumbed to the cold nights several weeks ago. No duckweed or other aquatic plants remain in the pond. Everything here is dormant, asleep for winter. A flotilla of sticks and debris bobs on ripples near the far bank.

Continuing on Deer Run Trail across the field, I note water standing in low places. Other than that, evidence of the severe flooding in these fields has disappeared now just four days after the whole area was inundated. However, the trail through the woods that previously led to the Gravel Bar has been reorganized by floodwater. New sandbars cover the

Winterberries (*Ilex* sp.)

original trail and water stands in pools where we hiked before.

Turning left at the stream, I walk a little way beside it. At a bank overhang about 8' (2.4 m) above the stream, I notice a large winterberry bush (*Ilex verticillata*). Its abundant red berries populate the limbs and add bright color to the otherwise drabness of the scene. Here in the woods beside the stream, birds are quite active today. In addition to woodpeckers and robins, there are cardinals, jays, swamp sparrows, Carolina wrens, and white-throated sparrows. I can hear other birds "muttering" in the thickets, but I can't get a clear view to identify them.

Backtracking to the Gravel Bar, I hear a flamboyant red-headed woodpecker and watch as it comes into view and lands atop a limb high up

Red-headed woodpecker (*Melanerpes erythrocephalus*)

in a tree not far away. I also saw a red-headed woodpecker (*Melanerpes erythrocephalus*) in this same area last month. With a black and white body and bright red head, these are striking birds. They are native, year-round residents in our area and live in mature deciduous woodlands that have plenty of oaks. They prefer riverbottom lands in open wooded swamps where there are numerous dead and dying trees. Red-headed woodpeckers are one of only four woodpecker species known to store food and cover it with wood or bark. They sometimes store grasshoppers alive, wedging them into bark crevices so well that the hapless insects can't escape. Red-headed woodpeckers are the most omnivorous of the woodpeckers. Their diet consists of insects, bird eggs, and even nestlings and mice, in addition to seeds, berries, acorns, and nuts. They build nests in holes of dead trees and lay four to seven eggs in the spring. Because of habitat loss, their numbers are declining over the breeding range, which includes the southern United States west to the

Chert found in the field near the Deer Run Trail

Mississippi River. They are more abundant in flooded areas and beaver meadows where there are large numbers of dead trees. Red-headed woodpeckers are beautiful to watch. I hope these will be permanent residents in the Sanctuary woods.

Walking back along the Deer Run Trail across the field, I notice the pervasive but delicate, onion-like scent of meadow garlic. The field appears to be carpeted in green velvet by this omnipresent, hardy winter plant. Meadow garlic (*Allium canadense*) belongs to the family Alliaceae and is native to North America. The bulb is edible and tastes much like domestic onion. But one should always be sure there is a definite onion scent before tasting because some non-edible plants resemble meadow garlic. Last May and June, I noticed their dome-shaped clusters of pinkish white, star-shaped blooms in the fields here. Pollinated by bees and other insects, the flowers produce small, black seeds that develop into the grass-like plants. Thriving in winter and able to survive sessions of flooding, meadow garlic is now the dominant plant in the Sanctuary's meadows.

As I continue on the Deer Run Trail through the field, I discover a rock in the middle of my path. I have not seen rocks like this in the Sanctuary before. This one is about the size of a grapefruit, has several flat surfaces and is heavy when I pick it up. I dip my finger into standing water nearby and wet a smooth surface to brighten the colors. Some areas are a translucent orange; other surfaces are grayish. The rock has several square corners where it has been chipped. Later, I check my *Field Guide to Rocks and Minerals*, consulted several Internet sources, and conclude that this is chert.

Chert is a common type of rock often found on gravel bars and in streambeds. Millions of years ago, what is now the southern United States was covered by water. Sediments were deposited and over time, silicon dioxide (SiO_2) infiltrated the sediments to form this hard, dense monocrystalline type of quartz. Usually light gray, chert can also be red, yellow, or brown depending on the type of organic matter and minerals incorporated when it was being formed. The presence of iron gives chert a reddish-brown color. This form is called jasper. Because of its hardness, chert was used by Indians to make arrowheads. I cannot be sure where the rock I find here today originated. It may have been uncovered during the recent floods, or humans could have brought it here from somewhere else. In any case, I put it down so other hikers can discover it and ponder how it came to be here.

I reverse course and walk back to the east end of Jobala Pond, then keep right and continue toward the Jobala Haven Observation Point. Looking north, I photograph the view across the broomsedge field. Broomsedge is not a sedge, but rather a bushy, herbaceous, perennial bunch grass. In fall and winter it turns red-brown and converts whole fields into a waving, three-foot-tall sea of grass. The most abundant broomsedge species in the southeast is broomsedge bluestem (*Andropogon virginicus*). While it can be a nuisance growing rampant in pastures and hayfields, it is useful in stopping erosion. Ground nesting birds such as quail build nests among its stems. Other birds and mammals eat its seeds in winter when food is scarce. Broomsedge belongs to the family Poaceae. This warm-season grass grows best when the temperature is between 60°F and 65°F (15.7°C and 18.3°C). Now in its winter brown, it persists here in the field, fringed by leafless trees and the mountains in the background. Broomsedge adds an ambiance and rich tone to the winter landscape.

Looking up the stream that runs into the pond at the Jobala Pond Observation Point, I notice that the banks, thick with undergrowth

Honeyvine milkweed (*Cynanchum laeve*) seedpod

and vegetation last month, are now sparsely covered. Effects of rapidly flowing floodwater are evident. More rain will come today. The weatherman has promised it by noon. It's now eleven o'clock and the sky is darkening. A restless breeze ruffles the leaves of a water oak nearby. I quickly make my way back around the end of the pond and along Hidden Springs Trail toward the car.

On the way, I notice tracks on a muddy section of trail. These appear to be beaver tracks. I passed a damaged beaver dam at the head of Jobala Pond when I began the hike today. These tracks in the mud reassure me that beavers still inhabit the area and are here in spite of the flooding. I also find deer tracks in the same area. I have not found insects today although I look carefully at tree trunks to see if the interesting green lacewing larvae I discovered in the Sanctuary in November might still be here.

In the thicket on my left as I walk along Hidden Springs Trail I notice a lone seedpod with silvery-white downy fluff on one side where the pod is split open. This pod is about 4" (10 cm) long and 0.75" (1.9 cm) wide. It hangs from a leafless vine in a tangle of other vines. By the shape of this pod and the seed fluff designed for wind travel, I believe it is that of a milkweed. But I didn't see milkweed blooming here last

summer, and the swamp milkweed I photographed in the field across from Jobala Haven Observation Point was a tall plant with clusters of pink flowers, not a vine.

When I search books and Internet soruces later, I make an interesting discovery. The seedpods are those of the vine, honeyvine milkweed (*Cynanchum laeve*). The probable reason I didn't find its flowers in this location last summer is that blooms are small and mostly whitish and would not have been easy to see among the tangle of other vines in this thicket. However, I did discover honeyvine milkweed in bloom and trailing over vegetation on the opposite side of the trail near Jobala Pond in July. I documented it again in August when I found a group of large, orange milkweed bug nymphs congregating on one of the seedpods in that same area. This plant carries an excess number of common names: bluevine, climbing milkweed, dog's-collar, Enslen's-vine, honeyvine, peavine, sandvine, smooth anglepod, and smooth swallow-wort.

Milkweed aphids suck juices from the foliage and monarch butterfly caterpillars eat the leaves of honeyvine milkweed just as they eat leaves of other milkweed species. I'm especially happy to have this vine growing in several locations in the Sanctuary since it will provide food for monarch butterflies. Deer and other herbivores do not eat the foliage probably because it is bitter and has toxic properties. Seedpods, like the one I discover today, linger into winter and some still shed seeds as late as February.

On my right as I walk along, I notice the catalpa trees on both sides of the pond. Now, hanging from the leaf-bare limbs, the seedpods contrast sharply against the muted gray of the winter sky. The pods of the southern catalpa (*Catalpa bignonioides*) are 6" to 20" (15 cm to 51 cm) long. Slender and almost cylindrical, they are brown now, and many will hang on these trees throughout the winter. Within each pod, there are numerous silvery gray, winged seeds. The wings have fringes at the ends and are designed for wind dispersal. Southern catalpas are native to the southeast, but they have adapted and spread to other regions of the country as well.

Bean-like catalpa (*Catalpa speciosa*) seedpods

There is a peacefulness about the marsh today and all is quiet as I walk past. The skeletal phyllaries (series of overlapping bracts) and fuzzy remnants of giant ironweed and goldenrod blooms are all that is left to remind us of the vibrant colors of last season's wildflowers. The alders around the pond have lost their leaves, but catkins still hang from their limbs. Deer tracks are everywhere on all the trails and in the fields where we have walked today. Other evidence of creature activity includes snail trails in the mud near the footbridge on Hidden

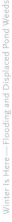

Phyllaries of giant ironweed (*Vernonia gigantea*)

Springs Trail, large and small raccoon tracks in muddy places in the field and on Deer Run Trail, and beaver tracks near Jobala Pond on Hidden Springs Trail.

Today, I did not walk where I think the bobcat usually travels beside the river, so I don't know what animals passed that way after the flood. I wonder if the Sanctuary's coyotes and mink weathered the flooding and if opossums, raccoons, mice, and other animals found safety in trees as the water rose. Deer obviously had no difficulty returning to the area afterward. They probably found higher ground nearby during the worst of the flooding. I wonder if the little muskrat waited, safe and dry in an underground den until the floodwaters receded. I will watch for evidence of these animals on my next trips to the Sanctuary.

Hidden Springs Trail winds into the distance ahead, and the wind is beginning to whisper louder in the trees. I had better hurry before the rain begins. At the red gate, I pause and look up as a flock of ducks flies overhead—dark silhouettes against a gray sky. The silence is momentarily broken by their calls carried on the cold wind. Winter is here. The darkening sky promises immediate rain; I sprint to the car as the first drops fall.

Hidden Springs Trail

December sky

SPECIES LIST: DECEMBER

Plants
Broomsedge bluestem (*Andropogon virginicus*)
Coontail (*Ceratophyllum demersum*)
Giant ironweed (*Vernonia gigantea*) phyllaries
Honeyvine milkweed (*Cynanchum laeve*) seedpod
Meadow garlic (*Allium canadense*)
Parrot feather watermilfoil (*Myriophyllum aquaticum*)

Trees and Shrubs
Common Winterberry (*Ilex verticillata*)
Southern catalpa (*Catalpa bignonioides*) seedpods
Water oak (*Quercus nigra*)

Mammals
Beaver (*Castor canadensis*) tracks
Raccoon (*Procyon lotor*) tracks
White-tailed deer (*Odocoileus virginianus*) tracks

Birds
American robin (*Turdus migratorius*)
Blue jay (*Cyanocitta cristata*)
Carolina wren (*Thryothorus ludovicianus*)
Northern cardinal (*Cardinalis cardinalis*)
Pileated woodpecker (*Dryocopus pileatus*)
Red-headed woodpecker (*Melanerpes erythrocephalus*)
Swamp sparrow (*Melospiza eorgiana*)
White-throated sparrow (*Zonotrichia albicollis*)

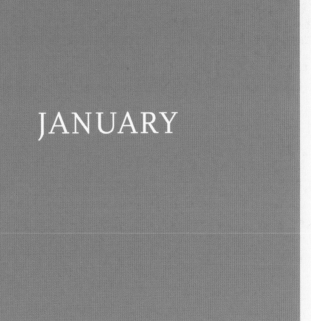

JANUARY

Snow, Ice, and a Bluebird Drama

Date: January 9
Begin: 11:30 A.M.
End: 1:25 P.M.
Weather: 11:30 A.M., 27°F (-3°C) cold, breezy, weak sun
    1:25 P.M., 30°F (-1°C)
Participants: Margaret Anne and Marian
Purpose: To visit the Sanctuary in snow

OVER HALF AN INCH OF SNOW fell two days ago and, with temperatures remaining below freezing, the snow has not completely disappeared. Today a weak sun shines—its frail rays do little to warm us as we begin our hike. We pause at the Boy Scout pavilion at Hidden Springs Overlook. Traces of snow highlight fallen trees across the swamp's expanse of mixed vegetation and ice-crusted water.

As we walk along Hidden Springs Trail toward Jobala Pond, I tell Margaret Anne about the snipe I flushed from this marsh yesterday. I was walking slowly and looking for animal tracks in the snow. As I came to the marsh just past the red gates, a movement at the marsh edge caught my eye. A long legged bird was scurrying away on top of milfoil frozen in the ice that coated the surface of the marsh. The bird

A common snipe (*Gallinago gallinago*) dancing across frozen milfoil

ran with a prancing motion. I had time for two quick shots before it took flight and went zig zagging low over the stream to disappear. Then I realized it was a snipe. I had never seen this bird in the wild, and I was thrilled. Though timid, snipe are common inhabitants of marshes and wet meadows along streams, rivers, lakes, and estuaries throughout North America. They are also found in Iceland, northern Europe, and Russia. These snipe winter in southern Europe and Africa. In North America, snipe spend the winter in the lower forty-eight states and Central America, and return to their northern range in Canada and Alaska in the summer, although some do not migrate to these extremes. The common snipe (*Gallinago gallinago*) is about 9" (23 cm) long with a wingspan of 17" to 18.5" (43 cm to 47 cm). They weigh 2.5 oz to 6.4 oz (72 g to 181 g). A member of the sandpiper family Scolopacidae, snipe exhibit cryptic coloration with buff, brown, chestnut, and black streaks and blotches that blend well with colors in the marsh. They are wading birds and probe the marsh with their bills, which can be 2" to 3" (55 mm to 75 mm) in length, in search of invertebrates, including insects, insect larvae, small crustaceans, snails, and spiders. A snipe's bill is equipped with nerves that allow it to function as a sensory organ. They can determine what type of object the bill is touching and whether it would be good to eat, even though the object is underground and unseen. I am

An ousted raccoon (*Procyon lotor*)

thrilled to have this special bird spending time here in the Sanctuary. Today, we walk quietly and scrutinize the marsh from side to side, but we do not find the snipe.

Our attention is diverted from snipe hunting when we hear growling and scuffling on the opposite side of the stream. Suddenly, about 20' (6 m) ahead, a raccoon surges from a large hole in the stream bank. Close on its heels, another raccoon rushes out but stops in the entrance. The first raccoon runs about 15' (5 m) upstream, away from the den, and stands up to look back, then drops down on all fours. It appears to

be agitated and half rises again and glances back at the bigger, fluffier raccoon that still stands at the den entrance. After waiting a moment longer and looking quite forlorn, the ousted raccoon turns and ambles up the small cut that drains into the stream and disappears into the broomsedge beyond. The possessor of the den goes back into the hole in the bank as Margaret Anne and I walk nearer. We now have verification that raccoons spend time in these dens in the far bank of the stream. We agree that the first fifteen minutes of our hike today have been quite exciting and eventful. We feel privileged to have witnessed this confrontation in the life of Sanctuary raccoons.

For months, I have wondered what animal occupies these dens in the stream bank. But raccoons may not be permanent residents. Perhaps the ones we see today were out foraging and sought shelter from the snow and cold. When I come here in the next months, I'll watch for muskrats and beavers in the hope that I may discover other occupants of the dens.

I've often wondered how denning animals stay safe and dry when their habitat floods as it has several times this winter. Here, the holes in the bank were probably made by muskrats, perhaps the one we saw swimming in the pond several times last year. Muskrats usually dig an entrance, about 3' (0.9 m) or more below water level, into a dam or stream bank to make a den. When it floods, animals tunnel further upward (as shown in the figure at right) and widen the den. As rising water reaches equilibrium between its level inside and outside the den, it does not rise higher inside. Muskrats may dig a network of tunnels and widen chambers at different levels. Thus, they always have an air space. But den animals can be in danger if flooding is severe. Sometimes the very young may perish.

Continuing along Hidden Springs Trail we find many of the tracks I discovered here yesterday, but now they are barely visible in the snow. Several animals are represented, including canid, rabbits, raccoon, and small birds. I note two sets of tracks side by side and wonder what story they tell. The larger prints appear to be those of a coyote trotting along.

Schematic of a muskrat den (illustration by Jenifer Rees, adapted
from Hyngstrom et al., Prevention and Control of Wildlife Damage;
courtesy of the Washington Department of Fish and Wildlife)

The longer, straight trail seems to have been made by an animal loping
and dragging its foot. I believe the two animals traveled here at different times. The straightness of their trails does not indicate a chase or
interaction. It is difficult to determine what animals may have made
these tracks now blurred in the softening snow.

There is another set of tracks on Hidden Springs Trail that I do not
recognize right away. Later after searching several sources and consulting a wildlife biologist, I realize that these tracks were made by
river otters. I am surprised and delighted to discover that river otters
came this way. I have not seen evidence of this animal in the Sanctuary before, and we can now add it to the list of mammalian species
found here.

Finding their tracks in the snow is one of the methods for determining presence of otters in an area. Otters may have been here previously, but we weren't aware of them until these two traveled beside
Jobala Pond after the snow fell two days ago. The home range of an
otter may encompass 5 mi to 40 mi (64 km), so they may not come our
way often. In the 1990s, river otter populations were in decline in some
areas of their range, which includes most of North America. But now,
primarily because of water quality regulations, their population trend is

River otter (*Lutra canadensis*) tracks in the snow

stable and their conservation status is listed as "least concern" according to the red list of the International Union for Conservation of Nature (IUCN), which monitors endangered species. River otters choose ponds with vertical banks where they can find semi-aquatic animal burrows, like the ones made by muskrats or beavers on the opposite bank of the stream. Females use these dens or a fallen tree near water as places to have their pups. River otters generally breed in winter and produce one to five pups between February and April. River otters mostly eat fish, but their diet also includes frogs, crayfish, small mammals, mollusks, reptiles, birds, and fruits. Predators in the Sanctuary may include coyotes, bobcats, and dogs.

The North American river otter or northern river otter (*Lutra canadensis*) is a member of the weasel family. These animals are agile, playful, fast swimmers, and gregarious. River otters are well adapted to their environment: they can drink underwater because of a specially designed valve in their nose; they can see well in murky water because of special lenses in their eyes; their sensitive whiskers help locate prey underwater; and all four feet are webbed. Adult otters weigh 11 lb to 33 lb (5 kg to 15 kg) and range in length from 3' to 4.5' (1 m to 1.4 m); 40 percent of that length is their muscular tail. If threatened, otters can run at speeds up to 18 mi (29 km) an hour. River otters probably live about ten years in the wild. I surely hope otters will visit Jobala Pond again and that we will have the opportunity to see them.

We continue across the footbridge and walk around Jobala Pond to the Tall Tupelo Trail. This trail follows the edge of the woods beside the field where a large patch of broomsedge stands bending with the breeze. Snow still blankets shady places in the woods, but in the fields it is almost gone now. At the Tall Tupelo Observation Point, I photograph the tupelo swamp in snow. The trees stand majestic—their broad bases disappear into a sea of white. Mountains visible in the background lend depth to the scene.

There are numerous tracks in the snow here in the tupelo swamp. I can make out mink, squirrel, and rabbit tracks. And the side-by-side front and back prints clearly show that a raccoon walked this way, too. We make our way through the woods toward the Flint River. This is no easy task because the trail is not clearly marked here and we are forced to bushwhack our way around small pools of icy water. The ground,

Tall tupelo swamp in snow

covered with leaves and ice needles, is uneven and not solid under us. Needle ice rises 3" or 4" (8 cm to 10 cm) in palisades. Our boots crunch and sink into it, breaking the needles. The going is slow and slippery as we make our way through these woods.

Needle ice forms when air temperature is below freezing and the temperature of the ground is above freezing, as conditions have been for several days here in the Sanctuary. Moisture under the surface of the ground is brought up by capillary action where it freezes in the colder air at the base of the ice needle. This causes the ice crystals to grow upward. These thin ice crystals can push up soil and leaves as they have done here where we are walking. The columns of needles usually extend upward only a few inches, but they may grow as tall as 16" (0.4 m) if conditions remain favorable. We will not surprise any wildlife in these woods today. Our footsteps make too much noise as we walk along.

When we near the Flint River, we come to the new bicycle trail recently cut through the woods. It is as wide as a motor grader blade. This bike trail will eventually be paved and connect with the one in the Hays Nature Preserve about a half mile away from the north entrance of the Sanctuary. Here, this trail will parallel or blend with the Deer Run Trail beside the Flint River and then diverge from the river back into the woods for some distance.

We walk beside the river a few hundred feet toward the break in the trees where I usually look for the great blue heron nests we found here last March and April. But now the branches of several trees, pushed down to make way for the bicycle path, screen the view and I'm having difficulty locating the nests. Finally, we move a few paces to our left and I can see several nests in the tall trees on the opposite side of the river. Herons usually return to the same location year after year, and they will be returning to this rookery soon. Last spring, I spotted four nests occupied by herons at this location.

The Flint River runs swiftly today. The limb of a fallen tree dips into the water and causes turbulence at the intersection of limb and current.

Eastern bluebird (*Sialia sialis*)

Nearer the bank, thick inch-long icicles cling to the underside of the limb where the sun does not reach. The icicles have formed from snow as it melted when the sun warmed the top of the limb.

We continue to the Gravel Bar Trail. Patches of snow in the field glisten in the sun and the woods brighten with snow-reflected light. At the Gravel Bar, we are happy to find several bluebirds (*Sialia sialis*) in the surrounding trees. They do not seem afraid of us and fly from the trees to sip water from the stream about 20' (6 m) away. Margaret Anne and I find ourselves incorporated into a scene of contrasting colors, sounds, and textures. The intense blue of the bluebirds splashes against a canvas of gray-brown tones of bare trees and vines, white snow, brown sand, and fallen leaves. The rough texture of pebbles on the sand bar contrasts with smoothly flowing water as it lilts hypnotically against the quiet of the woods here. We stand in reverence of the serenity and beauty of this place.

But this mood ends abruptly. Quicker than a heartbeat, the scene shatters, broken like those ice crystals crunched underfoot earlier today. Suddenly, out of the corner of my right eye, I glimpse motion. A

Stream at the Gravel Bar in winter

fast-moving object is flying toward us from upstream. It veers downward and flies low over the edge of the stream in front of us. I recognize it—a hawk. Its aim is sure; the bluebird at the water's edge has no opportunity to escape. I register a gasping cry, a raspy *shreeeeee*; and then all is quiet again except the singing water. The hawk has vanished, as if it never existed, into the island's deeper woods across the stream—its meal secure in its grasp.

The other bluebirds have scattered into the woods, and now, silent and completely still as if frozen, they wait high in the trees until they sense that danger has passed. Another of nature's small dramas has just played out before us—so sad for the bluebird, but a matter of survival for the hawk.

Although I did not get a good look because of the speed of its attack,

I believe this predator was a sharp-shinned hawk (*Accipiter striatus*) based on its small size and sudden, swift attack on the bluebird. However, it is difficult to distinguish between sharp-shinned and Cooper's hawks (*Accipiter cooperii*). Both belong to the family Accipitridae (small, short-winged, long-tailed, agile hawks). They behave much the same and their ranges overlap. Sharp-shinned hawks are about the size of a blue jay, whereas Cooper's are crow-sized. The hawk Margaret Anne and I glimpsed today is not as large as a crow. But male Cooper's hawks are smaller than the females of the species and similar in size to female sharp-shinned hawks.

Sharp-shinned hawks feed mainly on small birds. They are designed for sudden bursts of speed and agility in maneuvering around trees, limbs, and dense bushes in the woods. They depend on surprise in capturing prey. Sharp-shins are common winter residents here in North Alabama and throughout the southern states. They spend summers in their breeding range in the northern United States, across Canada and into Alaska. I find it interesting that this hawk ignored Margaret Anne and me in its pursuit of the bluebird. The drama played out not 20' (6 m) from where we stood watching. In its present state of development, this is truly a wildlife sanctuary.

We walk back through the woods and intersect Deer Run Trail at the edge of the field. Here we find the tracks of several turkeys in the snow. They have been out scratching through leaves and debris in the woods foraging for acorns, dogwood berries, and any seeds they may find. The eastern wild turkey (*Meleagris gallopavo silvestris*), one of five subspecies in North America, ranges from southern Canada and New England to northern Florida and west to Texas. Turkeys inhabit hardwood and pine-hardwood mixed forests that have open areas. They are found in bottomlands, such as the Sanctuary, as well as upland forests from North Alabama throughout the state south to the Mobile-Tensaw Delta. Their mating season in the Sanctuary begins early in March and lasts through April. After mating, hens select a nest site and lay ten to twelve eggs. The eggs hatch in about twenty-eight days. Poults, as the young are called, leave the nest site within twelve to twenty-four hours after

Ice and flowing water

hatching. They follow the hen to grassy openings in the woods, where they feed on insects and grass seeds. I am told that the best way to view wild turkeys is to be in place before daylight near their frequently traveled path. One must remain hidden and be very quiet and still. I look forward to trying this tactic on a cool morning next spring.

We make our way back to Jobala Pond and walk beside it on Hidden Springs Trail. A sprinkling of snow dusts the leaves and vegetation in the woods and blankets exposed banks around the pond. Wind ripples the water on unfrozen surfaces in the middle of the pond, but the still water near the banks is crusted with ice. Though remnants of the beaver dam remain, water rushes through several breaks in the structure. Twigs, limbs, and leaves at the edges of the flowing water are encased in ice, and the air bubbles at the foot of the dam appear to be frozen. They look like small, round ice cubes.

Cattails (*Typha latifolia*) in winter

At the head of the pond, we notice bedraggled downy masses on the cattails' spikes. Many of the seeds, packed so tightly into brown, cigar-shaped seed heads last fall, have been wind dispersed or washed into the marsh by winter rains. Cattails produce large numbers of seeds, an estimated average of 220,000 per spike. Although colonies increase and maintain size primarily by vegetative reproduction in which new plants develop from rhizomes, reproduction by seeding is important. Aided by the fluff attached, the tiny seeds travel by wind to initiate new colonies in locations distant from the original colony.

I wonder why some of the fluffy masses clinging to worn-looking spikes seem to be larger than others and why some stems have little or no fluff. My research later leads me to an interesting possibility. The caterpillars of some species of cattail moths feed on seeds in winter and spin silken, almost invisible webbing, which holds the spikes and fluff together. The caterpillars inside are well insulated during cold wintry days. I am not sure if the bedraggled cattails here in the marsh are boarding houses for these caterpillars, but the appearance of the fluff suggests that it may be so. Infested spikes tend to look more weather-worn and the fluff is grayer than that of other weathered spikes. In winter, chickadees, red-winged blackbirds, and other birds frequent marshes like this one. These birds are probably feeding on the resident caterpillars or other cattail-associated insects rather than on the tiny, hairy cattail seeds.

As we head for the cars, I look back toward the Sanctuary. A bright, red cardinal (*Cardinalis cardinalis*) is watching from a perch where the sun shines brightest through the vegetation in the thicket. Several Carolina chickadees (*Poecile carolinensis*) scold us as we walk by. With their feathers fluffed, they look twice their normal size.

I wonder how such small birds can endure freezing temperatures in winter. Later, I learned that they have several ways to keep warm. Even if the air temperature drops to 0°F (-17.8°C), the heat conserved by fluffing the feathers allows a chickadee's breast to maintain a normal temperature of 105°F (40.6°C). On very cold nights, birds can go into a state of torpor in which they lower their body temperature by about twenty degrees and shiver periodically. This allows them to use much less energy to keep warm during the night. A third adaptation that helps regulate body temperature in cold weather is a heat exchange system of blood circulation in the legs. Warm arterial blood flows from the body into the feet and releases its heat to the cool venous blood as it flows back to the heart. I was really surprised to learn that chickadees may also conserve heat by spending cold nights huddled together in holes in trees or other cavities. Bluebirds also roost communally. Now I worry much less about survival of birds in winter.

Northern cardinal (*Cardinalis cardinalis*)

We have had a drama-filled day in the Sanctuary. We witnessed conflict between raccoons and the capture of a bluebird by a hawk. I had the opportunity to photograph majestic tupelos in snow and colorful birds. Our discovery of river otter tracks in the snow beside Jobala Pond adds another animal to the list of wildlife I have confirmed in the Sanctuary. We gained health benefits while crunching our way through the icy woods on the rustic Tall Tupelo Trail. All in all, this has been an excellent wintry day excursion.

Species List: January

Plants
Common cattail (*Typha latifolia*) seeding
Parrot feather watermilfoil (*Myriophyllum aquaticum*)
Wooly dutchman's pipe vine (*Aristolochia tomentosa*) seedpod

Mammals
Canid, possibly coyote (*Canis latrans*) tracks in snow
Common raccoon (*Procyon lotor*)
Eastern cottontail (*Sylvilagus floridanus*) tracks in snow
Eastern gray squirrel (*Sciurus carolinensis*) tracks in snow
River otter (*Lutra canadensis*) tracks in snow

Birds
American robin (*Turdus migratorius*)
Blue jay (*Cyanocitta cristata*)
Carolina chickadee (*Poecile carolinensis*)
Carolina wren (*Thryothorus ludovicianus*)
Common snipe (*Gallinago gallinago*)
Eastern bluebird (*Sialia sialis*)
Eastern wild turkey (*Meleagris gallopavo silvestris*) tracks
Mallard (*Anas platyrhynchos*)
Northern cardinal (*Cardinalis cardinalis*)
Pileated woodpecker (*Dryocopus pileatus*)
Red-headed woodpecker (*Melanerpes erythrocephalus*)
Sharp-shinned hawk (*Accipiter striatus*)
Swamp sparrow (*Melospiza georgiana*)
White-throated sparrow (*Zonotrichia albicollis*)

Fungi
Lichen (spp.) in rosette patterns
Shelf fungus (spp.)

FEBRUARY

Manifestations of Spring and Bounding Deer

Date: February 27
Begin: 9:00 A.M.
End: 12:00 P.M.
Weather: 9:00 A.M., 33°F (1°C), windy, bright sun
    12:00 P.M., 43°F (6°C)
Participants: Margaret Anne, Clayton, Dee, Willard, Sam, Jerry,
    Jimmy, Guadalupe, and Marian
Purpose: February hike with the Sanctuary Artists

WE BEGIN TODAY AT THE Hidden Springs Overlook. Shoots of arrow arum (*Peltandra virginica*) are now visible in the swamp. This aquatic plant has overwintered in the form of submerged rhizomes. Now at the end of February, it has emerged to begin its spring growth cycle. Patches of parrot feather watermilfoil (*Myriophyllum aquaticum*) that lasted through the winter dot the marsh. Soon this milfoil will cover large areas of the swampy water.

As we near the marsh past the red gates, we notice that the beaver dam is almost dismantled, a result of winter floods. Flooding has also caused significant erosion on the banks of Hidden Springs Stream and

Jobala Pond. We continue across the footbridge and around the pond. Dee points to a tangle of vines. She tells us that these vines were covered with beautiful blue morning glory blooms last summer. I photograph the brown tangle so that we will not forget how bare vines appear at this time of year.

Walking on, we come to the Forest Glen Observation Point. We approach it quietly. Sometimes we find ducks in this small pond, but no ducks blast off to startle us today—all is quiet and still. There are no aquatic plants where duckweed carpeted the pond in green last summer. It's too early for sensitive fern to put up tender shoots where it flourished last season on the banks of the small ditch. Nature is slow to awaken here. We pause while Margaret Anne tells us how Jobala Pond got its name. The Pond is named for her three children—the first two letters of each of their first names, John, Barbara, and Laura.

We turn right and follow Deer Run Trail to the big field. Guadalupe and several others are walking a short distance ahead of Margaret Anne and me. Suddenly, Guadalupe stops and points toward the far side of the field. Looking in the direction she indicates, I spot several deer at the edge of the woods about 100 yd (91 m) away. A large buck notices us. His head goes up! He sniffs the air for messages—are we friend or foe? Before he bolts into the woods, I aim the camera and shoot. But I know the distance is too great to capture the deer's wonderfully exuberant spirit on this bright, sunny cool day in February.

Now, three deer, two bucks and a doe, spring from the woods and dash across the field. We notice that the lead buck has only one antler. The deer must be aware that we are watching, but they seem to take no notice of us. Their tails are not flagging the characteristic white of alarmed deer in flight. Instead, they appear to be playing, or perhaps the larger buck is defending his territory. February is still mating season for deer in the Sanctuary. After several minutes, they bound into the woods toward the tupelo swamp. Deer are fast runners and can bound at speeds of up to 30 to 40 mph (48 to 64 kmph) even through the woods.

A wary white-tailed buck (*Odocoileus virginianus*)

White-tailed deer (*Odocoileus virginianus*) are common in the Sanctuary, and I want to know more about their habits. My research later informs me that deer are good swimmers. This may explain the deer tracks leading through a narrow 18"-wide (0.5 m) pass down a steep bank where they disappear into a deep, slowly flowing section of the river. Apparently this is where deer enter the river to swim across.

Although we may encounter them at other times, deer are primarily crepuscular animals, and early morning and late afternoon are the best times to view them in the Sanctuary. On several occasions, I have seen them resting at the edge of the woods or strolling across the meadow in the middle of the day. I often wonder about deer activities at night and times when we are not in the Sanctuary to observe them. The City of Huntsville's Green Team kindly agreed to set up night-vision, motion-activated cameras in several locations. This allows visualization of deer and insight into their community structure and habits that would have otherwise remained a mystery.

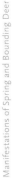

A white-tailed deer (*Odocoileus virginianus*) in early morning in the tupelo woods
(photographed with a stationary, motion-activated camera mounted
by Jim Poff, Goldsmith-Schiffman Wildlife Sanctuary Manager;
photo used by permission of the City of Huntsville Green Team)

In the early morning on a winter day, the motion-activated camera captured the image of a large buck as he walked through the woods near the tupelo swamp. The camera also documented a young buck in the same location as he reached above his head for tender twigs. Images acquired on different dates show solitary bucks and small doe herds indicating that deer browse and move through these woods on a regular basis.

Throughout the year, deer are selective feeders; they eat only a small number of the total plant species available in their habitat. Their long, pointed noses facilitate selection of specific leaves and other vegetation. Deer diet consists of young tree shoots, vines, and shrubs as well as fruit, including that of tupelo trees. Grasses and some agricultural crops are also favored. They eat many types of weeds and even lichen and fungi, but acorns or hard mast are their favorite foods, especially during winter. Now in February, they may nibble on bark when other food sources are scarce. Like cows, deer are ruminants; they have a four-chambered stomach and are cud chewers.

A mature buck can weigh as much as 300 lb (136 kg) and stand 3' to 5' (1 m to 1.5 m) high at the shoulder. Here in Alabama, bucks typically weigh 140 lb (64 kg) but may reach 250 lb (113 kg). However, many do not attain this size primarily because of hunters. Though not lethal, duels of dominance between bucks are common, and antlers are used during these dominance battles rather than for protection against predators. The large, one-antlered buck we saw earlier today may have lost his other antler fighting such a duel, or he may have lost it as the result of natural progression of the season. In Alabama, bucks usually shed their antlers in March and begin growing new ones in April or May. Growth is generally complete by September. Each year, the antlers will be larger than the year before until, by age five to seven, antlers will have reached maximum size.

Deer are sexually mature at two years old and can live for ten years. The best way to estimate the relative age of a buck is by the length of the nose and the color of the coat, rather than by counting the number of points or thickness of the antlers. The older the buck, the longer the snout and the grayer his coat will be. Bucks do not associate with does except during the breeding season. In other months, bucks live in bachelor groups or forage alone. Does either live alone or in matriarchal units with their new fawns and female yearlings.

Here in the Sanctuary, conception occurs in late November to mid-December but may also continue through early February. Mid- to late January is the peak breeding season. The gestation period is about six and a half months (two hundred days), and a healthy doe may have two to three fawns each year. Fawns are typically born in late July to mid-August, but occasionally birth occurs as early as April and as late as November. Fawns weigh 4 lb to 8 lb (1.8 kg to 3.6 kg) and are about 18" (46 cm) tall at the shoulder when they are born. During the first days of the fawn's life, the mother usually remains within 100 yd (91.4 m), but she does not stay with her fawn constantly. I have seen adult deer and many tracks of small deer here in the Sanctuary, but I have not seen a spotted fawn. This is largely because young fawns spend their first days lying with their necks outstretched, hidden in thickets.

Very young fawns have reddish coats with white spots. The spots provide protection from predators by blending with sunlight-dappled vegetation. Fawns lose their spots when they are three to four months old. They are weaned by four months and begin to forage with their mothers.

Deer can make several different sounds. Fawns bleat a high-pitched squeal when frightened or to call their mother. Does also bleat, and both does and bucks snort, a sound similar to a bark that is used to signal danger. Deer emit a guttural sound, or grunt, to get the attention of other deer in the area. Bucks can signal aggression and hostility by a grunt-snort-wheeze pattern. The sound pattern can be unique to each buck. White-tailed deer also communicate by body language. They signal danger with their tails. Raised, the underside of the tail is a white flag warning other deer to flee. Last summer, I photographed a buck bounding through the soybean field. Only its white tail was visible until he jumped up and over the rows of three-foot tall plants.

Another way deer communicate is by scent. During the rut or breeding season, bucks become intolerant of other bucks and bachelor groups dissolve. Hormonal changes occur, and mature bucks develop large, husky necks. They also produce a musky odor by a behavior known as rub-urination. Tarsal glands on the inside of the hind legs secrete a fatty substance, and when bucks urinate over this gland a distinctive odor is produced. Deer engage in this behavior throughout the year, but it is much more frequent during the breeding season. It notifies does of a buck's presence and marks territory to fend off other bucks. This method of communication allows deer to recognize other deer in the herd, and it gives information about their sex, reproductive state, and social status. Bucks also mark their territory by rubbing their antlers and preorbital gland (a scent gland on their forehead) against trees, saplings, and overhanging limbs. While doing this, they paw the ground to make scrapes, which they scent by urinating over the tarsal gland on the hind legs. Receptive does respond by leaving urine at the site. A buck uses his sense of smell to locate the doe with which he intends to mate.

Antlers of bucks are made of solid bone and are not hollow like horns of cows. During the first eight to nine months of a young buck's life, pedicles (skin-covered projections on the skull) appear. These pedicles are permanent and remain on the deer's forehead throughout his life. They are the point from which antlers grow and subsequently separate each year when the antlers are shed. As a buck matures, antlers increase in thickness, density, length, and point length. More points may be added each year, but this is not always the case. During times of new growth, antlers are covered with sensitive skin called velvet. This is rich in blood vessels that transport nutrients necessary for bone growth. Antler growth typically takes two to four months after which a hardened ring forms at the base of each antler. This is called a burr, and its function is to shut off blood supply to the velvet-covered antler. Deprived of nutrients, the velvet deteriorates and falls away. Bucks aid this process by rubbing the antlers against tree trunks. White-tailed deer shed their antlers after the breeding season. The shedding process takes only two or three weeks.

Several times here in the Sanctuary, I have seen bucks with unbranched antlers. This seemed odd, and I wondered why a deer that looked big enough to have branched antlers would have spikes about 4" to 5" (10 cm to 13 cm) long. When a friend, whose husband is a deer hunter, told me that this is a "spike buck" and that sometimes these bucks are eliminated from the herd, I became really interested in learning more about them.

A spike antlered buck is one that is one-and-a-half years old or older, whose antlers are not branched. Spike deer are not the same as male fawns six to twelve months old whose pedicles are beginning to appear during their first winter. The latter are called button or nubbin bucks. In Alabama, bucks may normally have spikes as yearlings, but in time, and if food is abundant, almost all of these will develop branched antlers as the deer matures. The Alabama Department of Conservation does not recommend spike buck elimination. Some hunters believe that spike deer are genetically inferior and that eliminating them will increase the genetic potential for production of large antlered deer.

Based on studies done by wildlife biologists in Alabama, this does not appear to be the case. (More information about spike deer management is available from the Deer Management Assistance Program, Alabama Department of Conservation and Natural Resources, Division of Game and Fish, 64 N. Union, Montgomery, AL 36130.)

In addition to deer, the Green Team's motion-activated camera mounted in the tupelo woods captured images of a pair of bobcats. I am delighted to see actual photographic evidence of these animals in the Sanctuary. In chapter 1, I expressed excitement at finding bobcat tracks on the trail beside the Flint River and wished for a night-vision, motion-activated camera to be mounted nearby. Bobcats are seldom seen in the wild. They are primarily crepuscular, but they can also be active during the day. It was at dusk one day last October when Clayton and Margaret Anne glimpsed a bobcat in a meadow not far from the river. I am grateful to the City of Huntsville's Green Team, and particularly to Jim Poff, for mounting the motion-activated camera in the tupelo woods. Now we have first-hand photographic proof that bobcats live in or frequent the Sanctuary.

Bobcats do not form lasting pair bonds and kittens may remain with the female through their first winter. In Tennessee, and probably in North Alabama, bobcats begin breeding in February and March, and kittens are born an average of sixty-two days later. A litter usually consists of two to four kittens, each weighing 10 oz to 12 oz (283.5 g to 340.2 g). At birth, kittens are blind and helpless and usually nurse for about two months before beginning to hunt with their mother.

Adults weigh between 13 lb and 25 lb (about 6 kg to 11 kg), but an adult male can weigh as much as 40 lb (18 kg). Males typically are 30 to 40 percent larger than females. The average height is 20" to 24" (51 cm to 61 cm) at the shoulder and they grow to lengths of 25" to 42" (0.6 m to 1.1 m). The tail is about 5" (13 cm) long. Fur is short, dense, and tan with black splotches scattered throughout the coat. The underbelly is white with black spots.

Bobcats are skilled climbers, swimmers, and runners. Their lung capacity is relatively small, thus they depend on sudden bursts of speed

Bobcats (*Lynx rufus*) at dusk (photographed with a stationary, motion-activated camera mounted by Jim Poff, Goldsmith-Schiffman Wildlife Sanctuary Manager; photo used by permission of the City of Huntsville Green Team)

rather than long chases to capture prey, usually rabbits, although they use stealth to capture small deer, too. Female bobcats make dens in logs and brush piles here in the Sanctuary and in caves and rock crevices in other locations. Bobcats are territorial but may range over large areas. They are usually silent, but during breeding season they may emit high-pitched screams or low growls. Once, on a dark night when I was camping in Georgia, I heard a bobcat's scream. It was the most otherworldly and eerie wail I have ever heard.

Bobcats habitually follow paths, animal trails, or logging roads, and this fact informs us about places we might have a chance to see them. They are beautiful animals and their presence adds to the biodiversity of species known to inhabit the Sanctuary.

The motion-activated camera also captured the image of wild turkeys meandering through the tupelo woods just after daylight one winter morning.

Now back to our hike today—we walk to the far edge of the field toward the Gravel Bar Trail. I notice a patch of low-growing weeds with ice crystals fringing the leaves. The ice appears to extend upward in

Hoar frost on ground cover

0.25" (0.6 cm) crystals from the leaf edges and dead stems. Back at home later, I research types of ice crystals and find that this interesting phenomenon is caused when cold air saturated with water vapor comes into contact with surfaces temperatures below the freezing point of water. The water vapor in the air condenses on these surfaces to form a type of large crystal frost known as hoar frost. Hoar frost forms on exposed surfaces such as grass blades, leaves, and tree branches. As we see here, it also forms around edges and surfaces of leaves and dead twigs. The crystals are larger than the small ice crystals of frost that we usually see on the ground. Hoar frost is not a common phenomenon. It forms only when air temperature and water content are optimal. We are very fortunate today to see the beauty of hoar frost ice crystals here in the Sanctuary.

At the Gravel Bar, we pause to photograph the stream and explore

A great blue heron (*Ardea herodias*) flies by overhead

the area. Then progressing farther on the Deer Run Trail, Margaret Anne leads the group to the pine tree overlook. Here the bank of the Flint River on our side is high and the sides are composed of colorful gray and yellow clay.

Back on the Deer Run Trail, we walk north beside the river to the location where I saw great blue heron (*Ardea herodias*) nests ten days ago. We did not see herons in the area then. Now, a heron is standing on the largest of the three visible nests. While we watch, another heron makes several passes overhead. Today, February 27, is an important date. It confirms nesting activities in progress during February. As the heron flies over us, we have an opportunity to view it from a different perspective.

We turn around and backtrack on Deer Run Trail to the Tall Tupelo Trail and then to the Tupelo Observation Point. In the woods here, we look for the dwarf wakerobin (*Trillium pusillum*) we found near the Tall

Tupelo Trail Loop in March last year, but this small spring wildflower has not yet braved the cold winter to venture above ground. Now in February after the rains of winter, the tupelos are standing in several feet of water. An ice film coats the surface here in the swamp where the sun has not reached to melt it.

We have been out for about two and a half hours, and several members of the group want to get home by noon, so we set a fast pace back toward the cars. On our way, we discover bobcat tracks in the big field near Deer Run Trail. Raccoon and turkey tracks are numerous here also. Patches of hairy bittercress (*Cardamine hirsuta*) are scattered throughout the field.

Hairy bittercress is a seedy winter annual that grows 4" to 16" (10 cm to 41 cm) tall. Here there are clusters of small, white, four-petaled flowers, and many plants have brown, erect fruits up to 1" (2.5 cm) long. These fruits, called siliques, rise above spent blooms and occur simultaneously with the flowers in the cluster. A silique is defined as a narrow, elongated, dry seedpod with two valves 0.75" to 1.25" (1.9 cm to 3.2 cm) long, usually containing many seeds, that fall away leaving a central partition. When mature, the siliques explosively release seeds that may spread as much as 10' (3 m) from the plant. Siliques are the characteristic fruit of plants in the mustard family (Brassicaceae).

As we reach Jobala Pond and walk beside it on Hidden Springs Trail, we notice developing catkins and cones on the alders bordering the pond. These are hazel alders (*Alnus serrulata*) in the family Betulaceae. Alders form thickets and have flexible stems and fibrous root systems, making them extremely useful and important in pond and stream bank stabilization and erosion prevention. They are monoecious with both pistillate and staminate flowers on the same plant. When mature in mid- to late March, the 1" to 1.5" (2.5 cm to 3.8 cm) long male catkins will produce pollen and seeds will develop in the 0.5" (1.3 cm) brown cones. This species of alder is native to the eastern United States from southern Maine to northern Florida and west to southeastern Oklahoma, Missouri, and Illinois. A deciduous shrub, alders are common

The tupelo swamp in late winter

Above: Hairy bittercress (*Cardamine hirsuta*)

Below: Hazel alder (*Alnus serrulata*) catkins and cones

A song sparrow (*Melospiza melodia*) searching for seeds

along stream margins and in bottomlands but can also be found in uplands that are well drained. In addition to stabilizing pond and stream banks, alders are beneficial as habitat for wildlife.

Farther along, we notice several song sparrows foraging for food on the frozen surface of the marsh at the head of Jobala Pond. One sparrow appears to be moving a small twig out of its way.

This has been an excellent day in the Sanctuary. We watched wild running deer, discovered ice films on standing water, saw hoar frost on plant leaves and stems, and observed great blue herons beginning nesting activities. We also found spring beauties blooming at the edge of the field beside Deer Run Trail. This wildflower as well as early saxifrage, spring cress, and hairy bittercress are the Sanctuary's earliest spring blooming wildflowers. Finding bobcat tracks today is exciting and the actual image of bobcats captured by the stationary motion-activated camera confirms their continued presence in the Sanctuary. We are back at the cars by noon.

Species List: February

Plants
Arrow arum (*Peltandra virginica*)
Duckweed (*Lemna* spp.)
Green algae (*Spirogyra* sp.)
Hairy bittercress (*Cardamine hirsuta*)
Meadow garlic (*Allium canadense*)
Parrot feather watermilfoil
    (*Myriophyllum aquaticum*)
Red buckeye (*Aesculus pavia*) buds
Spring beauty (*Claytonia virginica*)
Spring cress (*Cardamine bulbosa*)

Trees
Hazel alder (*Alnus serrulata*)
Pine (*Pinus* sp.)
Red maple (*Acer rubrum*) bloom buds

Mammals
Bobcat (*Lynx rufus*) tracks and motion-
    activated camera photo
Common Raccoon (*Procyon lotor*)
    tracks
White-tailed deer (*Odocoileus
    virginianus*) tracks

Birds
American robin (*Turdus migratorius*)
Brown thrasher (*Toxostoma rufum*)
Great blue heron (*Ardea herodias*)
Mallard (*Anas platyrhynchos*)
Song sparrow (*Melospiza melodia*)
Wild turkey (*Meleagris gallopavo*)
    tracks, photographed by a stationary
    motion-activated camera
Yellow-bellied sapsucker (*Sphyrapicus
    varius*), evidenced by freshly drilled
    holes circling a tree trunk

Pond Sliders, Great Blue Herons, and Spring Beauties

Date: March 19
Begin: 9:00 A.M.
End: 11:00 A.M.
Weather: 9:00 A.M., 45°F (7°C), sunny
   11:00 A.M., 60°F (16°C)
Participants: Keith, Margaret Anne, and Marian
Purpose: To visit the great blue heron rookery and discuss
   protection of nesting herons

TODAY WE WILL MEET WITH Keith to show him the great blue heron rookery and discuss the location of the planned bicycle trail that will run through heron territory near the Flint River. Margaret Anne and I arrive early, and I take a few minutes to photograph the scene at Hidden Springs Swamp. Although it's still too soon for trees to leaf out, aquatic vegetation adds tinges of green to the persistent winter gray-brownness of the swamp. Turtles have come out of their winter habitats and now compete for a place in the sun on a partially submerged log.

Keith arrives in his pickup, and Margaret Anne and I climb in. We

Turtles vie for space on a log in Hidden Springs Swamp

ride down Hidden Springs Trail, across the outflow stream at the far end of Jobala Pond and follow Deer Run Trail to the edge of the field. Even though we have had five days without rain, the water table is high and water still stands in low places in the field. Keith makes his way across as the truck splashes through mud and pools of water. We stop at the edge of the woods at the intersection of Tall Tupelo and Deer Run Trails. From here we will walk to the Flint River. Along our way, we find small patches of spring beauties (*Claytonia virginica*). I know spring has truly arrived in the Sanctuary when I see these delicate wildflowers in bloom. I found a few bedraggled spring beauties when I came this way in late February. Today their lavender striped white petals are a welcome contrast to the brown muddy soil in which they are growing.

Now walking along Deer Run Trail where it comes closest to the Flint River, we notice a mound about 20' (6 m) away in the woods on

Spring beauty (*Claytonia virginica*)

our left. The mound rises approximately 4' (1.2 m) above the surrounding terrain and has a diameter of about 15' (5 m). Keith says this is probably a midden used by Indians who camped here temporarily when on hunting and fishing forays near the river. The Creek Indians were the primary tribe living in the territory that is now Alabama, Florida, North Carolina, and South Carolina. Records date American Indian presence in these areas back to the sixteenth century. Later, Cherokees infiltrated Creek lands and, in the 1800s, settlers arrived to establish farms in the area.

Trees are growing in the middle of the mound now, and we notice several trilliums with mottled, dark green leaves also growing on and around the mound. This is *Trillium cuneatum*, the most common trillium in northern Alabama. Other names by which it's known include sweet Betsy, whip-poor-will flower, large toadshade, bloody butcher, and wakerobin. A native of the southeastern United States, *Trillium cuneatum* produces a dark, purplish-magenta bloom from March to mid-April. As we walk down the slope of the mound to leave we discover to

Early saxifrage (*Saxifraga virginiensis*) on the bank of the Flint River

our delight, several dwarf wakerobins (*Trillium pusillum*) in bloom. We found them in the tupelo swamp in the two previous years, but this is a location we did not know existed. These plants look strong and healthy here in the woods beside the Flint River.

We follow the graded bicycle path as it bends back toward the river and discover early saxifrage (*Saxifraga virginiensis*) on the riverbank. One of the earliest wildflowers to bloom in the Sanctuary, this perennial has a basal rosette of toothed leaves and hairy stems, 8" to 12" (20 cm to 30 cm) long. The stems bear branched clusters of small white blooms. Some say that young early saxifrage leaves may be used in salads.

Now we come to a section of trail that I have not walked before, and, looking toward the tall trees across the river, I am delighted to discover more heron nests in addition to the original ones we found south of here some months ago. A heron stands watching us from a nest high in the trees. We continue on the trail, and within a distance of about 0.4 mi (0.6 km) we count nineteen nests. Most are in trees on an island

A great blue heron (*Ardea herodias*) stands on its nest

formed where the river diverges into two streams. Herons fly from six of the nests as we approach. It's obvious from their behavior that our presence disturbs them even though we walk slowly and do not make sudden movements. I am concerned that the new bicycle path may come too close to the rookery.

If disturbed, great blue herons may abandon their nests. They are most likely to leave nests during pre-nesting and courtship activities. Once eggs are laid, herons are less likely to abandon nests. Several factors influence heron sensitivity to human presence. These include the size of the colony (the larger the colony, the less sensitive herons are to human presence), relative isolation (trees and bushes provide a buffer

and relative seclusion), and the degree to which the herons are accustomed to having humans around. I have seen herons nesting in trees bordering a stream near a ball park. They seemed to disregard human activity nearby. But because trail building in the Sanctuary is a new activity in heron territory, human presence is unfamiliar in this location.

Great blue herons nest in tall trees. From their high vantage they can watch for predators such as red-tailed hawks, raccoons, and American crows that might steal eggs or young herons from the nest. Nests are 2' to 3' (0.6 m to 0.9 m) across and about 20" (51 cm) thick. They are built of sticks and sturdy twigs and lined with pine needles, mosses, and lichens. Males bring building materials while females arrange and construct the nest. Many herons return to the same rookery year after year, but some may establish colonies elsewhere. Herons are communal and the number of nests per rookery (or heronry) may range from just a few to several hundred.

Adults remain together for one breeding season only and a new pair bond is formed each year. Herons reach maturity when they are two years old and can live fifteen to twenty years. With a wingspan of 6.5' (2 m) and a height of 3' to 4' (0.9 m to 1.2 m), the great blue heron is one of the world's largest birds. For such a large bird, its 5.5 lb (2.5 kg) body weight seems slight. Male and female herons are similar in appearance, but males are generally larger and have longer bills. Great blue herons lay an average of three or four eggs, but sometimes as many as seven in each clutch. The eggs are incubated for twenty-eight days. If eggs are destroyed by predation, or as a result of parent birds shuffling around on the nest in anxiety over a perceived threat nearby or human activity in the area, the females will lay another clutch. Each time an egg is laid, another twenty-eight days is added to the term of incubation diligence.

After eggs hatch, chicks require sixty days to develop before fledging. Both parents incubate eggs, and both bring food and regurgitate it to feed the chicks. After the first month, parents spend time away from the colony. They return only to feed the chicks and stand watch briefly. Even after young herons fledge, they come back to the nest in

A vigilant heron shown on left and a relaxed heron shown on right

the evening to be fed by parents for another two weeks. During this time chicks develop flying skills and learn to fend for themselves.

Because herons are particularly sensitive to disturbances during pre-nesting activities, it is important to be aware of signs of stress while we are in their territory. Great blue herons display distinct body language. An outstretched neck and eyes focused on the object they perceive as a threat, human or otherwise, indicates concern or stress. A relaxed heron holds its neck bent in the shape of an "S."

After checking information sources and observing herons in the rookery over several seasons, I offer the table below as a general guideline for heron watching in the Sanctuary.

It is important to remain at least 600' to 700' (183 m to 213 m) away from the nesting sites, especially from mid-January through mid-March. If we abide by the recommendations of biologists who have studied human impact on heron populations, the herons in the Sanctuary and adjoining areas will have an excellent chance to continue to

Table 1. Great Blue Heron Activity in the Sanctuary

Time of Year	Activity
Mid- to late January	Herons begin flying around rookery, selecting nests, and selecting mates.
February to mid-March	Herons begin bringing sticks, repairing nests, claiming location for new nests, conducting courtship activities, and laying eggs. Trees are not leafed out and nests are not secluded.
Mid-March through April	Herons fly in and out of colony, incubating eggs; some eggs begin to hatch. Trees are leafed out and nests are mostly secluded now.
May to early June	Most chicks should be fledging or nearly ready to fledge and leave nests.
July through August	Young herons are developed and look like adults.
August to January	Herons disperse throughout the Sanctuary and adjacent areas to forage in ponds and meadows.

Left: Dwarf wakerobin (*Trillium pusillum*), a fresh white bloom

Right: As they age, the blooms of dwarf wakerobins turn pink or lavender

thrive in their current location and will provide all of us spectacular views and insights into their lives.

Returning to Keith's truck, Margaret Anne and I bid him farewell and walk to the Tall Tupelo Observation Point loop where it diverges from the Tall Tupelo Trail. This is where I found dwarf wakerobins (*Trillium pusillum*) blooming in March last year. To our delight, we discover several of the plants, 3" to 5" (7.6 cm to 12.7 cm) tall, blooming here today in spite of our cold and snowy winter and generous spring flooding. When they first open, the blooms of dwarf trilliums are white, and as they age, the blooms turn pink to lavender. As I stand gazing at these diminutive plants, I am reminded again that it was the beauty and uniqueness of this small trillium that first inspired my decision to spend time exploring, documenting, enjoying, and sharing the beauty and diversity of life this place offers.

Common blue violets (*Viola sororia*) are also blooming here in the woods today. Their blooms have five petals, and the lateral petals are

Common blue violets (*Viola sororia*)

bearded with white hairs. These violets bloom from February to May in woods and fields throughout the southeast from Florida to Texas and north to Maine and North Dakota.

As we walk around the edge of the woods into the field on our way back to the cars, we note a number of tiny bluets (*Houstonia* sp.). Delicate, bright blue, four-petaled, and with reddish-centers, these tiny wildflowers bloom in March and April in open fields like the ones here in the Sanctuary. Continuing through the field, Margaret Anne and I also notice raccoon tracks and a canid print (coyote, perhaps) as we round the edge of the field and head toward Jobala Pond.

Now, back at the pond, we discover a small bird swimming among shadows cast on the water by the morning sun shining through trees. It's a pied-billed grebe (*Podilymbus podiceps*), so named because of the dark band around the bill visible during breeding season. Suddenly the grebe dives and, in less than a minute, pops up farther away from us near the opposite bank. Pied-billed grebes weigh 9 oz to 20 oz (255 g to 566 g). They rarely fly but they are excellent swimmers. Their diving

Pied-billed grebe (*Podilymbus podiceps*)

ability has earned them names such as hell-diver, dabchick, devil-diver, dive-dapper, and water witch. These little water birds are commonly found in freshwater ponds and marshes across the United States and eastern and central Canada. Their diet consists mainly of aquatic invertebrates, but occasionally grebes eat reptiles, amphibians, and fish. During the breeding season male and female grebes select a territory in shallow water where they build a floating nest of weeds pulled from the bottom of the stream or pond. Females lay two to ten eggs, which are then incubated by both parents. Incubation takes twenty-three to twenty-seven days. After hatching, chicks leave the nest within an hour and can already swim and dive. Sometimes chicks ride around on the parent's back. Within a month after hatching, chicks are on their own and independent of their parents. We hope this little grebe will select a mate and choose Jobala Pond for its home.

This has been one of our most informative trips into the Sanctuary. Today we discovered nineteen new great blue heron nests along the river. Most of these are in tall trees growing on the narrow island

Pond Sliders, Great Blue Herons, and Spring Beauties

formed by two branches of the Flint River north of the original site where we found heron nests last spring. We also discovered dwarf trilliums blooming in a new location near the Indian midden beside the Flint River, in addition to the ones in the tupelo woods we found last spring.

Before leaving the Sanctuary today, I pause to photograph Hidden Springs Swamp and notice that arrow arum has grown more than a foot since I first saw it barely above water level in February. Though the trees are still bare, buds have begun to swell and spring is really here.

And so in the newness of spring, another year begins with its progression of seasons and promises of abundant life ever changing in this microcosm of Earth's diversity.

Species List: March

Wildflowers and Plants

Arrow arum (*Peltandra virginica*)

Broadleaf cattail (*Typha latifolia*)

Common blue violet (*Viola sororia*)

Dwarf wakerobin (*Trillium pusillum*)

Early saxifrage (*Saxifraga virginiensis*)

Grape hyacinth (*Muscari botryoides*)

Parrot feather watermilfoil (*Myriophyllum aquaticum*)

Resurrection fern (*Pleopeltis polypodioides*)

Rue anemone (*Thalictrum thalictroides*)

Spring beauty (*Claytonia virginica*)

Swamp water pennywort (*Hydrocotyle ranunculoides*)

Tiny bluets (*Houstonia* sp.)

Trillium (*Trillium cuneatum*)

Trees

Red buckeye (*Aesculus pavia*) leaf and bloom buds

Red maple (*Acer rubrum*) winged, two-seeded samaras

Birds

Eastern bluebird (*Sialia sialis*)

Great blue heron (*Ardea herodias*)

Pied-billed grebe (*Podilymbus podiceps*)

Tufted titmouse (*Baeolophus bicolor*)

Other Species

Damselfly (Order Odonata, suborder Zygoptera)

Pond slider turtle (*Trachemys scripta*)

Smallmouth bass (*Micropterus dolomieu*)

CONCLUSION

Many changes have occurred in the Sanctuary since I began photo documenting its flora and fauna in 2009. Change is inevitable, but it is difficult to acknowledge that much of the natural world as we know it today may disappear. Encroaching residential developments, human population growth, and changes in the Earth's climate add to pressures imposed on wildlife habitats locally and globally.

The descriptions presented in this book establish a natural history of flora and fauna in a riparian habitat as it currently exists in the southern Appalachian region in the early twenty-first century. Future generations of students, scientists, environmentalists, and nature enthusiasts may wonder what wild areas once were like. Included within this book is baseline information, a starting point for future assessment of ecological change and shifts in populations of plants and animals as the Sanctuary is altered to better accommodate human visitation.

Mitigation of wetlands, altering stream flow, removing vegetation, and building trails and greenways will change the "naturalness" of the Sanctuary and alter habitats of the plants and animals that currently make a home there. Whether a species will remain in the Sanctuary over time will depend on how well that species adapts to environmental change and adjusts to the proximity of humans. We can foster our coexistence with wildlife if we respect and remain sensitive to the needs of plant and animal species as we modify and visit the wild places. I shall look forward to hiking in the Sanctuary in future years and finding beavers, muskrats, herons, bobcats, and other wildlife still living in this chosen location. It is my hope that students of ecology and natural history will monitor the Sanctuary in the years to come. Perhaps it will be a site for research projects, including in-depth investigations utilizing the tools of field and molecular biology to study the biodiversity of multitudes of aquatic and terrestrial plant, animal, insect, and fungal species that occupy this habitat.

The Sanctuary as it exists now will be further modified in the near future to better accommodate human use. This is a good thing when the modifications are accomplished with careful concern for protecting wildlife. Consideration of the balance between human use and preservation of habitat will be essential if the Sanctuary is to continue as a wildlife sanctuary where we can explore and learn about its denizens firsthand.

Outdoor opportunities and free play outside are in danger of extinction. At best, these have become restricted. Our propensity for urban and suburban dwelling sets us up for a nature deficit as described by Richard Louv in his book *Last Child in the Woods*. In our society today, children are increasingly tuned into virtual experiences. Simulated reality is not the same as actual experience that develops self-reliance, judgment, and concern for our "spaceship Earth." Many children will never know the freedom of running wildly through the woods or wading barefooted in a stream, but they can experience the thrill of discovering a camouflaged tree frog resting on a gray limb in a damp forest. In places like the wildlife sanctuary described in this book, they can learn about nature firsthand and enjoy being outdoors.

Change that is beneficial to the environment, to the wildlife, and to the welfare of our children and ourselves can be influenced through public awareness and participation in the preservation of wild places. Philanthropic gifts, such as donation of the land for the Sanctuary, can tip the balance of change toward the beneficial side for Alabama and the country as a whole. It is my sincere hope that this book will inspire nature enthusiasts, present and future, and individuals of all ages wherever they may be, to go on excursions into the sanctuaries, parks, and preserves of the Earth and to explore, enjoy, respect, and protect our natural world.

Appendix 1

LIST OF TREES COMMON TO SOUTHERN RIPARIAN HABITATS

The following is a list of trees one may expect to find in the riparian environment of the Goldsmith Schiffman Wildlife Sanctuary.

Note: The indicator statuses below are used to designate occurrence of plant and tree types in a wetland or upland. National indicators reflect the range of estimated probabilities expressed as a frequency. The data is drawn from the USDA Natural Resources Conservation Service's Plant Database "Wetland Indicator Status," http://www.plants.usda.gov/wetinfo.html.

Status Categories

OBL Obligate Wetland: Occurs almost always (estimated probability 99 percent) under natural conditions in wetlands.

FACW Facultative Wetland: Usually occurs in wetlands (estimated probability 67 percent to 99 percent), but occasionally found in non-wetlands.

FAC Facultative: Equally likely to occur in wetlands or non-wetlands (estimated probability 34 percent to 66 percent).

FACU Facultative Upland: Usually occurs in non-wetlands, but may occur in wetlands.

UPL Obligate Upland: Almost never occurs in wetlands

Oaks

Black oak (*Quercus velutina*) family
Fagaceae; widespread, FACW
Cherrybark oak (*Quercus pagoda*)
family Fagaceae; dominant
bottomland species, FACW
Overcup oak (*Quercus lyrata*) family
Fagaceae; OBL
Shumard's oak (*Quercus shumardii*)
family Fagaceae; FACW
Southern red oak (*Quercus falcata*)
family Fagaceae; widespread but
tending toward uplands, FACW
Swamp chestnut oak (*Quercus
michauxii*) family Fagaceae; FACW
Water oak *(Quercus nigra)* family
Fagaceae; widespread but abundant
in bottomlands, FAC
Willow oak *(Quercus phellos)* family
Fagaceae; FACW

Other Species of Trees and Shrubs

Hazel alder, smooth alder (*Alnus serru-
lata*) birch family Betulaceae; OBL
American hornbeam, blue beech
(*Carpinus caroliniana*) family
Betulaceae; FAC
American sycamore, plane tree,
buttonwood (*Platanus occidentalis*)
family Platanaceae; FACW
Bitternut hickory (*Carya cordiformis*)
family Juglandaceae; FACU
Black cherry (*Prunus serotina*) family
Rosaceae; widespread, FACU
Black locust (*Robinia pseudoacacia*)
family Fabaceae; FACU

Black walnut (*Juglans nigra*) family
Juglandaceae; FACU
Black willow (*Salix nigra*) family
Salicaceae; OBL
Box elder (*Acer negundo*) family
Aceraceae; FAC
Buttonbush (*Cephalanthus occidentalis*)
family Rubiaceae; OBL
Common elderberry (*Sambucus
canadensis*) family Adoxaceae; FAC
Common paw paw (*Asimina triloba*)
family Annonaceae; FAC
Cottonwood, eastern cottonwood
(*Populus deltoides*) family Salicaceae;
bottomlands, FAC
Dogwood, silky dogwood (*Cornus
amomum*) family Cornaceae; FACW
Eastern redbud (*Cercis Canadensis*)
family Fabaceae; FACU
Green ash (*Fraxinus pennsylvanica*)
family Oleaceae; bottomlands,
FACW
Green hawthorn (*Crataegus viridis*)
family Rosaceae; FACW
Honeylocust (*Gleditsia triacanthos*)
family Fabaceae; FAC
Pine (*Pinus* sp.) family Pinaceae;
wetland status depends on species
Red buckeye (*Aesculus pavia*) family
Hippocastanaceae, FAC
Red maple (*Acer rubrum*) family
Aceraceae; widespread, FAC
River birch (*Betula nigra*) family
Betulaceae; FACW
Shagbark hickory (*Carya ovata*) family
Juglandaceae; FACU

Slippery elm (*Ulmus rubra*) family
Ulmaceae; FAC

Southern catalpa (*Catalpa bignonioides*)
family Bignoniaceae; FACU

Sugarberry; southern hackberry (*Celtis laevigata*); FACW

Swamp dogwood (*Cornus foemina*);
FACW

Sweetgum (*Liquidambar styraciflua*)
family Altingiaceae; widespread,
bottomlands, FAC

Water hickory (*Carya aquatica*) family
Juglandaceae; OBL

Water tupelo (*Nyssa aquatica*) family
Cornaceae; OBL

Winged elm (*Ulmus alata*) family
Ulmaceae; tends toward uplands,
FACU

Yellow-poplar, tulip poplar
(*Liriodendron tulipifera*) family
Magnoliaceae; widespread, FACU

Exotics and Invasives

Chinese privet (*Ligustrum sinense*)
family Oleaceae; major woody
invasive, FACU

Mimosa, silktree (*Albizia julibrissin*)
family Fabaceae; wetland status not
given

Paulownia empress tree, royal
paulownia (*Paulownia tomentosa*)
family Scrophulariaceae; UPL

Tree-of-heaven (*Ailanthus altissima*)
family Simaroubaceae; FACU

Appendix 2

Physical Characteristics of the Goldsmith Schiffman Wildlife Sanctuary

The Goldsmith Schiffman Wildlife Sanctuary is located in the Wheeler Watershed of the Tennessee River Valley. The Sanctuary is bordered on the east by the Flint River as it meanders through the northeastern part of Madison County, Alabama. Geologically, the area that includes the Sanctuary is in the Cumberland Plateau Section of the Appalachian Plateau Province. This physiographic section is the southernmost part of the Appalachian Highlands Region.[1] Beneath the soils of the Sanctuary lie rock fragments and weathered bedrock (regolith) dating back to the Tuscumbia Limestone of the Mississippian Age lasting from about 360 to 320 million years ago. Under the Tuscumbia limestone is a layer called Fort Payne Chert. This is made up of abundant chert beds and nodules in fossiliferous limestone. The primary rock type is limestone with chert as the secondary type. Other rock types are siltstone, shale, and claystone. All of these are bioclastic (rock consisting of very small pieces of animals and plants) sedimentary formations, each with characteristic light to olive-gray or bluish gray to green, mostly fine to coarse-grained layers in medium-bedded (relative layer thickness) striations.

The Sanctuary encompasses four major habitat areas.[2] The first consists of five agricultural fields, about 64.7 acres of the total 447.7-acre property. Some farming continues, but these fields will eventually be restored to wetland status. A second environmental area encompasses about 38.6 acres and includes second growth, opportunistic trees, and some invasives, notably Chinese privet. Stands of desirable swamp chestnut oak, overcup oak, and willow oak also grow here. The third habitat type is a 7.5-acre wetland in which water tupelo trees dominate. These trees grow in a depression slightly lower than the surrounding land.

The fourth and largest portion of the Sanctuary consists of approximately 336.9 acres. The west and southwest sections include mixed, second-growth successional stands that were affected by cutting or farming in the 1940s. Successional trees include red maple, sweetgum, green ash, sycamore, and tulip poplar. The east-northeast section of this large area contains older growth trees and does not appear to have been farmed historically. A few unique stands, including water, chestnut, overcup, willow, and swamp chestnut oaks, as well as water tupelos, are scattered throughout the property.

The hydrology of the area is affected by several tributaries of the Flint River that run through the Sanctuary, as well as beaver dams located along the western boundary and two springs in the north central section. Surface water from flooding also contributes to the saturated conditions of the wetlands. During a one-year period in 2009 and 2010, Flint River overbank flooding occurred several times, as shown in Table 2.

Rainfall also contributes to the hydrology of the Sanctuary. Measurements for rainfall in the Huntsville area from July 2009 through June 2010 are shown in Table 3.

The soil types in the Sanctuary were defined in a survey of Madison County in 1958 by the US Department of Agriculture's Soil Conservation Service. There are two types of soil associations listed. One is the Huntington-Lindside-Hablen on the east side. This includes bottomlands along the Flint River that are subjected to river overflow. The

Table 2. Flint River Overbank Flooding Dates

2009	2010
August 1	January 23
September 13	March 25
October 6	April 23
November 10	May 2
December 8	

Source: Goldsmith Schiffman Wildlife Sanctuary Mitigation Banking Instrument, August 2011; used by permission of OMI Engineering, Inc., Huntsville, Alabama, and the City of Huntsville Green Team

second association is the Holston-Tupelo-Robertsville on the west side. Here the soils consist of low, flat areas of old, alluvial plain that shallowly overlies limestone bedrock.

Hydric soil types make up the majority of the individual soils in the Sanctuary. These are the Melvin silty clay loam and the Prader fine sandy loam types (Table 4). Dunning silty clay is also listed as a hydric soil. According to the United States Department of Agriculture Natural Resources Conservation Service, "a hydric soil is a soil that formed under conditions of saturation, flooding or ponding long enough during the growing season to develop anaerobic conditions in the upper part."[3]

The type of soil in an area affects natural drainage, soil permeability, and the types of plants growing there. The upper portion of hydric soil

Table 3. Rainfall Measurements in the Huntsville Area

Year	Month	Rainfall (inches)
2009	July	6.75
	August	5.44
	September	5.96
	October	8.17
	November	3.01
	December	8.16
2010	January	5.21
	February	3.26
	March	4.97
	April	0.54
	May	4.87
	June	2.75
Total twelve-month rainfall		59.09

Source: National Oceanic and Atmospheric Administration, Huntsville International Airport

Table 4. Soil Types Identified in the Goldsmith Schiffman Wildlife Sanctuary

Soil ID	Soil Type
Br	Bruno fine loamy sand
Dw	Dunning silty clay
Eg	Egam silty clay loam
Ha	Hamblen fine sandy loam
Hv	Holston fine sandy loam
Hx	Huphreys silt loam
Lk	Lindside silty clay loam
Me	Melvin silty clay loam
Pr	Prader fine sandy loam
Sf	Sequatchie fine sandy loam
Ta	Taft silt loam
Tu	Tupelo silt loam

Source: *Goldsmith Schiffman Wildlife Sanctuary Mitigation Banking Instrument, August 2011;* used by permission of OMI Engineering, Inc., Huntsville, Alabama, and the City of Huntsville Green Team is anaerobic (absence of oxygen); thus, hydric soils only support plants and microbes that are adapted to grow without oxygen or under conditions of low oxygen. Examples of such plants are cattails and sedges.

An indication of the wetland quality of the Sanctuary was obtained by evaluating ground water levels at ten sites and comparing values with ground elevation at each site. Measurements taken on a monthly basis from July 2009 through June 2010 indicate that much of the Sanctuary is composed of hydric soils. Ground elevations at the sites tested measured approximately 582' to 588' above sea level.

1. Encyclopedia of Alabama, *Cumberland Plateau Physiographic Section*, http://www.encyclopediaofalabama.org/face/Article.jsp?id=h-1301.

2. *Goldsmith Schiffman Wildlife Sanctuary Mitigation Banking Instrument, August 2011.* Used by permission of OMI Engineering, Inc., Huntsville, Alabama, and the City of Huntsville Green Team.

3. For further information about soil types, see the US Department of Agriculture/Natural Resources Conservation Service, *Technical Soil Services Handbook*, http://www.nrcs.usda.gov/wps/portal/nrcs/detail/soils/home/?cid=nrcs142p2_053400.

Appendix 3

Taxonomy and Measurements

Basic Taxonomic Hierarchy

Kingdom
Phylum
Class
Order
Family
Genus
Species

Basic Convention for Scientific Nomenclature

Capitalize names of Kingdom, Phylum, Class, Order, Family, and Genus. Do not capitalize species names.

Italicize names of *Genus* and *species*. Do not italicize names of Kingdom, Phylum, Class, Order, and Family.

Useful Measurements

1 inch (in) = 25.4 millimeters (mm)
1 inch (in) = 2.54 centimeters (cm)

1 foot (ft) = 30.48 centimeters (cm)
1 foot (ft) = 0.3048 meter (m)

1 yard (yd) = 91.44 centimeters (cm)
1 yard (yd) = 0.9144 meters (m)

1 mile (mi) = 1.609 kilometers (km)

1 ounce (oz) = 28 grams (g)
1 pound (lb) = 0.4536 kilogram (kg)
1 centimeter (cm) = 0.394 inch (in)
1 millimeter (mm) = 0.039 inch (in)
1 meter (m) = 39.4 inches (in)
1 meter (m) = 3.28 feet (ft)
1 meter (m) = 1.1 yards (yd)
1 centimeter (cm) = 0.0328 feet (ft)

1 kilometer (km) = 3,281 feet (ft)
1 kilometer (km) = 0.621 miles (mi)
1 gram (g) = 0.035 ounces (oz)
1 kilogram (kg) = 2.2 pounds (lb)

0°F = -17.77°C
Conversion formula: (°F - 32) x 5/9 = °C

0°C = 32°F
Conversion formula: °C x 9/5 + 32 = °F

Resources

BIRDS

Butler, R. W. "Great Blue Heron (*Ardea herodias*)": *The Birds of North America,* no. 25, eds. A. Poole, P. Stettenheim, and F. Gill. Philadelphia: Academy of Natural Sciences; Washington, DC: American Ornithologists Union, 1992.

Johnsgard, Paul A. *Waterfowl: Their Biology and Natural History.* Lincoln: University of Nebraska Press, 1968.

Kaufman, Kenn. *Birds of North America.* Boston: Houghton Mifflin, 2000.

Kroodsma, Donald. *The Singing Life of Birds.* Boston: Houghton Mifflin, 2005.

Peterson, Roger Tory. *Birds of Eastern and Central North America.* 5th ed. New York: Houghton Mifflin, 2002.

Robbins, Chandler S., Bertel Bruun, and Herbert S. Zim. *Birds of North America.* Racine, WI: Western Publishing, 1983.

Sibley, David Allen. *The Sibley Field Guide to Birds of Eastern North America.* 2nd ed. New York: Alfred A. Knopf, 2014.

FUNGI

Lincoff, Gary H., and Carol Nehring. *National Audubon Society Field Guide to North American Mushrooms.* New York: Alfred A. Knopf, 1981.

McKnight, Kent H., and Vera B. McKnight. *Peterson Field Guides: Mushrooms.* Boston: Houghton Mifflin, 1987.

Weber, Nancy Smith, and Alexander H. Smith. *A Field Guide to Southern Mushrooms.* Ann Arbor: University of Michigan Press, 1985.

INSECTS AND OTHER INVERTEBRATES

Beadle, David and Seabrooke Leckie. *Peterson Field Guide to Moths of Northeastern North America.* Boston: Houghton Mifflin Harcourt, 2012.

Bright, Sara, and Paulette Haywood Ogard. *Butterflies of Alabama.* Tuscaloosa: University of Alabama Press, 2010.

Burris, Judy and Wayne Richards. *The Life Cycles of Butterflies.* North Adams, MA: Storey Publishing, 2006.

Burton, Maurice, and Robert Burton. *Encyclopedia of Insects & Arachnids.* New York: Crescent Books, 1975.

Dunkle, Sidney W. *Dragonflies through Binoculars: A Field Guide to Dragonflies of North America.* New York: Oxford University Press, 2000.

Evans, Arthur V. *Field Guide to Insects and Spiders of North America.* New York: Sterling Publishing, 2008.

Nikula, Blair, Jackie Sones, Donald Stokes, and Lillian Stokes. *Beginner's Guide to Dragonflies.* New York: Little, Brown, 2002.

Opler, Paul A. *Peterson Field Guides: Butterflies and Moths.* Boston: Houghton Mifflin, 1992.

Paulson, Dennis. *Dragonflies and Damselflies of the East.* Princeton, N.J.: Princeton University Press, 2011.

Pennak, Robert W. *Fresh-Water Invertebrates of the United States.* New York: John Wiley and Sons, 1978.

Wright, Amy Bartlett. *Peterson First Guides: Caterpillars.* Boston: Houghton Mifflin, 1993.

LICHENS

Brodo, Irwin M., Sylvia Duran Sharnoff, and Stephen Sharnoff. *Lichens of North America.* New Haven, Conn.: Yale University Press, 2001.

Purvis, William. *Lichens.* Washington, DC: Smithsonian Institution Press, 2007.

MAMMALS

Bowers, Nora, Rick Bowen, and Kenn Kaufman. *Mammals of North America.* New York: Houghton Mifflin, 2004.

Elbroch, Mark, and Kurt Rinehart. *Behavior of North American Mammals.* Boston: Houghton Mifflin Harcourt, 2011.

Reid, Fiona. *Peterson Field Guide to Mammals of North America*. 4th ed. Boston: Houghton Mifflin, 2006.

Wilson, Don E., and Sue Ruff, eds. *The Smithsonian Book of North American Mammals*. Washington, DC: Smithsonian Institution Press, 1999.

PLANTS AND WILDFLOWERS

Brandenburg, David M. *National Wildlife Federation Field Guide to Wildflowers of North America*. New York: Sterling Publishing, 2010.

Brown, Lauren. *Grasses: An Identification Guide*. Boston: Houghton Mifflin, 1979.

Bryson, Charles T., and Michael S. DeFelice, eds. *Weeds of the South*. Athens: University of Georgia Press, 2009.

Carman, Jack B. *Wildflowers of Tennessee*. Tullahoma, TN: Highland Rim Press, 2001.

Common Weeds of the United States. Agricultural Research Service of the United States Department of Agriculture. New York: Dover Publications, 1970.

Dean, Blanch E., Amy Mason, and Joab L. Thomas. *Wildflowers of Alabama and Adjoining States*. Tuscaloosa: University of Alabama Press, 1973.

Fassett, Norman C. *A Manual of Aquatic Plants*. Madison: University of Wisconsin Press, 1957.

Foote, Leonard E., and Samuel B. Jones Jr. *Native Shrubs and Woody Vines of the Southeast*. Portland, OR: Timber Press, 1989.

Gibbons, Whit, Robert R. Haynes, and Joab L. Thomas. *Poisonous Plants and Venomous Animals of Alabama and Adjoining States*. Tuscaloosa: University of Alabama Press, 1990.

Miller, James H., and Karl V. Miller. *Forest Plants of the Southeast and Their Wildlife Uses*. Athens: University of Georgia Press, 2005.

Mohlenbrock, Robert H. *This Land: A Guide to Eastern National Forests*. Berkeley: University of California Press, 2006.

Newcomb, Lawrence and Gordon Morrison. *Newcomb's Wildflower Guide*. Boston: Little, Brown, 1989. Revised name changes list by Steve Young, https://docs.google.com/document/preview?id=1kbhzZy1xjNDE7VS_WqqrswkcP-DqdD_5DM8Fv4kEA44o&pli=1.

Rickett, Harold. *Wild Flowers of the United States: Southeastern States*. New York: New York Botanical Garden, 1967.

REPTILES

Mount, Robert H. *The Reptiles and Amphibians of Alabama*. 2nd ed. Tuscaloosa: University of Alabama Press, 1980.

TRACKS

Eiseman, Charley, and Noah Charney. *Tracks & Sign of Insects and Other Invertebrates*. Mechanicsburg, PA: Stackpole Books, 2010.

Halfpenny, James C., and Jim Bruchac. *Scats and Tracks of the Southeast*. Guilford, Conn.: Falcon Guides, 2002.

Murie, Olaus J., and Mark Elbroch. *Peterson Field Guide to Animal Tracks*. 3rd ed. Boston: Houghton Mifflin Harcourt, 2005.

TREES

Brockman, C. Frank and Rebecca Marrilees. *Trees of North America: A Guide to Field Identification*. 2nd ed. New York: St. Martin's Press, 2001.

Sibley, David Allen. *The Sibley Guide to Trees*. New York: Alfred A. Knopf, 2009.

Williams, Michael D. *Identifying Trees: An All-Season Guide to Eastern North America*. Mechanicsburg, PA: Stackpole Books, 2007

ADDITIONAL RESOURCES

Campbell, Louis W. *The Marshes of Southwestern Lake Erie*. Athens: Ohio University Press, 1995.

Canfield, Michael R., ed. *Field Notes on Science and Nature*. Cambridge, Mass.: Harvard University Press, 2011.

Colburn, Elizabeth A. *Vernal Pools: Natural History and Conservation*. Blacksburg: McDonald and Woodward Publishing, 2004.

Duncan, R. Scott. *Southern Wonder: Alabama's Surprising Biodiversity*. Tuscaloosa: University of Alabama Press, 2013.

Eastman, John. *The Book of Swamp and Bog*. Mechanicsburg, PA: Stackpole Books, 1995.

Gosse, Philip Henry. *Letters from Alabama: Chiefly Relating to Natural History*. Tuscaloosa: University of Alabama Press, 1993.

Haskell, David George. *The Forest Unseen: A Year's Watch in Nature*. New York: Penguin Group, 2012.

Leopold, Aldo. *A Sand County Almanac: and Sketches Here and There*. New York: Oxford University Press, 1949.

Louv, Richard. *Last Child in the Woods: Saving Our Children from Nature-Deficit Disorder*. Chapel Hill: Algonquin Books, 2008.

Phillips, Doug. *Discovering Alabama Forests*. Tuscaloosa: University of Alabama Press, 2006.

———. *Discovering Alabama Wetlands*. Tuscaloosa: University of Alabama Press, 2002.

Pough, Frederick H. *A Field Guide to Rocks and Minerals*. 5th ed. Peterson Guide Series. Boston: Houghton Mifflin, 1988.

Sanders, Jack. *The Secrets of Wildflowers: A Delightful Feast of Little-Known Facts, Folklore, and History*. Guilford: Lyons Press, 2003.

Young, Jon. *What the Robin Knows*. Boston: Houghton Mifflin Harcourt, 2012.

Useful Websites

Animal species

International Union for Conservation of Nature and Natural Resources (IUCN) Red List of Threatened Species
http://www.iucnredlist.org/search
http://eol.org/data_objects/18920057

Bugs and insects

BugGuide
http://bugguide.net/node/view/504
Butterflies and Moths of North America
Collecting and Sharing Data about Lepidoptera
http://www.butterfliesandmoths.org/

Fungi

Glossary of Mycological Terms
http://www.mushroomexpert.com/glossary.html#saprobe
How to Recognize and Control Sooty Molds by Kenneth J. Kessler
http://www.na.fs.fed.us/spfo/pubs/howtos/ht_sooty/ht_sooty.htm

Great Blue Heron

The Great Blue Heron by Clara Johnson
http://northwestwildlife.com/wp-content/uploads/2013/12/Great-Blue-Heron.pdf

The Heron Working Group
    http://www.sfu.ca/biology/wildberg/hwg/aboutherons.html

Reptiles
Outdoor Alabama (snakes)
    http://www.outdooralabama.com/watchable-wildlife/what/reptiles/snakes
Reptile Database
    http://reptile-database.reptarium.cz

Tracks
Wildlife Tracker Jonah Evans
    www.naturetracking.com

Trees and plants
Alabama Plant Atlas
    http://www.floraofalabama.org
Photographs and Information for the Plants of Alabama
    http://alabamaplants.com
Physiographic Sections of Alabama
    http://www.encyclopediaofalabama.org/face/Article.jsp?id=h-1362
Treasure Forest
    http://www.atfa.net
Trees of Alabama and the Southeast
    https://fp.auburn.edu/sfws/samuelson/dendrology
USDA Plants Database
    http://plants.usda.gov/java
Wildflowers of the United States
    Reference List for Alabama Wildflower Identification
    https://uswildflowers.com/stateref.php?State=AL

Index

American bald eagle, 180

American black elderberry, 115, 146. *See also* elderberry

American hornbeam, 39, 47, 256

American lady. *See* butterfly

American robin. *See* robin

American sweetgum, 180. *See also* sweetgum

American sycamore, 22. *See also* sycamore

Amorpha fruticosa. See false indigo

Ampelopsis arborea. See peppervine

anaerobic, 261, 264

Anas platyrhynchos. See mallard (duck)

Andropogon virginicus. See broomsedge bluestem

annulus (of mushroom), 56

Anthocharis midea. See falcate orangetip butterfly

antlers, 225–27

ants, 93, 128, 173. *See also* imported fire ant; native fire ant

Apiaceae. *See* carrot family

Apios americana. See groundnut

aposematic, 61, 145

Appalachian Plateau Province, 259

Appalachian, 20, 251, 259

Araceae (Arum family), 33, 64

Araneus marmoreus. See marbled orbweaver spider

Ardea herodias. See great blue heron

Arisaema dracontium. See green dragon

Aristolochia tomentosa. See wooly dutchman's pipe vine

Armillaria tabescens. See ringless honey mushroom

arrow arum, *10*, 21, 47, 64, 70, 77, 93, 119, 146, 151, 164, 167, 221, 236, 250; family (Araceae), 64

arrowhead: broadleaf arrowhead, 115, *133*, 146; common arrowhead, 146. *See also* sagittaria

arrowheads (Indian), 192

arum family (Araceae), 32, 33. *See also* arrow arum; green dragon

Asclepiadaceae. *See* milkweed

Asclepias incarnata. See swamp milkweed

Asiatic dayflower, 1, 122, *123*, 146

Asimina triloba. See common paw paw

aster family, 12, 111, 120, 122, 137, 157; family (Asteraceae), 12, 76

Asteraceae. See aster family

Asterocampa celtis. See hackberry emperor butterfly

bacteria, 38, 41, 132; nitrogen fixing 82–83. *See* Rhizobia. *See also* cyanobacteria

Baeolophus bicolor. See tufted titmouse

barred owl, 17, 22

Bartram, William, 26

Battus philenor. See pipevine swallowtail butterfly

beaked cornsalad, 13, *14*, 21, 39, 47

beard lichen. *See* lichen

beaver, 28, 154, 169, 198, 204, 252; dams 169, 186, 193, 213, 221, 260;

yellow bellied sapsucker, 236

yellow poplar, 57, 257. *See also* tulip poplar; tuliptree

Zonotrichia albicollis. See white-throated sparrow